BEST
BIDS

BEST BIDS

THE INSIDER'S GUIDE
TO BUYING
AT AUCTION

Dana Micucci

VIKING
STUDIO

VIKING STUDIO
Published by the Penguin Group
Penguin Putnam Inc., 375 Hudson Street,
New York, New York 10014, U.S.A.

Penguin Books Ltd, 80 Strand,
London WC2R ORL, England

Penguin Books Australia Ltd, Ringwood,
Victoria, Australia

Penguin Books Canada Ltd, 10 Alcorn Avenue,
Toronto, Ontario, Canada M4V 3B2

Penguin Books (N.Z.) Ltd, 182–90 Wairau Road,
Auckland 10, New Zealand

Penguin Books Ltd, Registered Offices:
Harmondsworth, Middlesex, England

First published in 2002 by Viking Studio,
a member of Penguin Putnam Inc.

10 9 8 7 6 5 4 3 2 1

The following photographs—Tang horse and Ming-style vase in Chinese Ceramics, and Mayan
plate in Pre-Columbian Art—are © Sotheby's, Inc.

All illustrations courtesy Christie's, New York, are copyright Christie's Images, New York, 2002.

Robert Motherwell, Untitled. © Dedalus Foundation, Inc./Licensed by VAGA, New York.

Jonathan Borofsky, *Duck Dream Painting with Chattering Man at 2,847,789,*
courtesy the artist and Paula Cooper Gallery, New York.

Edward Weston, *Hands of Harold Kreutzberg,* © 1981 Center for Creative Photography,
Arizona Board of Regents.

Library of Congress Cataloging-in-Publication Data

Micucci, Dana, 1961–
Best bids : the insider's guide to buying at auction / Dana Micucci
p.   cm.
Includes bibliographical references.
ISBN 0-670-89383-8
1. Art auctions—United States. 2. Art—Prices—United States. I. Title.

N8603.M53   2001
381'.17'0973—dc21   2001026882

Printed and bound by Dai Nippon Printing Co., Hong Kong, Ltd.

CONTENTS

Acknowledgments

I WOULD LIKE TO THANK the many auction house specialists and personnel, dealers, and collectors who generously contributed their time, expertise and enthusiasm to make this book possible. Invaluable public relations assistance was supplied by Andrée Corroon and the press staff at Christie's; Matthew Weigman and the press staff at Sotheby's; Cynthia Tashjian, director of public relations at Skinner; Levi Morgan and the press staff at Butterfields; Jackie Insel, director of public relations at Phillips, de Pury & Luxembourg; Louis LeB. Webre and the press staff at Doyle New York; Caroline Birenbaum and the press staff at Swann Galleries; Valerie Flowe, director of public relations at Sloan's; Jane Padelford and the staff at Christie's Images; Elizabeth Burns at Sotheby's; Patty Fox at Sothebys.com; Phillip Rinehart at ehammer.com; Jennifer Chu at ebaypremier.com; Cathleen Weber at ewolfs.com; Andrea Schnoor at artnet.com; and Meredith Mendelsohn at icollector.com.

Expertise on the auction process came from Ronald Pook of Pook & Pook; Deborah Seidel, president of Sloan's; David Rago of David Rago Auctions; Scot Levitt, director of fine arts at Butterfields; Donald Treadway of Treadway Gallery; Ronald Bourgeault, auctioneer at Northeast Auctions; Barbara Strongin, director of operations and auctioneer at Christie's.

For their contribution to the chapters on live and Internet auctions, I would especially like to thank Richard Madley, president of Christie's East; Christopher Thomson, chief executive officer of Phillips, de Pury & Luxembourg, U.K.; Lawrence DuMouchelle of DuMouchelle Art Galleries; Ronald Pook of Pook & Pook; Katie Hobas, vice president at Neal Auction Company; Carol and Larry Farley of Dargate Auction Galleries; David Rago of David Rago Auctions; Roger Reed of Illustration House; Richard Wright of Wright; Peter and Shannon Loughrey of Los Angeles Modern Auctions; Larry Gottheim of Be-hold; Gary Guyette and Frank Schmidt of Guyette & Schmidt; Mike Clum; Robert Emberlin of Bradford Auction Gallery; Susan and Richard Wacht of Canton Barn; Craig Moffett of sotheby's.com; Geoffrey Iddison, general manager of ebaypremier.com; Hans Neuendorf; chief executive officer of artnet.com; Karen Amiel, vice president of artnet.com; Uta Scharf, formerly of artnet.com; Delores Gardner, attorney at the Federal Trade Commission; Holly Anderson of the National Consumer's League; Dr. Michael Schlossberg; Robert Lehrman; Matthew Bruccoli; Michael Wolf, founder of ewolfs.com; Kerry Shrives, auctioneer and appraiser at Skinner; Clint Cantwell, executive vice president of icollector.com; Fred Giampietro, founder of ehammer.com; Ronald Capobianco; Mary-Anne Martin of Mary-Anne Martin/Fine Art; Russ Goldberger of the Russ and Karen Goldberger Gallery; Paul Gray of Richard Gray Gallery; Frank Levy of Bernard & S. Dean Levy; Leon Dalva of Dalva Brothers.

I am also grateful to Nancy Druckman and John Nye of Sotheby's; Patrick Bell of Olde Hope Antiques; Laura Fisher/Antique Quilts & Americana; Merrilee J. Possner at Northeast Auctions; Dr. Robert Booth; Martha Hamilton and Stephen Fletcher of Skinner; Frank Maresca of Ricco/Maresca Gallery; Wayne Pratt of Wayne Pratt Antiques; Dean and Frank Levy of Bernard & S. Dean Levy; and Daniel Checki, all of whom contributed to my chapters on American folk art and American furniture.

Thank you to books and manuscripts experts Natalie Bauman of Bauman Rare Books; Catherine Williamson of Butterfields; George Lowry, Christine Von Der Linn and Jeremy Markowitz at Swann; and Matthew J. Bruccoli; Chinese ceramics and furniture specialists Eric Zetterquist of Zetterquist Galleries; James Lally of J. J. Lally & Company; Allan Chait of Ralph M. Chait Galleries; Marcus Flacks of MD Flacks Ltd.; Theow H. Tow of Christie's; and Leon Wender of China 2000 Fine Art. Expertise in contemporary art came from Robert Lehrman; Philippe Segalot of Christie's; Joseph Helman of Joseph Helman Gallery; Michael Maloney at Butterfields; and Richard Gray of Richard Gray Gallery.

For their contribution to the chapters on European ceramics and furniture, I gratefully acknowledge Jody Wilkie of Christie's; Stuart Slavid at Skinner; Leon Dalva of Dalva Brothers; Jill Fenichell of Fenichell-Basmajian Antiques; Karen Cangelosi at Phillips, de Pury & Luxembourg; Mark Jacoby of Phillip Colleck; Andrea Blunck Frost at Doyle New York; George Subkoff of George Subkoff Antiques; and Michael Connors of Michael Connors Inc.

I would also like to thank Japanese art specialists Joan Mirviss of Joan B. Mirviss Ltd.; Sebastian Izzard of Sebastian Izzard LLC Asian Art; Toshiyuki Hara, Susan Lewis and Jeffrey Olson of Christie's; and Jeffery Cline of Kagedo Japanese Art; as well as Howard Rutkowski of Phillips, de Pury & Luxembourg; David Norman of Sotheby's; Richard Feigen of Richard L. Feigen & Company; Anthony Crichton-Stuart of Christie's; Vance Jordan of Vance Jordan Fine Art; Myron Kunin; Thomas Dedoncker of Butterfields; Mary-Anne Martin of Mary-Anne Martin/Fine Art; and Lawrence Salander of Salander-O'Reilly Galleries, all of whom contributed to the chapter on paintings.

My sincere appreciation also goes to photographs specialists Denise Bethel of Sotheby's; Daile Kaplan of Swann; Howard Greenberg of Howard Greenberg Gallery; Jan Kesner of Jan Kesner Gallery; W. M. Hunt of Ricco/Maresca Gallery; Pre-Columbian art experts Stacey Goodman of Sotheby's; Spencer Throckmorton of Throckmorton Fine Art; and David Bernstein of David Bernstein Fine Art; and rugs and carpets authorities F. J. Hakimian; Mary Jo Otsea of Sotheby's; Jo Kris of Skinner; Samy Rabinovic; and rug restoration experts at Woven Legends Restoration, Inc., The Textile Conservation Center at The American Textile History Museum, The Textile Conservation Laboratory at The Cathedral of St. John The Divine, Restoration by Costikyan, and the American Institute for Conservation of Historic and Artistic Works.

For their contribution to the sculpture chapter, I would like to thank G. Max Bernheimer of Christie's; Jerome Eisenberg of Royal-Athena Galleries; Jean Fritts of Sotheby's; Eric Robertson of Eric Robertson African Arts; and Dr. Bernard Wagner. I would also like to express my gratitude to 20th-century decorative arts specialists David Rago of David Rago Auctions; Beth Cathers of Cathers & Dembrosky Gallery; Eric Silver of Doyle New York; Nancy McClelland of Christie's; Anthony DeLorenzo of DeLorenzo; Robert Aibel of Moderne Gallery; Peter Loughrey of Los Angeles Modern Auctions; John Sollo of David Rago Auctions; and Rosalie Berberian of ARK Antiques.

Special thanks to Todd Weyman at Swann; Dr. Nancy Bialler of Sotheby's; Gerald Peters of Gerald Peters Gallery; Dr. Michael Schlossberg; Meredith Harper Wiley of Christie's; Christopher Gaillard of Sotheby's; Joni Moisant Weyl of Gemini G. E. L. at Joni Moisant Weyl; and Susan Reinhold of Reinhold-Brown Gallery for their contribution to the works on paper chapter, and to all others who helped to bring this book to fruition, including Cyanne Chutkow of Christie's, Friederike Ringe, Margaret Cameron, my agent Stuart Bernstein, and my editor Cyril Nelson for his wise guidance and support.

Part One

AUCTIONS

Chapter 1
THE PROCESS

It is no secret that auctions are more popular now than ever. The past two decades have seen an unprecedented number of private buyers bidding for art and antiques at auction, once the domain of dealers. A robust national economy and the increasing availability of information through publications, the Internet, blockbuster museum exhibitions, and the PBS hit television series *Antiques Roadshow* have helped to make auctions more accessible to the public at large—everyone from the casual weekend shopper to the serious collector.

The new phenomenon of Internet auctions (see page 151) and glamorous headliner sales at Christie's and Sotheby's, which have offered everything from Marilyn Monroe's dresses to Jackie Onassis's jewelry, also have fueled interest in traditional live auctions. (Christie's reported a 15 percent increase in worldwide sales from 1998 to 1999 while Sotheby's reported an 18 percent increase in its North American sales for the same period.) As a result, more family heirlooms are finding their way out of the closet and onto the block. And auction fever is on the rise.

Yet the auction process still can be mysterious and intimidating to the uninitiated first-time bidder. You may ask Why buy at auction when there are plenty of reputable art and antiques dealers eager to cater to your acquisitive whims? Some collectors will tell you that they are addicted to the thrill of the hunt and the adrenaline rush of competing against other bidders in the saleroom. Dealers find auctions to be a good source of a wide variety of material from which they can build inventory, although many are increasingly bidding on behalf of private collectors, who are driving what were once considered wholesale prices into the retail realm. Auctioneers themselves point to the fair market-value allure of the saleroom, where you can buy objects that aren't subject to dealer markups. And then there is the comfort level of knowing that

Auction in progress (Courtesy Sotheby's, New York)

Auction in progress (Courtesy Doyle New York)

others, too, are visibly interested in your object of desire, seemingly confirming its worth.

"Auctions give you the opportunity to view a huge selection of objects at a single place in time, making it more convenient than visiting a lot of different galleries. You can look and touch and ask the experts questions. Auctions also allow you to set your own price in a competitive market environment," says former dealer Ronald Pook, owner of Pook & Pook auctions in Downingtown, Pennsylvania. "With so much information now available about art and antiques, people are more educated and feel more empowered about what they're buying. They want to be in control."

The auction process works for a very simple reason: A seller wants to sell an object at the highest possible price, while a buyer wants to buy it at the lowest

Auction in progress (Courtesy Skinner, Boston)

Auction in progress (Courtesy David Rago Auctions, Lambertville, NJ, ragoarts.com)

possible price. Of course, the ultimate value of an object is whatever price someone is willing to pay for it. When egos and emotions are involved, however, bidding wars ensue, and prices can skyrocket beyond reasonable levels, challenging the fair market-value premise. But for many this kind of competition makes auctions fun and exciting.

"Auctions are great entertainment," says Deborah Seidel, president of Sloan's Auction Galleries in Bethesda, Maryland, and Miami, Florida. "They're a participatory sport, live theater, and a social event all rolled into one. Once people overcome their initial trepidation, they find that their dollars are more effective when they buy at auction."

Indeed, you can still find some good buys at auction.

"Almost all the material we sell is fresh to the marketplace, directly from estates," notes Stephen Fletcher, head of Americana, auctioneer, and appraiser at Skinner Auctioneers and Appraisers in Boston and Bolton, Massachusetts. "The rare things will always bring high prices, but you can find a lot of good 18th- and 19th-century furniture at auction for reasonable prices compared to what you'd pay for modern store-bought pieces. That's great value, when you consider that many antiques are beautifully designed and handmade from extraordinary lumber that will last another hundred years or more. Even restored pieces offer good value at lower prices. Don't ignore the 18th-century candlestand or drop-leaf table that may be refinished or have a new base, reconfigured drawers, or replaced brass."

Perhaps you've just bought a new home, and you can't wait to furnish it. Maybe you're in search of a special gift, or you've begun a collection that you'd like to expand. You've thought about attending an auction, but it seems too complicated. You're not familiar with auction parlance and etiquette. Or you're afraid that a mere head nod or nose scratch will inadvertently commit you to a multimillion-dollar Picasso and land you in bankruptcy court.

Actually, the auction process is not as mystifying as it seems. And you certainly don't have to be a millionaire to participate, an illusion created by the press frenzy for record-breaking works of art and antiques. Whether you're in the market for a Tiffany lamp, a Chippendale chair, a contemporary painting, or a first edition of a Dickens novel, you need only follow a few simple steps.

Suppose you're redecorating and looking for some beautiful antiques for your living room or dining room. You've noticed an advertisement in the newspaper about an auction of American furniture at an established auction house in your region, and it's piqued your curiosity.

The first thing you need is an illustrated catalogue of the various lots being offered for sale. A lot may be one item or a group of items sold together. Lots are numbered in the order in which they will be auctioned. Available several weeks before a sale, a catalogue can be purchased at the auction house or by annual subscription. In this online age, many auction houses now display their catalogues on Web sites (a more cost-efficient option). Prices vary depending on the size and stature of the auction house.

Large auction houses such as Christie's and Sotheby's hold several sales each week between September and June. Their sales of American furniture and decorative arts, for example, are traditionally held each January and June, and their major Contemporary and Impressionist and Modern art sales take place in May and November.

For each lot identified, auction catalogues usually list the artist's or maker's name, a date or period, and dimensions. They may also include detailed descriptions for specific lots as well as *provenance* (ownership

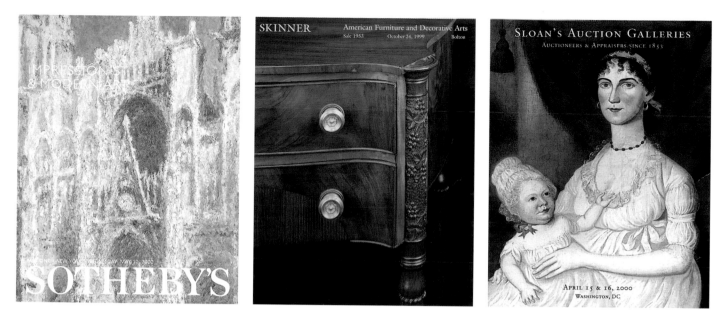

Catalogue cover (Courtesy Sotheby's, New York)   Catalogue cover (Courtesy Skinner, Boston)   Catalogue cover (Courtesy Sloan's Auction Galleries, Washington, D.C.)

history), exhibition and publication history, and a *pre-sale estimate*—the price range the object is expected to fetch at auction. Estimates are based upon prices recently paid at auction for similar works. The quality, rarity, condition, and provenance of a particular work also affect its estimate.

The catalogue's title page usually lists the collections of property represented in the sale. Some lots may have belonged to a well-known collector or interior designer, which often enhances their value. A good provenance helps to establish the authenticity and art-historical importance of the lots being sold, as does their inclusion in significant exhibitions. That does not mean, however, that lots listed under a "various owners" heading or those without a detailed exhibition history are necessarily of lower quality.

Some sales may be entirely devoted to single-owner collections—Sotheby's sale of Impressionist and Modern art from the collection of Mr. and Mrs. John Hay Whitney, for example, or the personal property of Marilyn Monroe, auctioned by Christie's. Of course, not all single-owner sales are the domain of the rich and famous. Also keep in mind that the sometimes exorbitant prices realized at celebrity sales do not accurately reflect market value; many buyers are paying as much for the name as for the object. After all, would a box containing a piece of wedding cake have sold for $29,000 had it not belonged to the Duke and Duchess of Windsor?

Catalogues also may indicate whether or not a lot carries a *reserve*—a confidential minimum price agreed upon prior to the sale by an auction house representative and a consignor, below which the lot will

not be sold. In Christie's sales, for example, the majority of objects sold are subject to a reserve. A small black dot printed next to a lot description in Christie's catalogue means that lot is *not* subject to a reserve.

Standard practice at most auction houses, reserves serve as protection for the seller. At some auction houses, such as Northeast Auctions of Portsmouth and Manchester, New Hampshire, few if any lots carry reserves, meaning that an item will be sold to the highest bidder no matter how low the bid. Proponents of this approach say it allows for purer market dynamics and encourages more people to bid because they hope to walk away with bargains.

Whichever auction you decide to attend, read the catalogue carefully. It usually contains additional information about buying and selling at auction, conditions of sale, and warranties on the authenticity and, in some cases, the condition of the objects being auctioned—all of which vary from one house to another. Established auction houses stand behind their offerings with published guarantees that hold them responsible for authenticity (as defined in their catalogues) for a specific period of time. In many cases, auction houses guarantee only the information published in capital letters or boldface type in their catalogues. Although auction houses generally operate with the caveat that "all sales are final," should you determine after the sale that an item has been miscatalogued or misrepresented, you may be eligible for a refund within a specific period of time. At Pook & Pook, for example, items may be returned within fifteen days if you are able to prove an error on the part of the auction house. Such returns are rare, however, especially for reputable auction houses, who strive to be responsible to buyers.

Most auction houses state that merchandise will be sold "as is," which means that it is the responsibility of the buyer to evaluate condition. Some auction houses, such as David Rago Auctions in Lambertville, New Jersey, which specializes in 20th-century decorative arts and design mostly from the Arts and Crafts period, pride themselves in standing behind both the condition and authenticity of their offerings.

"An auction catalogue is an invaluable research tool both for its art-historical information and estimates, which keep you abreast of the market," says David Rago. "It's a good idea to subscribe to catalogues in your area of interest well before you place your first bid."

You also should pay close attention to the glossary of terms listed in the catalogue, which varies from one house to another. At Doyle New York, for example, a lot identified as a *Regency Desk, First Quarter 19th Century,* is different from a lot identified as a *Regency Desk,* which may have undergone substantial alterations such as new drawers, or legs that do not date from

Auction preview (Courtesy Doyle New York)

the Regency period. A *Regency-style* desk is one that has been manufactured after the Regency period. A painting listed as "signed" by the artist is not the same as a painting described by the phrase "bears signature," which means that the signature *might* be that of the artist. Obviously, a simple misreading could lead to a very expensive mistake.

Research. Research. Research. It's the rally cry of the experts. The more you educate yourself before the auction about your particular area of interest, the better your bids will be.

"My advice to first-time buyers at auction is to take at least a year and go to as many galleries, auctions, and museums as possible. Read a lot. Ask questions about the art and antiques that appeal to you. Just like you would spend time researching a new car or a new house," says Scot Levitt, director of Fine Arts and an auctioneer at Butterfields in San Francisco and Los Angeles. "You'll have developed your eye so that you'll be able to make a more educated purchase. If you come prepared, there's no need to be intimidated by auctions."

Auctions are free and open to the public. And you don't have to bid to attend.

"Before buying anything, take your catalogue to a few auctions and keep track of the prices brought by pieces that interest you," advises Skinner's Fletcher. "Study several pieces in some detail. Compare prices and estimates, noting why a particular object sold above, within, or below the estimate. Did the high-priced chest of drawers have a wonderful patina and its original brasses intact?"

So you've done some homework and narrowed your choices to three antiques illustrated in the catalogue—a pair of red-painted Windsor side chairs estimated at $3,000 to $5,000; a Queen Anne carved cherrywood tea table estimated at $4,000 to $6,000; and a Federal inlaid-mahogany sideboard estimated at $8,000 to $12,000. Although you can call the auction house to ask questions about your selections, you should make every effort to inspect them in person at the *preview*—also referred to as a *viewing* or *presale exhibition*—which is free and open to the public for several days before the auction. Catalogue photographs can be deceiving. Sometimes the colors are inaccurate, and condition problems such as scratches and replacements are rarely visible.

"Going to an auction exhibition is not like going to a museum. You're not behind a velvet rope. You can handle the art and antiques, and

Auction preview (Courtesy Doyle New York)

examine them closely. Auction experts are available to answer questions about each piece as well as the auction process. It's an interactive, educational experience," notes Louis LeB. Webre, a vice president and director of marketing at Doyle New York. "I always advise bringing a notebook listing the dimensions that you require in your home. If you're looking for a chair, you'll want to know the height of your desk or dining-room table. If you want to buy a painting to hang above your sofa, how large should it be? If you're looking for a chandelier, what is the height of your ceiling? Will your freight elevator accommodate the sideboard you plan to buy? You may also want to bring some photographs of your interior, a measuring tape and a Polaroid camera to snap some shots of your favorite pieces. It's hard to know what something will look like in your home."

According to the collector's guide published by the Art Dealers Association of America, the key criteria when considering a potential purchase are quality, authenticity, rarity, condition, provenance, and value. In addition to asking the advice of auction specialists at the preview, it's always a good idea to consult dealers and restoration experts, particularly if you plan to bid on an important item. Dealers will accompany collectors to previews and auctions and bid on their behalf for a modest commission, usually about 10 percent of the sale price of an object. Their expertise is an added comfort for many collectors and especially invaluable to first-time bidders.

At the preview, ask the auction specialists to show you catalogues and price lists from previous sales so that you know what similar objects have fetched. Ask how they arrived at the pre-sale estimates and what price range they think your selections will bring at the upcoming sale.

It is important to remember that estimates do not necessarily predict final prices. They are sometimes set low to attract bidding, and depending on the competition in the saleroom, some lots may sell for much more than the high estimate, somewhere between the high and low estimates, or for less than the low estimate. Since many sellers negotiate reserve prices, some lots may be *withdrawn* or *bought-in,* which means that they did not meet the reserve and therefore failed to sell. While state laws vary, reserves generally are not permitted to exceed the low estimate. You may also want to consult dealers or published price guides such as Kovels', or log on to artprice.com for current market values in various collecting categories.

Since everything is sold "as is" at most auction houses, pay special attention during the preview to

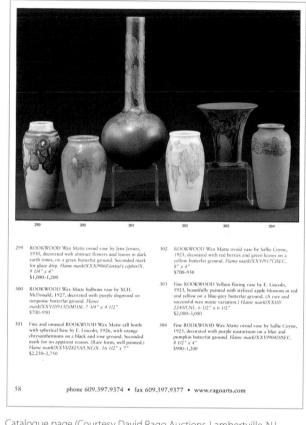

Catalogue page (Courtesy David Rago Auctions, Lambertville, NJ, ragoarts.com)

Catalogue page (Courtesy Skinner, Boston)

Absentee bid form (Courtesy Doyle New York)

the lots that have caught your eye. Are the Windsor chairs refinished? Are there cracks in the sideboard? Has the tea table been repaired in any way? Although a certain amount of wear and tear is to be expected with antiques, you'll want to know how much it affects value, which in turn will enable you to determine more accurately how much you want to spend on a particular piece. If you're in the market for a painting, ask whether it was examined under ultraviolet light for repairs and inpainting, meaning damaged areas that have been retouched. Ask whether it has been lined (also referred to as relined in the trade), which means that a second canvas has been applied to the back to stabilize it. The most desirable art and antiques are those that have remained as close as possible to their original state.

Auction catalogues often don't contain information about the condition of their offerings. The major auction houses, however, will provide you with written condition reports upon request. This information is prepared by auction specialists and offered as a courtesy only. With some exceptions, auction houses generally do not hold themselves responsible for the accuracy of these reports. Again, a second opinion from a dealer is recommended, especially if you can-

not attend the preview in person. Should an item need repairs, refinishing, or reupholstering, most auction houses will provide you with a list of restorers and other specialists who will give you a free estimate. Dealers also can recommend professional restorers.

After a thorough inspection of the three pieces that have caught your eye at the auction preview, you've decided to bid on the sideboard. It has a few scratches, but the auction specialist has assured you that it is in otherwise good condition. It meets your size requirements, and its spare, elegant aesthetic and rich mahogany make it the perfect centerpiece for your dining room. Now it's time to bid. You should first decide on the top price you are willing to spend, also known as your ceiling price. Depending upon your attachment to the sideboard, you may be prepared to bid one or two increments higher. Of course, there's no telling how you'll react in the heat of the moment once the bidding begins.

"The first thing I recommend to bidders is to know what you're buying. Don't rely on the auction house to do all the background research for you. Of course, some houses are more thorough than others," says Donald Treadway of Treadway Gallery in Cincinnati, Ohio, which holds auctions of 20th-century art and design in Oak Park, Illinois, in association with John Toomey Gallery. "Then you have to determine how important the object is to you. Are you going to be comfortable paying more for an unusual or rare piece? Some people get caught up buying objects that aren't top rate and think they've landed bargains when they really haven't. Many mediocre objects bring higher prices than they deserve. If you don't know what you're looking at, you may end up spending more than you should."

Auction specialists, dealers, and collectors always advise buying the best you can afford.

"Don't expect to find a lot of bargains. If you see a great piece, be prepared to pay a great price," says Ronald Pook. "And don't go for quantity over quality. You're better off buying one piece that's the best of its kind rather than seven average examples."

Nevertheless, it pays to be prepared and know your price limit.

"There is such a thing as auction fever once you're in the saleroom. And no auction house wants its clients to experience what we call 'buyer's remorse,'" Deborah Seidel adds.

Experts also agree that you should never buy art and antiques for investment, whether at auction or from dealers. It is easy to fall prey to this temptation when the market is hot and prices are rising. If you are a beginning collector and buy art and antiques on the basis of price only, you most likely will amass a mediocre collection that will not hold its value over time.

"Buy with your heart. If you don't love a piece, you won't enjoy it," Rago counsels. "While you may wish to think of your collection as an investment, you're better off making money another way. Ultimately, you're buying art because financial profit is not your primary concern. That is not to say that you shouldn't keep your eyes open for good value. You can do this by buying ahead of the market, paying attention to trends as they begin to happen. A good bet is to determine which maker's work was important when made but has not seen more than a negligible increase in price in a ten-year period."

When determining your price limit before the auction, remember that the *hammer price* (sometimes referred to as the *knockdown price*)—the successful bid price for which a work of art is sold when the gavel falls—does not include the *buyer's premium* and state and local sales tax, which may add as much as 25 percent. A percentage of the final bid price, which the buyer pays as a commission to the auction house, buyer's premiums vary from house to house and are stated in auction catalogues.

At Sotheby's, for example, the buyer's premium is 20 percent of the hammer price up to $15,000; 15 percent on the next $85,000, up to $100,000; and 10 percent on any amount over $100,000. Sloan's and Butterfields charge a buyer's premium of 15 percent on the first $50,000 of the successful bid price, and 10 percent on amounts over $50,000. Sales tax varies from state to state, and you will also want to figure shipping charges and potential restoration fees into your projected cost.

You have several options when bidding at traditional live auctions. Many people choose to bid in person at the sale, which insiders say is preferable if you want the complete auction experience. Auctions are, after all, live events that can be both fun and exciting. At most auction houses, if you cannot attend, you can bid by telephone and arrange for a representative to call you when your lot is to be auctioned. Or you may authorize the auction house to bid on your behalf in your absence. An *absentee bid,* also called an *order bid,* is a written maximum bid that you must submit in advance of the sale, either by mail, phone, fax, or electronically via an Internet Web site, depending upon the auction house's preferred methods of receiving absentee bids.

Absentee-bid forms are often included in auction catalogues. Read the instructions carefully; they vary

slightly from house to house. Many absentee-bid forms require that you list the lot number and description of the item on which you want to bid, as well as your top bid price (which does not include the buyer's premium and sales tax). You also may be asked to note whether you wish to bid one increment above your top price in the event that there is a tie bid with someone in the audience. Bidding *increments,* which are called out by the auctioneer during a sale, gener-

Bidding paddle
(Courtesy Sotheby's, New York)

ally do not exceed 10 percent of the previous bid. Auction houses sometimes list their particular bidding increments in their catalogues. In most cases, an absentee bid of $1,000 plus one increment means that you're willing to pay $1,100 at the most.

When an auction house receives identical absentee bids, the first bid received takes preference. In the case of ties between live, telephone, and absentee bids, check with the auction house to determine which is given priority. At Christie's and Butterfields, for example, absentee bids take priority over live bids and telephone bids.

Before submitting your absentee bid, ask the auction house how it will be treated. Some auction houses may consider it a "hard" bid, meaning that you will pay your top price regardless of the price at which bidding stops in the room. Other auction houses will try to purchase your lot or lots for the lowest price possible. In the latter case, if the bidding in the room stops at $1,000, for example, and you have placed a top bid of $1,500, you will win the lot for $1,100 ($1,000 plus one increment), not including buyer's premium and state and local sales taxes.

"Auction houses offer different bidding options for the buyer's convenience and to reach as wide an audience as possible," says Ronald Bourgeault, auctioneer at Northeast Auctions, which is known for its Americana and estate sales. "Of course, when you're bidding in the room, you are more a part of the action, and you get a better sense of your competition. You can also be more spontaneous. Since the object is right there in front of you, you may decide at the spur of the moment that you want to go a few bids higher. When you bid by telephone, you're bidding live with the audience, but it's harder to feel the pulse in the room and make a quick decision. One advantage to absentee bids is that you've already set your limit, so you won't get carried away by your emotions or the auction fever in the saleroom."

Many collectors who want to remain anonymous choose to bid by telephone or send someone to bid for them at a live auction, particularly if they are planning to spend a lot of money. Many people simply can't attend an auction and appreciate the convenience of telephone and absentee bidding. Perhaps you live in California, and the auction is happening in New York, or you don't want to take the time to sit through it. Skinner's Fletcher recalls that a doctor once bought a pair of Queen Anne side chairs by telephone during surgery—an option, however, that the patient most likely would not recommend. There is always the possiblity of a technical glitch when you aren't bidding in person—telephone busy signals, for example, or an overlooked absentee bid. Auction houses usually do not hold themselves responsible for errors in executing such bids.

You've decided to bid in person on the sideboard. If you don't want to sit through the entire auction, plan to arrive at least a half hour before your lot is to be auctioned. Many auctions last about two to three hours, with sixty to one hundred lots sold per hour. You can judge by the sideboard's lot number approximately when it will come to the block. Auctions are open to everyone. It costs nothing to participate, and you are not required to bid. If you plan to attend one of the high-profile evening sales of Impressionist and Modern art held each May and November at Christie's and Sotheby's, you will need to call in advance for a free ticket. These sales are often standing-room only, so a limited number of tickets are available.

At the auction house, you register to bid and receive a numbered bidding paddle, though you often can speed up the process by calling in advance to pre-register. If you are a first-time bidder, you will have to supply identification and a credit reference. Ask what form of payment the auction house accepts. Some houses offer a credit line to good customers.

Bidding paddle and catalogue in hand, you enter the saleroom and find a seat at the rear, where you will have a good view of the bidding action. Don't be nervous. From the podium the auctioneer gazes down upon the afternoon crowd with intense concentration and a slightly benevolent smile. (No need to intimidate anyone.) He calls out increments on the tea table you decided not to pursue. The hammer falls, and he notes the bid price and the paddle number of the successful bidder in his ledger. Two runners carry the next lot to the block. The auctioneer announces the lot number, identifies the piece, and opens bidding below the confidential reserve, or below the low estimate if the lot is unreserved. Some auction houses also display their offerings on a large video screen positioned at the front of the saleroom. At Christie's and Sotheby's all bids appear on a conversion board in several different currencies.

Fortunately, you've arrived early enough to acclimate yourself to the auctioneer's pace and style of calling.

"Every auctioneer has a different style, the way he or she opens and closes bids and plays the crowd. Some auctioneers proceed quickly, others allow a little more time between each bid or give you more time to make up your mind at the last minute. We have to appear to be fair to everyone," notes Barbara Strongin, director of operations and an auctioneer at Christie's. "Auctions are like live theater, and the auctioneer is the director. We have to keep track of absentee bids, phone bids, and bids in the room. We learn to read the room well, taking note of who is bidding aggressively or who has dropped out. There is a lot of body language and eye contact. It's my job to encourage people to spend more money. With a glance I can try to persuade someone to go another bid higher."

The more time you spend observing an auctioneer's style, the more comfortable you'll feel when bidding. It is standard practice in America for auctioneers to announce the next increment—"I have $5,000, do I hear $5,500?" To avoid confusion they may also point to bidders and describe what they are wearing or where they are sitting in the saleroom. "Two thousand from the gentleman in front . . . $2,200 to the lady in black on the aisle . . ." Some auctioneers say *fair warning* before the hammer falls, while others say "any advance," "any further bidding," or "last call," which means that it's your last chance to bid. The auctioneer says *bought-in* or "pass" or "withdrawn" to indicate that bidding on a lot has not reached the reserve price. Having failed to sell, the lot will be returned to the consignor.

Absentee bids are executed by either the auctioneer or a clerk in the saleroom and are usually identified as such. Auctioneers, however, may or may not announce that they are bidding on behalf of the consignor up to the reserve price, a common practice that is often stated in the auction catalogue or elsewhere. If an auctioneer chooses to announce that he is bidding on behalf of the consignor, he may say, for example, "I have $10,000 with me." Auction catalogues may state that the auctioneer will not place bids on behalf of the consignor at or above the reserve, a dishonorable practice that colloquially has been referred to as *chandelier bidding*—unfairly "running-up" bidders to obtain the highest possible price.

"Very few auctioneers will run up bids over the reserve. It's not in our best interest," Butterfields' Levitt says. "The goal at the end of the day is to make a sale. If we get caught running up bids, and all the other bidders drop out, then we're stuck with the object. The term 'chandelier bidding' is sometimes used to describe situations where the auctioneer knows that a rich collector is present, and he tries to make him or her pay more by calling out fictitious bids."

A disreputable auction house may also run up bids by engaging a shill—a third party, whether a dealer, collector, or an auction-house representative, who agrees to place bids with the intention of driving up the price against the competition (a marked dealer or collector). Auctions often proceed at a brisk pace, particularly when bidding is heated, so it is difficult to identify such questionable practices. Auction houses say foul play is rare, however, because it alientates their customers and compromises their reputation.

Auction practices and laws vary from state to state, so read auction catalogues carefully, and ask questions before you bid. In New York State, for example, it is against the law for consignors to bid on their own property. Sometimes dealers agree not to bid against one another and pool their funds in an effort to keep prices down on a number of lots, which they later divide among themselves for resale. Pools are illegal because they restrain trade. But they don't affect the buyer whose heart is set on a particular lot; he or she will bid as high as his or her funds permit, regardless of the activity in the room.

As you listen to the auctioneer and wait for your lot to come up, you admire the beautiful diamond ring on a woman sitting next to you. Across the room, you recognize one of your neighbors, clad in jeans and a T-shirt, gazing intently at his catalogue. You had no idea that he also was an auctiongoer. Careful, you're getting distracted. Your sideboard is now being carried to the front of the saleroom. You glance again at your catalogue, noting that the lot number the auctioneer has announced is not your lot number. The sideboard on the block is similar to the one you came to buy, but you will have to wait until another five lots are auctioned. You write down the successful bid price (remembering to add the buyer's premium and sales tax) in your catalogue. This lot sold for a bit more than what you were prepared to bid on your sideboard. But it is similar in style, of the same period, and carries the same estimate. You reread the catalogue notes you took during the preview and adjust your ceiling price, knowing that your budget can accommodate it.

The auctioneer announces your sideboard, lot 226, and calls for bids. Simply raise your paddle when you want to bid, and the auctioneer will record your bid number. Most people hold up paddles; some raise their hands. Don't worry. As mentioned previously, you are in no danger of mistakenly acquiring an expensive artwork by rubbing your nose or scratching your ear. That only happens on television. Just don't wave wildly to your friend across the room. When the competition is intense, bidding can last up to four or five minutes for a lot. Each person has his or her own bidding strategy, ranging from aggressive to discreet, depending upon the action in the saleroom. Insiders say there is no surefire strategy that will increase your chances of being the highest bidder.

"There are a lot of different bidding styles, but they seldom make a difference in the end. If you really want something, you'll bid until you get it. Maybe you feel more comfortable jumping in right away to show that you're serious, or maybe you want to keep a low profile as you size up your competition," Christie's Strongin observes. "Some people use the 'Statue of Liberty' method and continuously hold up their paddles, hoping to intimidate other bidders. Others like to be anonymous and arrange secret bidding signals with the auctioneer in advance, which is rare. They may nod or take their glasses off. Sometimes prearranged signals backfire. I remember a man who chewed on his pen to signal that he was bidding.

But it turned out to be a nervous habit, and he made a lot of unintentional bids."

Big-ticket works of art such as Vincent van Gogh's *Self-Portrait Without Beard,* which sold at Christie's for $71.5 million in 1998, the third-most-expensive work ever sold at auction, are sometimes the subject of elaborate bidding strategies that protect the anonymity of the buyer and inadvertently provide some added saleroom drama. The anonymous buyer of the van Gogh reportedly had instructed several people to bid for him in a "relay bid" in which someone nodded to a Christie's representative, who then nodded to another Christie's representative, who then signaled the auctioneer.

The auctioneer will question you if he or she is unsure of your signal.

"Make sure you're visible to the auctioneer. If you're going to use a special signal like nodding your head, it should be clear, particularly if you jump into the bidding late, and I haven't recognized you as part of the initial bidding group," advises Rago, who is also an auctioneer.

"If you haven't been bidding from the beginning, don't think you're going to get in under the gun when you hear, 'last call.' There's always the risk that the auctioneer will miss you," Doyle New York's Webre adds.

Of course, there's also the risk that you will fall prey to auction fever, or become engaged in an emotional bidding war and wind up spending much more than you intended. Auction specialists, dealers, and collectors agree that the best bids are the most rational bids. The best advice is to take your time and be patient. Don't shoot from the hip. And don't feel that you're going to be closed out by a strong showing of dealers. Since they are buying for resale, they want to pay wholesale prices when possible. Your main competition usually will be private collectors, who are more likely to drive prices to the retail level.

"It's easy to get carried away by the drama of an auction," says Treadway. "Everyone is on a treasure hunt, and they want to get there first. Very few people go to a sale and not buy what they came to buy. The competition is an adrenaline rush for some bidders. When a few big egos get involved, they battle it out, and the next thing you know is that the price has gone way beyond the high estimate. That's exactly what the auction house and consignor want."

The bidding war hasn't yet begun for your sideboard. The auctioneer opens bidding below the reserve and progresses in standard increments at his discretion. He may slow down or speed up, skipping increments when necessary, depending on the momentum of the bidding. You notice that your competition so far is one person in the room and one person on the telephone, who is bidding through an auction-house representative standing near a bank of phones at one side. The auctioneer calls out, "$6,000 on the phone, do I have $6,500?" Your pulse quickens as you raise your paddle high so the auctioneer can see you. He records your bid and moves to the next increment.

The bidding heats up, and you pause for a moment before raising your paddle again at $8,000, the low estimate on the sideboard. Your hopes of bargain hunting have diminished, but you are secretly enjoying the thrill of the pursuit. A bald man in the third row raises his paddle at $8,500. You imagine the polished sideboard stunningly commanding center stage in your dining room and the complimentary dinner conversation that ensues. You ignore the whispers of the couple seated behind you and the faint rustle of catalogue pages. Your palms are slightly moist.

The bidding has reached $9,500. You have decided that you are not going home without that sideboard, then hesitate, reminding yourself not to let your emotions take over. When the sideboard reaches $10,000, the bidding increments increase to $1,000. The phone bidder beat you to $11,000. You raise your paddle at $12,000, the sideboard's high estimate. Your rivals don't respond. There's a brief silence in the room. "Fair warning," the auctioneer calls. The gavel falls. "Sold! To you madam, at the rear!" You smile triumphantly and breathe a sigh of relief. That was your top price. You had already taken into consideration the added costs of the buyer's premium, sales tax, and shipping charges.

You will have to pay for and collect your sideboard promptly. Inquire about methods of payment and a specific time frame for removing property, which differs for each auction house. If you exceed the time limit for pickup, you most likely will be charged a storage fee. Doyle New York, for example, requires that you pay for and remove your property within forty-eight hours of the sale. Sloan's charges a storage fee of $25 per lot per month for purchases not paid for and removed within ten days of the sale. Some auction houses offer valued buyers the option of extended payments. Credit terms should be arranged before the sale. Although you are responsible for shipping and insurance expenses, many auction houses will assist you with packing and shipping arrangements (an administrative fee may be involved) or provide a list of shippers for you to contact.

After the sale, many auction houses offer buyers an opportunity to purchase lots that have bought-in. In such cases, the auction house acts as a liaison between buyer and seller to negotiate a price.

"Sometimes we call underbidders on an item to see if they want to buy it after the sale, or people call us," Skinner's Fletcher says. "You may be able to get some good deals, especially if the reserve was too high. But for the most part, items that buy-in are often not the best of their kind. There's a reason why they didn't sell."

As you admire your new purchase at your next dinner party, you may decide that the thrill of its pursuit was so simple and painless that you are ready to do it all over again. Or you may find yourself wondering what to do with an old painting that has been gathering dust in your attic for years.

If you're interested in *selling* at auction, the first step is to have the painting appraised by the appropriate auction-house specialist. Most auction houses offer free auction estimates by appointment and may conduct special appraisal days. You can also send photographs and digital images (in some cases) with accompanying information including a description, medium, dimensions, physical condition, artist's signature or maker's mark, historical details, provenance, how the item was acquired, and any other relevant information. You usually can bring easily transportable items directly to the auction house for an appraisal. Many auction houses will also provide, for a fee, detailed, written appraisals for estate, tax, and insurance purposes. Keep in mind that insurance appraisals reflect the replacement value of an item and not its fair-market value, which is typically lower.

If you decide to consign your painting for sale, you will have to deliver it to the auction house well in advance of the auction so that it can be catalogued and researched. The *consignor* (seller) is usually responsible for shipping and insurance fees, which may be flexible, depending upon the value of the item or items consigned. The auction house may assist you with shipping arrangements and often will store your property free of charge. In most cases, you will also have to pay for photography, should you want your painting illustrated in the catalogue, as well as for any restoration that may be required. There are always exceptions, of course. David Rago Auctions, for example, does not charge for photographs and insurance.

You should also expect to pay a *seller's commission,* which varies according to the potential auction value of the property consigned. Each auction house has its own sliding scale of charges. For example, Doyle New York charges 10 percent of the hammer price for individual lots that sell above $5,000, and 15 percent for lots that sell for $5,000 and under. Suppose your painting, attributed to a minor American landscape artist, sells for a $25,000 hammer price. Acting as your agent, Doyle would pay you $22,500 minus fees for services such as insurance, shipping, and catalogue illustration.

If you are consigning a valuable item or collection for sale, you may want to ask for extras such as free advertising in auction-house publications and promotional literature. International auction houses such as Sotheby's and Christie's offer a broad range of marketing services including traveling exhibitions, and print and television publicity through a global network of salerooms. For valuable collections, some auction houses also provide financial guarantees in which a seller receives a guaranteed minimum price. The auction house is required to inform potential buyers when it has a financial interest in property to be auctioned. In Sotheby's catalogues, guaranteed property is designated by a circle symbol. Some auction houses also broker private sales between buyers and sellers, which are known as private-treaty sales. These transactions usually involve high-priced works of art.

Other auction houses purchase property outright and offer it for sale, a good choice if you are moving, for example, and need to sell items quickly without risking a buy-in fee at auction. Many auction houses also offer a range of estate-liquidation services ranging from detailed written appraisals to packing, shipping, marketing, and accounting. When deciding where to auction your property, you may want to consider the advantages of regional marketing. For example, Philadelphia Chippendale furniture is popular with northern buyers, but Victorian furniture tends to command higher prices in the South.

Before the sale, an auction specialist will recommend an estimate and, in some cases, a reserve price for consigned property. Suppose your painting is estimated at $16,000 to $20,000, and you agree to a reserve of $9,000—the confidential minimum price below which the painting will not be sold. If the bidding stops below $9,000, and the painting fails to sell, the auction house may charge you a buy-in fee, which is typically a small percentage of the reserve. Buy-in fees cover overhead costs such as cataloguing and printing.

"My advice to consignors is to agree to reasonable estimates and reserves. Don't be greedy. You'll scare buyers away if you overestimate your property," Levitt says. "Lower estimates generally breed higher prices; it's part of the marketing. Remember, the goal is to encourage people to bid, and to sell your property."

Generally, it's best to sell an item the first time

around, when it's fresh to the market. If it buys-in, and you put it up for auction again, you may not be successful. It may be perceived as flawed.

"Unrealistic high reserves and estimates are inappropriate to a successful sale at auction. They not only affect the saleability of that particular item in the future but also that of similar items on the market," Webre observes. "People remember what doesn't sell. When reserves and estimates are used appropriately to protect an item, they won't have any impact on what the buyer is willing to pay. Trust the expertise of the auction specialists."

The auction house notifies you after the sale that your painting fortunately sold above its high estimate, for $25,000 (not including buyer's premium). Now, all you have to do is wait for your check. Each auction house has its own payment schedule. Christie's, for example, will pay you approximately thirty-five days after the sale, provided the buyer has paid promptly. Remember, the amount you receive is the final bid price minus the auction house's commission and any other charges you may have incurred.

When you know these basics, the auction process is really quite simple. And once you've perfected the art of the bid or experienced the thrill of a quick sell, you may even develop a habit.

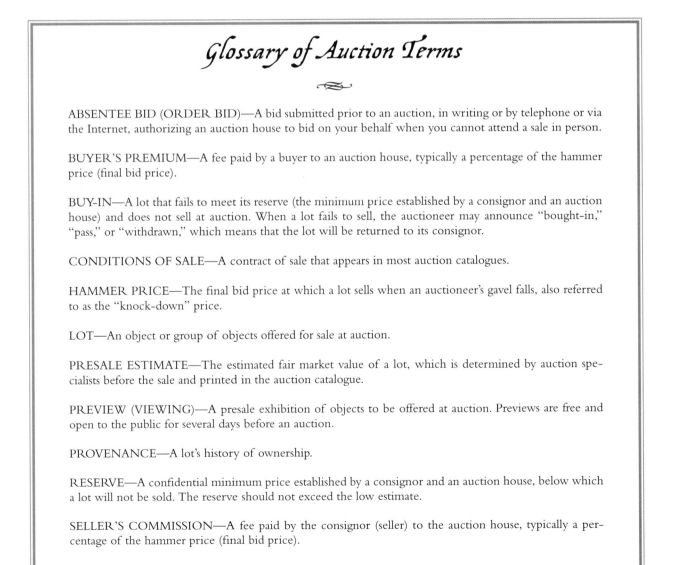

Glossary of Auction Terms

ABSENTEE BID (ORDER BID)—A bid submitted prior to an auction, in writing or by telephone or via the Internet, authorizing an auction house to bid on your behalf when you cannot attend a sale in person.

BUYER'S PREMIUM—A fee paid by a buyer to an auction house, typically a percentage of the hammer price (final bid price).

BUY-IN—A lot that fails to meet its reserve (the minimum price established by a consignor and an auction house) and does not sell at auction. When a lot fails to sell, the auctioneer may announce "bought-in," "pass," or "withdrawn," which means that the lot will be returned to its consignor.

CONDITIONS OF SALE—A contract of sale that appears in most auction catalogues.

HAMMER PRICE—The final bid price at which a lot sells when an auctioneer's gavel falls, also referred to as the "knock-down" price.

LOT—An object or group of objects offered for sale at auction.

PRESALE ESTIMATE—The estimated fair market value of a lot, which is determined by auction specialists before the sale and printed in the auction catalogue.

PREVIEW (VIEWING)—A presale exhibition of objects to be offered at auction. Previews are free and open to the public for several days before an auction.

PROVENANCE—A lot's history of ownership.

RESERVE—A confidential minimum price established by a consignor and an auction house, below which a lot will not be sold. The reserve should not exceed the low estimate.

SELLER'S COMMISSION—A fee paid by the consignor (seller) to the auction house, typically a percentage of the hammer price (final bid price).

Part Two

HOW TO BUY

Chapter 1
AMERICAN FOLK ART

Prized for its direct beauty, simplicity, and authentic handmade quality, American folk art has attracted growing interest over the past twenty-five years. More recently, the spectacular success of Sotheby's $12 million sale in 1994 of American folk art from the collection of the late Bertram K. and Nina Fletcher Little, longtime preeminent New England collectors, along with a host of publications and museum exhibitions, have brought indigenous American art forms such as quilts, needlework samplers, painted furniture, folk portraits, weathervanes, and decoys into the spotlight and onto the market in increasing numbers.

"While the best material is becoming scarce, there's a plentiful supply of quality, affordable American folk art at auction," says Nancy Druckman, Sotheby's director of American folk art. "What's great about this field is that it's accessible, not intimidating. People feel very comfortable with these objects because they are homegrown."

The majority of authentic handmade American folk art on the market was created from the mid-19th century to about 1945, by formally untrained artisans often for utilitarian purposes. You'll find good examples at large auction houses like Sotheby's (which has a separate department devoted to the field), Christie's, and Skinner, as well as at smaller regional houses like Northeast Auctions of Portsmouth, New Hampshire; Garth's Auctions in Delaware, Ohio; and Pook & Pook, which holds auctions in a small firehouse in Downingtown, Pennsylvania.

"American folk art, whether textiles, furniture, portraits, or sculptural objects, has strong visual appeal," says Patrick Bell of Olde Hope Antiques in New Hope, Pennsylvania. "It's colorful and whimsical, highly personal and expressive. It's also a powerful link to America's social and cultural history. People are attracted to it for all these reasons."

A certain amount of buyer's savvy will of course make your pursuit of the perfect piece of Americana even more pleasurable and rewarding.

If you're in the market for a quilt, one of the most popular American collectibles, you'll want to take note of the quality of the design and workmanship, where it was made and by whom, the type of material used, and its condition. Quilts are made from many different pieces of fabric—usually cotton, wool, or silk. They have a top layer, a center or batting to pro-

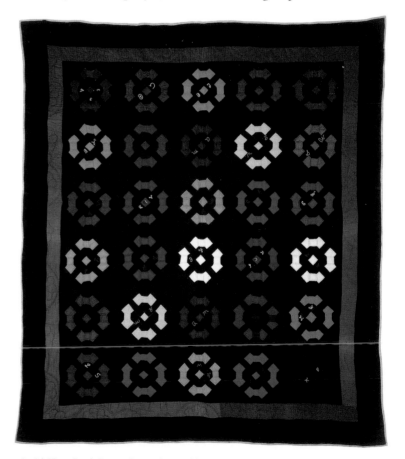

Amish "Four Patch/Bowtie" pieced Friendship quilt, Holmes County, Ohio, cotton, 1920s–1930s. (Courtesy Laura Fisher: Antique Quilts & Americana, New York) "Quilts like this one, executed in jewel tones against a dark background, are the Rolls Royces of midwestern Amish quilts," Fisher says. "They are noted for their beautiful artistry and striking colors. And they are reasonably priced at around $2,500 to $10,000, which is cheap, cheap, cheap compared to contemporary art. Friendship quilts are usually embroidered with the initials or names of the people who contributed the blocks. They are often given as gifts or made for special occasions."

vide warmth, and a backing. These layers are joined together with stitching, which is the quilting. Antique quilts at auction typically date from the mid-19th to mid-20th centuries.

"There are several different ways to collect quilts," says New York City dealer Laura Fisher, one of the nation's leading dealers in antique American textiles. "You may want to collect by region, for example, in which case you would learn to distinguish early-20th-century Amish quilts made in Lancaster County, Pennsylvania, which have bold, graphic designs, from, say, mid-19th-century East Coast album quilts, which display blocks of diverse floral and pictorial designs created by different individuals. These quilts are a bit like autograph albums and are noted for their extraordinary workmanship."

You can also collect by color—blue-and-white or red-and-white, for example—or by image. There are star designs such as the Star of Bethlehem and those that depict broken stars or eight- or six-point stars, among other variations. Log cabin quilts, of which there are about a dozen variations, incorporate a center square around which strips are added to simulate the process of building a log cabin.

Quilts are especially appealing for their versatility. They don't have to function solely as bed coverings. They can be used decoratively as accents of texture and color around a room or hung like art on the walls—a more affordable option than the tens of thousands you'd spend on a large Contemporary painting.

"The first thing to look for with any quilt is the successful execution of the design and the harmony of color, materials and composition," says Fisher. "It's the artistry of a quilt that brings the highest prices, whether the quilt has a unique design with pictorial elements like people, buildings and specific landscapes, or it's a classic quilt with a traditional pattern that's wonderfully made with pieced geometrics or appliquéd florals. While some rare quilts have sold for over $200,000, you can find a lot of visually stunning examples with great designs, beautiful materials, brilliant colors, and wonderful workmanship for less than $5,000 at auction."

The rarest quilts date from around the mid-18th century, most of which are in museums and important Americana collections, or display pictorial elements that tell a specific story. These quilts, which sometimes depict people in period costumes, names, dates, buildings, and other historical details, also rarely come on the market.

Condition, as always, distinguishes the better from the lesser examples.

"Quilts in the best condition have never been washed. Some of the great old quilts were so highly valued by their makers that they were stored in blanket chests, passed down as heirlooms, and never used," says Druckman. "You will, of course, find many quilts at auction that have been used. Those with faded colors, stains, and bleached or torn areas are less desirable."

You should also be able to distinguish antique quilts from new quilts, which sometimes find their way into auctions, catching buyers unaware.

"Nowadays, a lot of quilts that copy old quilt designs are being made cheaply overseas in countries like China, India, and Haiti," Fisher cautions. "If you want an antique, you should make sure that you're not paying old-quilt money for a brand new quilt. The colors and patterns on new quilts will look slightly off to eyes that are knowledgeable about antique quilts. For example, an antique quilt will have a mellowness of color that comes with age, as well as different stitching, density, and surface feel. A quilt that's been laundered will lie down differently from one that's been freshly made. And it's hard to reproduce the centuries-old appearance of folded edges and combination of materials."

In addition to reproductions, beware of new quilts made from old quilt fragments and alterations that make a piece more trendy or collectible. For example, quilts that have been cut down or reduced in size may be missing an element such as a border that contributes to the overall balance of the design.

"At the auction preview, spread out the quilt and hold it up to the light," Fisher advises. "Is the composition harmonious? Check for eroded material, restorations, and gaps. A quilt that has been laundered a lot may show gaps or shifts in the batting, which is an indication of use. Have parts of the quilt been newly patched? New fabrics don't blend with the weathered look of an old quilt. Some restoration is appropriate and necessary to stabilize the quilt. If skillfully done with period fabric, it should not affect the value significantly. Depending on the quilt, restitching is acceptable if it's well executed, as are commonly replaced edge bindings, which are often worn from years of handling. Some quilts may have such extensive fabric erosion, however, that restoration would not bring it back to its original condition."

If your heart is set on a folk portrait, you'll want to inspect it with similar care and caution before you cast your first bid. Throughout America's history, wealthy families commissioned portraits of their loved ones for posterity, particularly before the invention of the daguerreotype (the first photograph) in 1839.

Folk portraits were created mainly during the 18th and 19th centuries by nonacademic artists, many of them anonymous. Although these artists did not attend traditional art schools, they trained as apprentices to accomplished professionals. The most sought-after examples are those by well-known painters such as John Brewster, Jr., who worked in Connecticut and Maine during the late-18th and early-19th centuries; Ammi Phillips of Connecticut, Massachusetts, and New York; and Joseph Steward of Connecticut. Prices range from a few thousand dollars for a good-quality single portrait to several hundred thousand for family groupings and exceptional examples by noted painters.

"As with any art form, a folk portrait should first of all please your sense of aesthetic," says Patrick Bell. "Some sitters are more physically appealing than others. Many collectors prefer portraits that depict small children in period costume holding an animal, toy, flowers, or other accessory. In descending order of preference and price are, generally, pretty young women in elegant period costume, followed by young men and older folks. That said, I'd rather have an attractive old man than a hideous child. I'd also rather own a great portrait by an anonymous artist than a poorly executed signed piece."

The best folk portraits exhibit a certain freshness and purity of vision, an unselfconscious naïveté that is lacking in other types of paintings. Once you've made an aesthetic judgment, you'll want to ascertain that the painting is in original condition.

"Ask the auction expert to show you the work under ultraviolet light," Druckman advises. "The paint fluoresces darker in areas if it's been retouched."

"But ultraviolet light is not foolproof," Bell adds. "A painting may be glazed over time with layers of varnish, which conceals restorations. Look at it under bright sunlight. The shinier the finish, the more suspect the painting is."

Certain defects like fine cracks are to be expected on old paintings and are useful indicators of authenticity.

"You should see some honest wear and tear, whether it's surface grime, a small area of paint loss or abrasion around the edges of the canvas where it's been framed," says Merrilee J. Possner, an American folk-art specialist at Northeast Auctions. "These aspects help to distinguish the real thing from a fake."

Portrait of a boy, attributed to Joseph Whiting Stock (American, 1815–1855), the subject shown full-length wearing a striped green shirt with white ruffle collar and blue pants holding a whip in his right hand, his black dog at his left, in an ornate interior, c. 1840. Unsigned, identified on exhibition label on the stretcher. Oil on canvas, height 49", width 40", in a period-style frame. Condition: Good, lined/re-stretched, scattered retouch, craquelure. Provenance: Collection of Edith Gregor Halpert; Nathan S. Kline. Exhibitions: Initial Loan Exhibition of the Museum of Early American Folk Arts, New York, October 5–November 18, 1962. Auction estimate: $15,000–25,000. Price realized: $18,400. (Courtesy Skinner, Boston) The word attributed is used in the catalogue description because this painting is unsigned, although Skinner folk-art specialists believe it to be the work of Joseph Whiting Stock, a well known folk portraitist who worked in Connecticut, Massachusetts, and Rhode Island during the early-19th century. This portrait is desirable for several reasons. Children depicted in personalized settings with pets and other accessories are often the most sought-after folk-portrait subjects. The painting's exhibition history enhances its value, as does its provenance. Edith Gregor Halpert was a major collector, dealer, and leader in the American folk-art movement during the 1920s. Additionally, this portrait was part of a single-owner sale of folk art from the collection of Marna Anderson, herself a noted American folk-art dealer and collector. Single-owner sales of notable collections attract attention because of the generally high quality of the offerings. The condition is listed as good. The term lined means that a backing has been added to the canvas to stabilize it. Unlined canvases are rare and more desirable. This canvas also needed to be restretched or flattened. The term craquelure refers to the small cracks on the paint surface that indicate age and do not generally alter the value of an old painting.

Painted furniture, another common American folk-art form, is particularly susceptible to faking.

"The market for painted tables, chairs, blanket chests, cupboards, and boxes has been glutted with fakes since the early 1980s," Bell says. "Some forgers have repainted stripped pieces using 19th-century paint formulas. Skilled restoration, on the other hand, is acceptable. Sometimes it's necessary to enhance the original color, since pieces that have retained most of their original paint are rare. If you want a true antique, you may want to pay for the advice of an expert who will analyze the piece before you bid on it."

Painted furniture was constructed of modest woods such as pine and poplar, by either local cabinetmakers or untrained artisans, and painted with bright colors to enliven the dark interiors typical of old rural American homes. The most desirable pieces have retained most of their original paint. Some forms, such as blanket chests, may also be decorated with geometric, floral, or pictorial patterns, or graining to resemble wood, which often enhances their

Painted and decorated chest over
drawer, New England, c. 1830. The hinged top opens
to an interior with molded lidded till above a single drawer
on bracket feet with shaped sides, original vinegar-grained red and yellow surface,
replaced brass, height 31", width 36⅝", depth 18¼". Auction estimate:
$4,000–$6,000. Price realized: $7,475. (Courtesy Skinner, Boston) "This is a fine
example of folk-art furniture," says Martha Hamilton, an American folk-art specialist
at Skinner. "Its wonderful form, vibrant colors, and grain-painted decoration make
it aesthetically pleasing. Applying a grained-wood pattern on a solid ground was
an inexpensive way to simulate expensive imported woods like mahogany. The
replaced brass pulls are appropriate because they closely approximate the form of
the original pulls and fit in the original holes."

value. Painted furniture can be classified according to period, region, and style.

"Furniture made by the Dunlap family of New Hampshire at the turn of the century is noted for its faux graining and unique cornices and carvings on the aprons and drawers," Possner says. "Schoolgirl-painted furniture usually depicts baskets, flowers, and shells. Painted furniture made in the Connecticut River Valley during the 18th and 19th centuries displays representational motifs like suns and flowers, which imitate early carved pieces, while 19th-century painted furniture from Maine is noted for its flamboyant colors."

Auction prices for painted furniture range from a few thousand dollars up to $100,000, depending on the size of the piece, whether or not it can be attributed to a specific maker or region, and the extent of vibrancy and decoration.

"Red is the most common color. Blue-and-yellow painted pieces are more scarce," notes Bell. "Read the auction catalogue descriptions carefully. A 'blue-painted blanket chest' is not as desirable as a 'blanket chest with original blue paint.' You should always look for the word 'original.' Original hardware also enhances the value. Another thing to look for is whether or not the piece you desire has a noteworthy provenance. If it's part of a well-known collection like the Little collection of American folk art, which sold at Sotheby's, it's more likely to be legitimate and good than if it's listed under a 'various owners' heading in the catalogue. This applies to all areas of art and antiques, not just folk art."

Sotheby's Druckman notes that the market for sculptural American folk-art forms like cigar-store figures, carved ships' figureheads, and weathervanes has recently been strong because of their bold, graphic quality and compact size, which make them adaptable to a variety of interiors.

"Many of the best weathervanes on the market are three-dimensional copper-molded or flat sheet-iron forms made by New England factories like A. L. Jewell and J. Howard and Company from the mid- to late-19th century," Druckman says. "The most common forms are horses and barn animals like chickens, roosters, and cows. Rare subjects like tennis players, for example, or a centaur, American Indian, or Statue of Liberty, bring higher prices."

The value of a weathervane is also determined by the quality of its surface.

"If you plan to bid on a weathervane, look for evidence of its original surface," Bell advises. "Weathervanes are easy to regild. There are a lot of weathervanes on the market that have been overly re-

Rooster weathervane, molded and sheet copper with an old weathered-paint finish, anonymous American maker, c. 1875. $9,500, (Courtesy Olde Hope Antiques, Inc., New Hope, PA) While roosters are not a rare weathervane form, this example is desirable because of its large size (height 36") and detailed surface embellishment. Most weathervanes were painted after years of weathering. This rooster has a visually interesting surface that shows both paint weathering and a copper patina. Its resoldered tail is an old repair made while the weathervane was still in use.

stored and made to look like they have old gold finishes. Some have fake green surfaces meant to imitate a naturally oxidized copper patina."

Early weathervanes with rare form and in good condition will bring the highest prices. Three-dimensional copper-molded vanes are generally more expensive than two-dimensional iron vanes. Although a horse-and-rider weathervane by J. Howard and Company with its original surface sold at Sotheby's in 1990 for a record $770,000, you can still find authentic antique weathervanes at auction for several hundred to a few thousand dollars.

Decoys are another indigenous American art form that is rapidly increasing in value. Long collected by hunters, conservationists, and wildfowl enthusiasts, they have begun to attract folk-art collectors who value the carvings' agrarian, grassroots history and sculptural quality. A sleeping Canada Goose by the renowned carver Elmer Crowell of East Harwich, Massachusetts, circa 1917, set an auction world record for a decoy when it sold for $684,500 at Sotheby's in early 2000.

Other types of American folk art available at auction are needlework samplers made by young schoolgirls during the 18th and 19th centuries, many of which are signed and dated; hooked rugs in lively floral, geometric, and pictorial patterns; wool and cotton handwoven coverlets (bed coverings); salt-glazed, cobalt-blue-decorated stoneware vessels; 19th-century carved and painted wooden gameboards; and tramp art—frames, boxes, furniture, and other utilitarian objects decorated with multiple layers of chip-carved wood.

Whether you are buying a single American folk-art object or beginning a collection, any collector will tell you that the process of identifying, evaluating, and pursuing your object of desire is, first of all, a labor of love.

"You should buy things that make you smile," says Dr. Robert Booth of Philadelphia, an orthopedic surgeon, past president of the American Folk Art Society, and, along with his wife, Katherine, an avid American folk-art collector. "I work in a dreary realm of stainless steel and operating-room efficiency. But coming home to folk art is like walking into a new world. It's colorful and fun, and adds a whimsical dimension to our lives. True collectors are emotionally attached to the objects they collect. They'd almost rather forsake their firstborn child than a prized antique."

Dealers and collectors agree that even if you don't plan to collect, education is the best weapon when buying at auction.

"When we first started going to auctions, we bought a lot of lesser examples by great artists, and then learned to trade up, or sell off those pieces and acquire better examples," notes Booth, whose world-class collection of folk portraits, quilts, fire-fighting-related items, and Shaker furniture is constantly evolving. "But it's always 'caveat emptor' at auction houses. They stand behind their offerings for the most part, but it's important to view the object in person before the sale, touch it, and discuss it with the auction specialist, and even call in a dealer, curator, or restoration expert to confirm its authenticity. You're more likely to find fakes among the rarest, most sought-after antiques, because they bring the highest prices."

"I have seen grievous errors in auction-house catalogues. Don't buy anything without sufficient knowledge of its history, condition, and market value," Bell adds. "If it seems like too good a deal, it's usually not a good deal."

✦✦✦✦✦✦✦✦

SALES OF AMERICAN FOLK ART AT SELECTED AUCTION HOUSES:

- SOTHEBY'S—January, October; June sale on Sothebys.com
- CHRISTIE'S—January, June, October
- NORTHEAST AUCTIONS—March, August, November
- SKINNER—February, June, August, October
- GARTH'S AUCTIONS—twelve to fifteen times per year
- POOK & POOK—five to eight times per year

RECOMMENDED MUSEUM COLLECTIONS:

- Museum of American Folk Art, New York, NY
- New England Quilt Museum, Lowell, MA
- Shelburne Museum, Shelburne, VT
- New York State Historical Association, Cooperstown, NY
- Abby Aldrich Rockefeller Folk Art Center, Williamsburg, VA
- The National Museum of American Art, Smithsonian Institution, Washington, D.C.

Market Watch
AMERICAN VERNACULAR ART

An extension of the American folk-art tradition, American vernacular art, which includes self-taught and outsider art, has been attracting a growing number of collectors since the early-20th century, when the French artist and collector Jean Dubuffet began to popularize what he called "art brut" or raw art.

Self-taught art refers to art made by individuals without formal art training who exist outside the art historical continuum. Outsider art refers more specifically to work made by those who are mentally challenged. Dubuffet's original definition of *art brut* encompassed art created by all sorts of culturally isolated and marginalized individuals, including prisoners, visionaries, and religious eccentrics.

Although groundbreaking exhibitions such as those organized in the 1930s by New York art dealer Sidney Janis and the Museum of Modern Art and "Black Folk Art In America," presented in 1981 by Washington's Corcoran Gallery of Art, brought renewed recognition to the field, the market for American vernacular art is still in its infancy.

"This art is the new truth," says Frank Maresca of New York City's Ricco/Maresca Gallery, one of the first to exhibit self-taught and outsider art. "And it's affordable. You can buy a world-class masterpiece by a blue-chip artist for around $75,000. That's a bargain when you consider that you'd spend millions for a work of comparable quality in fields like Modern and Impressionist art."

Among the most notable self-taught artists are Bill Traylor, an ex-slave from Montgomery, Alabama, who began making drawings of local street life on pieces of discarded cardboard in 1939 at age eighty-five, and William Hawkins, who in his seventies began painting architectural, figurative, and biblical scenes with enamel paint on masonite and cardboard. Their best

Eddie Arning, *Three Girls,* c. 1972, crayon/craypas on paper, height 19", width 25". (Courtesy Ricco/Maresca Gallery, New York)

works are now worth up to $200,000 and $50,000, respectively. Eddie Arning of Texas, who makes drawings based on magazine and newspaper advertisements, and Dwight Macintosh, noted for his powerful portrait drawings and watercolors, are outsider artists whose work can be found at auction from about $2,500 to $8,000.

Chapter 2
AMERICAN FURNITURE

The market for antique American furniture is stronger than ever, as established and new collectors alike compete for top-quality pieces from all periods, whether it's a Queen Anne chest of drawers, a Chippendale tea table, a Federal sideboard, or a Windsor chair. A robust national economy, along with numerous books, exhibitions, and the popular PBS television program *Antiques Roadshow* have made American antiques more accessible to an increasingly educated public. And there is always the added allure of owning a piece of American history.

"While American antiques of great quality and condition bring extraordinary prices, there are still many affordable pieces waiting to be discovered at auction," says Stephen Fletcher, head of Americana at Skinner in Boston. "If you're willing to settle for some minor restorations, you could spend less than $5,000 for, say, a refinished Chippendale birch bureau with replaced brasses. The same bureau with its original surface and brasses would be worth about $10,000 or more. The type of wood used also affects the price. Birch and maple, for example, are generally less expensive woods than cherry and mahogany. My advice to new collectors is to buy the best you can afford and be eclectic in your tastes, meaning don't confine yourself to one period or style. When you have more to choose from, you are more likely to find something within your budget."

Whether you want to collect American antiques or simply decorate your home with a few choice pieces, experts agree that quality of craftsmanship and design, rarity, authenticity, and condition are the most important criteria to consider when evaluating the object of your desire, whatever the style or period. But first you must train your eye and sharpen your judgment.

"If you want to buy at auction, you should compile a library of references on the type of antiques that interest you. Then you should visit museums and galleries, and attend auctions for at least a year before bidding on anything, so that you can develop a men-

tal library," advises John B. A. Nye, director of American furniture at Sotheby's. "And talk to as many curators, collectors, dealers, and auction specialists as possible. When you're looking at a piece of furniture at the auction preview, you'll want to know how, when, and where it was made, and who made it. Although the majority of American furniture is anonymously crafted, some pieces are attributed to well-known cabinetmakers such as the Seymours of Boston or Goddard and Townsend of Newport, Rhode Island, which increases their value. But a labeled and signed object is only worth more when the craftsmanship and condition are first rate. Knowledgeable collectors won't pay a premium just for the label."

American furniture is categorized according to style, period, and the region or city in which it was made. Formal Queen Anne and Chippendale furniture made for wealthy families in the thriving colonial cities of Philadelphia and Newport, which produced many skilled craftsman, have traditionally been among the most sought-after and expensive American antiques. Early-20th-century collectors such as Henry Francis du Pont and Henry Ford were among the first to recognize the historical importance of these pieces, which have brought some of the highest prices at auction.

In general, American Queen Anne furniture, which dates from about 1730 to 1760, was made mostly of walnut, maple, and cherry, and is characterized by graceful S-curves and elegant cabriole legs in less opulent expression than its English counterpart. Chippendale furniture, which dates from about 1750 to 1790, was made mostly of expensive mahogany and is distinguished by rich carving and claw-and-ball feet. Each colonial cabinetmaking center produced its own stylistic innovations.

Replacing the Rococo curves of the Chippendale style was the more restrained furniture of the Federal period, which dates from about 1790 to 1830. Federal furniture is an interpretation of English and French designs of the mid- to late-18th century that were inspired by classical Greco-Roman forms. Although furniture from these periods is among the best known and most easily recognized, there are of course other styles both before Queen Anne and after Federal that you will also want to research.

Auction houses such as Christie's, Sotheby's, Skinner, Northeast Auctions, Garth's, and Pook & Pook offer among the broadest and finest selections of antique American furniture in all forms, including chests of drawers, sideboards, bookcases, secretaries, highboys and lowboys, and a variety of tables and chairs.

"With any type of American furniture, you should always ask the same basic questions," Fletcher says. "Has there been any restoration? If it's a table or a sideboard, are the legs and the top original? If it's a highboy or a secretary, do the drawers work? Are the same woods used for the top and bottom components, or is the unit a 'marriage,' meaning that it's been constructed from two different pieces of furniture? Are the brasses original, or have they been replaced? Has the piece been recarved? Is it well-proportioned? All these factors affect the value."

"The line and design of the furniture is very important. The first thing I look at is the proportion, the overall aesthetic harmony of the piece," notes American-furniture dealer Wayne Pratt of Woodbury, Connecticut, and Nantucket, Massachusetts. "Then I look at the surface. An original old surface or patina that hasn't been tampered with increases the value of American furniture from all periods. Of course, some people don't like rustic old surfaces, so they buy stripped pieces that have been refinished with new varnishes. But many collectors prefer the old patina and avoid refinished pieces. Enhancing the surface of an antique with a little cleaning and rewaxing is acceptable, however, and won't significantly affect the value."

Chippendale tea tables are a popular form that turns up frequently at auction. They were made throughout the colonies in different shapes and sizes ranging from about 20 to 36 inches in diameter. New England tea tables are usually rectangular in shape, while tea tables made in New York and Pennsylvania are circular. The region in which a piece was made can affect its value. Collectors generally will pay more for Chippendale furniture from Philadelphia or Newport, homes to some of the finest colonial cabinet-makers. A Boston collector, however, may choose to collect only homegrown pieces. The majority of tea tables date from 1730 to about 1790, when tea drinking among wealthy colonists became less popular.

Chippendale mahogany tilt-top tea table, southern New England, c. 1780, the circular top tips on a baluster-box support and vase-and-ring-turned post ending in tripod cabriole-leg base on claw-and-ball feet, old refinish, (imperfections), height 29", diameter 34¾". Auction estimate: $1500–$2500. Price realized: $2,070. (Courtesy Skinner, Boston) This tea table has nicely carved claw-and-ball feet and an attractive grain. However, condition flaws such as cracks and a wood patch on the top contributed to the low price.

"The quality of a Chippendale tea table is reflected in the proportion, the type of wood used, and the extent of carving. Is it made from domestically grown walnut or first-rate, dense, imported mahogany? Mahogany tea tables are more desirable to many collectors and bring higher prices," Nye advises. "Assuming graceful proportions, harmony of design, and quality craftsmanship, the more carving there is, the more valuable the tea table. Circular tabletops, for example, with elaborate piecrust edges bring more than those with molded edges or no embellishment at all. Does the table have an undecorated standard—the columnar support—or one that is highly turned and carved? Does it have plain cabriole legs or carved knees and claw-and-ball feet? Expertly carved feet show a tension between the claw and ball."

You'll also want to know whether the table has a stationary top or a tilt top. The most sophisticated examples tilt and revolve on a support called a "bird-cage." Remember that auction specialists are available at the preview (presale exhibition) to answer your questions. They'll point you to the best examples, help you improve your collection, inform you about items of interest that will be offered in future sales, apprise you of the market, and advise you on consigning objects for sale.

Once you've determined that a particular tea table meets all your aesthetic requirements, you'll also want to examine its condition before you place your first bid.

"As with other forms, make sure that the top and legs haven't been replaced, that the legs haven't been shortened, and that parts of the table haven't been re-carved, or carved for the first time at a later date," says Frank Levy of New York City's Bernard & S. Dean Levy, longtime American-furniture dealers. "A table with its original finish shows its age and authenticity. Original finishes generally enhance value, particularly on furniture made during early periods like Chippendale and Queen Anne."

The integrity of a piece's form is crucial to its value. A replaced leg on a rare tea table of impeccable quality may not reduce its value dramatically, whereas the same restoration on a tea table of lesser quality will be much less tolerable. You should expect to see chips, cracks, scratches, and some shrinkage, however, on all antiques. These acceptable blemishes are good indicators of age and authenticity and do not affect value significantly.

"If you're willing to compromise on condition, you're likely to find some incredible buys," notes Fletcher. "Don't feel excluded from the market just because you may not be a collector or don't wish to begin a collection. You can pick up a good tea table with minimal carving and a major restoration like a replaced leg for a small fraction of the price of a top-quality example. Pieces with minor restorations like wood patching will also bring lower prices. You have to decide whether you can live with the flaws. With any piece of furniture, don't look at what's missing; look at what's left. If a significant amount of the piece is original, go for it."

The best approach to buying any piece of antique American furniture is to ask yourself whether it's believable, and therefore authentic. Do all the parts make sense? Each form has its own pitfalls.

"With tea tables, the top and base should be made of the same wood. You don't want to see a mahogany top on a walnut base, for example, which indicates that one part was added later," Nye counsels. "There should also be evidence that the top and base have been interacting together for a long time, evidence of years of friction, which points to an authentic antique table. One way to determine this is to look for circular bruises made by the columns of the bird cage on the underside of the top. Another indication of age is that the top will be what we call 'out of round,' mean-ing that the diameter across the grain will measure slightly smaller than the diameter with the grain. That's because wood shrinks with age across the grain. This disparity is almost impossible to spot with the naked eye, so you should bring a measuring tape with you to the preview, or ask the auction specialist to measure the table for you. The turned standard also becomes out of round with age; it should not feel completely circular when you rotate your hand around it. This is true of lathe-turned elements on furniture from any period."

It's always a good idea to come prepared to the auction preview, where you'll want to inspect as closely as possible the pieces that interest you. In addition to a measuring tape, you may want to bring a magnifying glass, a flashlight, or even a high-intensity photography lamp such as dealers often use. Some dealers and collectors bring screwdrivers so that they can disassemble furniture. A tea-table top, for example, is attached to its base with cleats. When you unscrew the cleats, you should see screw holes that have become deformed or out-of-round with age. Even a simple straight pin can help you evaluate the authenticity of furniture. An old piece often has small wormholes on its surface. If you put a pin into one of these holes, and it slides straight in, you'll know that the holes have been fabricated. Worms don't make straight holes.

"When buying American furniture, it's as important to see with your hands as it is with your eyes," Nye observes. "Don't be afraid to touch the pieces, turn them around, lift them up, and even take them apart. One of the benefits of the preview is that you can study the furniture from the inside out, back to front, bottom to top. That's how you'll start to notice restorations."

You should also read the auction catalogue carefully. The more complete the description, the more likely it is that the object has remained relatively unchanged since the day it was made. In Sotheby's catalogues, for example, a piece described as a *Chippendale Mahogany Tea Table, Philadelphia, circa 1760–80* means that in the opinion of the auction house the piece is "of the period indicated with no major alterations or restorations." A piece listed as a *Chippendale Mahogany Tea Table,* without a date, means that, while of the period, it has undergone a significant restoration such as a replaced leg, or may have been constructed from old parts. A piece listed as a *Chippendale-Style Mahogany Tea Table* indicates that it is an intentional reproduction of an earlier style. In general, the closer a piece is to its original state, the higher its value.

As with most art and antiques, provenance (ownership history) can also enhance value. If an object's provenance is known, it is usually listed in the catalogue description. All things being equal, a Chippendale tea table that has come from an important collection such as that of the late Henry Francis du Pont, for example, or has descended from an historically important family or a famous American president, is more desirable than a tea table with a less significant provenance or no provenance at all. Since the exact ownership history of an object is often difficult to trace, the majority of American antiques at auction do not carry noteworthy provenances. In some cases, the catalogue description includes an object's exhibition and publication histories, which also adds to its cachet.

Auction-house catalogues may or may not describe the condition of their offerings. Sotheby's catalogues, for example, list major condition problems in italics at the end of a catalogue entry. Some descriptions may mention, for example, that a piece "appears to retain original cast-brass hardware and finish." For a more detailed description of an object's condition, you should request a written condition report, available at most established auction houses.

Many auction houses sell merchandise "as is," meaning that they do not hold themselves responsible for the condition and authenticity of their offerings, although they try to research each object as accurately as possible. Some auction houses guarantee for a limited period of time the information that appears in bold print in their catalogues (usually a simple identification of the object such as *Chippendale Mahogany Tea Table.*) Be sure to read the conditions and terms of sale printed in the auction catalogue.

Because of the large quantity of items that must be researched and catalogued for an auction, mistakes are sometimes made. As in most collecting fields, you may discover an occasional fake, particularly when prices begin to increase significantly for certain objects. But experts say a fake American antique is extremely difficult to manufacture.

"You really can't make new wood look old, although fakers have tried everything from hammering wood to burying it underground or tossing it into the ocean. When wood ages properly, it mellows and often takes on a darker hue from oxidation," notes Levy.

While you may never come into contact with a fake, you should proceed with caution when buying at auction. Consult a knowledgeable dealer, especially if you're planning to spend a large sum, and you're a first-time bidder.

"It is not uncommon for an auction house to allow items of questionable quality into their sales in order to increase volume," Levy says. "And the fact that some items are withdrawn before a sale should indicate that you should seek other opinions about your potential purchase."

Many dealers are willing to accompany you to a preview and even to bid on your behalf for a small fee, usually a percentage of the hammer price. A dealer will help you distinguish better from lesser examples, identify sleepers or undervalued items, provide you with information on the marketplace, and advise you on the price you should expect to pay.

"I only advise clients to buy pieces at auction that I would be interested in owning," Pratt says. "And I will recommend a reasonable purchase price so that the client will be able to resell the item in the future if necessary. I've watched a lot of people pay more than they should."

While an exquisitely carved Chippendale piecrust tea table in the Philadelphia Rococo style sold at Christie's in 1995 for $2.4 million, a good-quality uncarved Chippendale tea table with cabriole legs (versus the more sophisticated claw-and-ball foot) and made of indigenous woods (versus the more expensive imported mahogany) can be bought at auction for $1,000 to $3,000.

As more collectors compete for the best American antiques, certain forms such as Philadelphia Chippendale piecrust tea tables and Newport block-front and shell-carved furniture are becoming increasingly rare, and prices have skyrocketed as a result. A Chippendale mahogany block-and-shell desk-and-bookcase crafted by John Goddard, which sold at Christie's in 1989 for $12.1 million, holds the record auction price for American furniture.

If your heart is set on a Federal sideboard as the perfect pièce de resistance for your new dining room, you can breathe a sigh of relief that you won't have to break your bank. While the same general criteria of connoisseurship already mentioned apply to all American antiques, each form has its own specific value determinants. Many sideboards were made along the East Coast during the Federal period, when dining rooms began to appear in American homes, and they turn up frequently at auction.

"During the Federal period, the aesthetic shifted from the heavily carved furniture of the preceding Chippendale period to lighter, more streamlined pieces embellished with inlay and highly figured veneers. Since decoration takes the form of surface ornamentation, proportion is more obvious, and it's crucial to the success of a Federal sideboard," says Nye. "A sideboard is essentially a large storage cabinet supported by narrow legs. There must be a harmonious balance between the size of the case and the height and thickness of the legs. And the inlay should accentuate the design. When you see this symphony of successful design elements, the sideboard really sings."

Federal mahogany inlaid sideboard and butler's desk, Boston area, early 19th century, the elliptical top with an inlaid edge overhanging a case of veneered cockbeaded drawers, and end cupboards outlined with stringing and having bone-inlaid escutcheons as well as a central hinged drawer opening to an interior of small drawers and open compartments with a feltlined writing surface, above a working drawer and an arched skirt outlined with patterned inlay, set on square tapering legs outlined with stringing and ending in cuff inlays, original surface, replaced brass, height 41", length 62", depth 24". Auction estimate: $8,000–$12,000. Price realized: $14,950. (Courtesy Skinner, Boston) "For the price, you can't beat this piece," says Fletcher. "It's relatively plain, with beautifully matched mahogany veneers."

The amount and type of inlay on a sideboard affects its value. Assuming quality craftsmanship, desirable proportions, and good condition, intricately embellished sideboards often fetch higher prices than pieces with minimal decoration. Pictorial inlays depicting urns, flowers, and eagles, among other motifs, are generally more rare and desirable than geometric inlays. Most Federal sideboards are made of poplar or pine covered with mahogany veneers. Highly figured crotch-mahogany veneers are more desirable than dull, flat mahogany and will enhance a sideboard's value, as will the use of an unusual wood such as tiger maple, which has a beautiful, striped grain.

"While it's usually preferable to buy an American antique with its original finish intact, this factor is not as critical to the value of Federal furniture as it is to earlier pieces," Levy notes. "Federal sideboards were often cleaned and revarnished over the years, because successive owners wanted the decoration to be as visible as possible. So their surfaces may not appear as old as they actually are."

Federal sideboards were made in different shapes and sizes, with either four, six, or eight legs. You will see rectangular, bowed, and serpentine cases. While small sideboards, which average about six feet in width, have always been sought after, larger sideboards have become more popular as people seek to decorate large homes. Diminutive sideboards, about five feet in width, are rare and tend to fetch the highest prices because they adapt to a variety of spaces.

As with American furniture of every form and period, there are certain condition pitfalls that you will want to avoid when deciding which sideboard to buy at auction.

"Be wary of sideboards with replaced tops and legs, which can reduce the value by as much as half or more. Also beware of legs that have been extended or cut down from their original height," Nye advises. "A sideboard in original condition may have cuffs at the base of the leg that generally wrap around three sides. If you see a four-sided cuff, it may be hiding a seam where the leg has been extended. Be sure that the wood grain above and below the cuff looks the same. Since not every sideboard was crafted in high style, you may also come across minimally decorated pieces that were inlaid at a later date. It takes a lot of knowledge and a fine-tuned eye to recognize these alterations. Don't be afraid to ask the auction specialists for advice at the preview."

While Federal sideboards have sold for more than $200,000 at auction, you can find a simple but elegant period example for less than $10,000. The best sideboards are expertly crafted, show a harmony of design and proportion, are imaginatively inlaid with superior woods, and have retained their original patinas. Priced as low as $4,000 to $6,000, oversize sideboards of good quality are still an excellent buy, according to Fletcher, as are minimally decorated pieces made around 1820 during the late Federal period. Sideboards crafted outside urban cabinetmaking centers in rural areas throughout the East Coast and Midwest also bring lower prices. Formal city furniture was more labor intensive, displays more decoration, and

Painted fan-back Windsor armchair, probably Connecticut, c. 1790–1800, the serpentine crest with scroll-carved ears above seven spindles continuing through the arm crest, with carved, scrolled, knuckled handholds on vase and ring-turned supports, the carved, incised saddle seat on splayed vase and ring-turned legs joined by turned swelled stretchers, old green paint, height 42", seat height 17 1/2". Provenance: Samaha & Son Antiques, Milan, Ohio. Auction estimate: $20,000–$25,000. Price realized: $51,750. (Courtesy Skinner, Boston) "This is the best fan-back Windsor we've auctioned in years," Fletcher says. "It has a beautiful form, wonderful vase and ring turnings, a nicely carved saddle seat, and splayed legs. And it still has its original worn green paint. It brought a strong price, but deserved it. The fact that it was once owned by a reputable Americana dealer made it even more desirable."

weight pine or poplar was often used for the seat, while strong hickory was used for the spindles; and maple was chosen for the leg and arm supports because it is easily turned (carved) on a lathe.

There are several different forms of Windsor chair, including bow-back, sack-back, fan-back, and comb-back, one of the most sought-after forms that is considered by many experts to be the quintessential expression of the mid-18th-century Philadelphia Windsor aesthetic. You'll want to evaluate the Windsor chair you plan to bid on with the same attention to craftsmanship and design that you would apply to other American antiques.

"Windsor chairs usually have ring-turned legs and stretchers. Look at the quality of the turnings. Are

Painted sack-back Windsor armchair, attributed to Amos D. Allen, Windham, Connecticut, c. 1780, the bowed crest rail joining eleven spindles and shaped arms resting on vase and ring-turned supports, the saddle seat on splayed vase and ring-turned legs joined by bulbous stretchers, old black paint with gilt striping, height 35", seat height 15 1/2". Auction estimate: $2,500–$3,500. Price realized: $4,025. (Courtesy Skinner, Boston) "This is a great example of a Windsor sack-back chair. The fact that it is attributed to a specific maker enhances its value," notes Fletcher. "This chair carried a lower estimate and brought a much lower price than the Windsor fan-back because sack-backs are a more common form. It's also slightly heavier and plainer than the other chair, and its stretchers aren't as finely carved."

incorporates more expensive woods such as mahogany.

Perhaps you're in the market for a Windsor chair, another sought-after American antique that is plentiful at auction. A version of an English form, the American Windsor chair was first made in Philadelphia in the mid-18th century, and continued to be made throughout the colonies until the mid-19th century. Unlike Queen Anne chairs, for example, which were crafted entirely of either mahogany, walnut, or birch, Windsor chairs were made from different types of wood that were best suited to different structural parts. These chairs were always painted, so it was not essential for the wood to be uniform. Light-

they dramatic? The best chairs have exaggerated bulbous sections and equally exaggerated concave sections with razor-sharp edges—what we call 'thick thicks,' and 'thin thins,'" Nye observes. "Is the seat simply a large slab of wood, or is it shaped and scooped out? The more dramatic the curves, the more visually interesting and desirable the chair. Do the hand-holds or arm terminals look like amorphous paddles, or do they have beautifully carved knuckles that turn out and sweep away from the chair?"

One of the most important value determinants for Windsor chairs is the extent to which they have retained their original paint. Red-, green-, and black-painted Windsor chairs are more common than yellow- and blue painted examples. The more visible the original paint (or layers of paint that may have accumulated over the years) the more valuable the chair. Although paint loss due to normal wear and tear on the seat, hand-holds, legs, and stretchers is acceptable, chairs that have been entirely stripped of their paint are less desirable.

"During the mid-20th century when Scandinavian teak and other blond woods were popular, stripping Windsor chairs became fashionable," says Nye. "Then people became skilled at repainting the stripped chairs. Fakers got carried away with creating the illusion of wear. Remember that original Windsor chairs were intentionally painted to create a uniform surface to disguise the different woods used. You need to look closely at the paint. Is it believable? Go with your gut instinct. If you see a dent that has been painted, you know it's not right. A true dent would show paint loss. Look at the wear patterns on the chair. You would only want to see paint loss in areas that have been touched by the human body."

You'll also want to avoid Windsor chairs with extended legs; replaced spindles, crests, and seats; and false labels on the undersides of seats. Some fakers have branded recognized chairmakers' names on later chairs.

Windsor chairs are not only plentiful at auction, they are also affordable. While top-quality examples such as a Philadelphia comb-back Windsor with most of its original paint have brought $50,000 and more, you can find a good, period Windsor for less than $5,000. Refinished Windsors (without their original paint) sell for less than $2,000; some refinished Windsor sidechairs can be bought for a few hundred dollars.

Among the many other affordable American antiques available at auction are simple, country Queen Anne and Chippendale side chairs from the second half of the 18th century, which sell for a few hundred dollars. Plain Federal inlaid-mahogany card tables, which can be used as side tables, bring from $1,500 to $3,500, whereas you would pay double or triple that price range for a card table with a serpentine front and more inlay. If your taste tends more toward the ornate, Victorian furniture such as Rococo Revival parlor tables and ladies' and gentlemen's chairs can be bought for less than $1,000, a real bargain, according to Fletcher. Perhaps you're restoring a Victorian home. You'll find good-quality marble-topped Rococo or Renaissance Revival bedroom sets at auction for $2,500 to $5,000.

"People always say they can't afford to buy antiques," Fletcher says. "But the truth is that you can furnish your entire home with antique American furniture, albeit not necessarily collector's items but simple, finely crafted pieces, for less than you would spend on new furniture."

Says New York businessman and American-furniture collector Daniel Checki: "When I first started collecting years ago, I focused on a period that I could afford. Federal pieces at that time were less expensive than earlier Queen Anne and Chippendale furniture. I also tried to go after things that no one else seemed to want, like Chippendale sidechairs made in New York, which are generally less expensive than Philadelphia Chippendale chairs. A dealer once advised me to 'zig when others are zagging.' Auction houses tend to market certain types of furniture more aggressively than others. If you pay attention, you can find some good buys among periods and styles that aren't being hyped at a particular moment in time."

Now that you've done your research and consulted the experts, you're ready to bid on the Chippendale tea table, Federal sideboard, or Windsor chair of your dreams.

"My first few times at auction, I bid with a paddle like most people, but then I realized I had a habit of leaving my paddle up, and spending more than I had intended, so I changed to bidding with my hand or a pen. If you're not in control of your body language, you could make an expensive mistake," Checki notes. "Make definitive gestures. Remember that auctions move quickly. Auctioneers like to play with you and try to push you to bid higher. They're very personable up there on the podium, but they are not your friends. They want to get the highest possible price. My friend once pointed to the seat in front of him, and the auctioneer took it as a bid. Auctions are also fun. I like the bidding competition and trying to find the sleepers, pieces that others have overlooked. The worst thing, though, is to buy something and then hear the audience applaud. That usually means that you got caught up in the drama and overpaid."

Savvy auctiongoers also caution neophyte buyers against falling into the underbidder security trap. Just because several bidders really wanted that Windsor chair does not mean that you should feel confident that you won a gem. The fact that you emerged as the highest bidder also does not mean that the chair deserves the price you paid. In the heat of competition, there is always a chance that egos and emotions will prevail over good judgment.

And don't think that you landed a good buy because you outbid a dealer. It is true that when dealers buy for stock they will not bid beyond a certain level because they have to resell those antiques at mark-up prices. But dealers also bid for private collectors, some of whom know no limit when it comes to acquiring a coveted object.

"It's important to set your price limit before you start bidding, and stick to it. Know what you should pay and why you should pay it, and be willing to let the piece go when prices escalate beyond your level," Pratt counsels. "Don't be competitive just because you may have a lot of money to spend, and don't buy anything that you haven't examined in person before the sale, or have not had an expert examine for you."

RECOMMENDED MUSEUM COLLECTIONS:

- The Metropolitan Museum of Art, New York, NY
- Philadelphia Museum of Art, Philadelphia, PA
- Winterthur Museum & Gardens, Winterthur, DE
- Museum of Fine Arts, Boston, MA
- Bayou Bend, Museum of Fine Arts, Houston, TX
- Shelburne Museum, Shelburne, VT
- The Henry Ford Museum and Greenfield Village, Dearborn, MI

SALES OF AMERICAN FURNITURE AT SELECTED AUCTION HOUSES:

- SOTHEBY'S—January, October
- CHRISTIE'S—January, October
- SKINNER—February, June, August, October
- NORTHEAST AUCTIONS—March, August, November
- GARTH'S—10 to 12 sales per year
- POOK & POOK—6 to 8 sales per year

✤✤✤✤✤✤✤✤✤

Daniel Checki on the Rules of the Game

The first step to being successful at auction is to do a lot of research. Initially, you should focus on a specific form or period, and learn as much as you can about the furniture that interests you. Look at a piece critically, and assume there's something wrong with it. Some dealers and collectors use auctions to get rid of inferior or incorrect pieces. And fakes do show up, especially among lower-priced items. Never buy anything unless you've examined it at the preview, before the sale. Just because something looks attractive on the auction block doesn't mean that it is free of flaws and repairs. I almost always ask a dealer to look at a particular piece before I bid on it. You have to be careful. I remember once when an auction house featured a sofa on its catalogue cover, but something didn't look right to me. The frame was an inch too long on each side. It turned out to be a marriage, meaning that the piece was constructed of a frame from one sofa and a seat from another. So you have to be a detective when buying antiques at auction. Try to go to the previews during the middle of the week, when you can watch the dealers shining bright lights on the furniture and taking it apart. Look for modern nails and screws that don't belong. If the woods don't match, there's probably something wrong with the piece. Look for refined dovetails and mortise-and-tenon joinery. If something looks wrong, walk away from it.

Market Watch
AMERICAN CLASSICAL FURNITURE

A renewed aesthetic appreciation and the practical appeal of reasonable prices have contributed to a growing interest in American Classical furniture made from about 1790 through the 1830s. The American Classical style, sometimes also referred to as neoclassical or Federal, was an interpretation of English and French designs of the mid- to late-18th century that were inspired by revived interest in classical antiquities as a result of new excavations at Pompeii, Herculaneum, and other archaeological sites.

Early Empire card table, attributed to Duncan Phyfe or comparable workshop, New York, c. 1815, mahogany, brass lion's-paw feet, brass capitals, height 30", width 36", depth 17½". $18,500. (Courtesy Bernard & S. Dean Levy, New York)

The Hepplewhite and Sheraton styles, which are characterized by light, clean lines and contrasting wood inlays, represent the early phase of Classical furniture in America, and the more elaborate Empire style, which derived from the Napoleonic Empire style in France, dominates the late Classical period. Early Empire furniture is often characterized by ormolu (gilded metal mounts), white marble tabletops, winged supports, lion's paw and Egyptian dog's-paw feet, and chairbacks with lyre splats. More massive forms, gilding, painting, and heavier carving are features of the late Empire period in America. Among the prominent early-19th-century American cabinetmakers were Duncan Phyfe, Charles-Honoré Lannuier, and Michael Allison of New York, and John and Thomas Seymour, and Isaac Vose and Sons of Boston.

"While Classical furniture has increased in value within the past decade or so, and some of the best pieces by noted makers have brought over a million dollars, you can still put together a good collection for a lot less than you would spend on Queen Anne and Chippendale pieces of similar quality," says Dean Levy of New York dealers Bernard & S. Dean Levy. "There are dozens of Classical chairs, sofas, and tables that sell in the $5,000 to $20,000 range. You could spend from $8,000 to $10,000 for a good, early Empire marble-top table, for example, and as little as $5,000 for a Phyfe tilt-top table, or $7,500 for a Hepplewhite or Sheraton card table."

As with American furniture of any period, prices are dependent on condition, rarity, and quality of design and craftsmaship. There is an ample supply of desirable Classical furniture because the rapid growth of American cities during the early-19th century brought with it a proliferation of cabinetmakers and an increased production of furniture made at affordable prices for the middle class.

Chapter 3
BOOKS AND MANUSCRIPTS

What bibliophile wouldn't thrill to the sight and touch of a first edition of F. Scott Fitzgerald's *The Great Gatsby* or Walt Whitman's *Leaves of Grass?* Perhaps you're an American history buff with a penchant for old books about the Wild West or the Civil War, or you have begun a collection of letters and manuscripts signed by American presidents. Whatever your cultural and historical tastes, you will find a vast array of books and manuscripts at auction for affordable prices.

"While books and manuscripts of all types have certainly increased in value over the past five years, they still offer very good value when compared to other collecting fields," says Natalie Bauman of Bauman Rare Books in Philadelphia and New York. "You can find the greatest examples of their kind for $10,000 to $60,000, whether it's a first edition of Darwin's *On the Origin of Species* or James Joyce's *Ulysses,* of which only 750 copies were printed. You can also find some very good books for under $5,000, including less-rare modern first editions by well-known authors and beautiful leather-bound volumes by Dickens and other 19th-century writers. Letters signed by certain American presidents or by other historical figures like Albert Einstein or Thomas Edison can be bought for a few thousand dollars."

Auction houses that specialize in books and manuscripts, such as Swann Galleries and Pacific Book Auctions, hold a number of sales throughout the year ranging from Americana and 19th- and 20th-century literature to books about travel, art and architecture, science and medicine, private press and illustrated books, and children's books. Larger auction houses such as Butterfields, Christie's, and Sotheby's hold general books-and-manuscripts sales that include examples from these categories.

A broad selection of material, detailed auction catalogues that serve as valuable reference books, and the free advice of experts make auctions an appealing source for rare books and manuscripts. Many auction-savvy collectors also find themselves addicted to the thrill of the chase and the possibility of landing a bargain.

If you're in the market for 20th-century literature, one of the most popular collectibles among book aficionados, you'll want to buy books that are as close as possible to their original published form.

"You should look for first editions in the best available condition," says Dr. Catherine Williamson, director of fine books and manuscripts at Butterfields. "A first edition is the total number of copies produced in the first impression or printing of a book. Each publisher has its own system for identifying first editions; sometimes the term first edition appears on the back of a book's title page, or a certain symbol is used. Bibliographies will tell you how first editions are marked and how many were printed. Generally, the fewer first editions printed, the more valuable they will be."

Bibliographic terms can be confusing because they are sometimes used interchangeably. Before you begin bidding on first editions by 20th-century authors like Hemingway, Faulkner, Fitzgerald, Steinbeck, Salinger, and others that are also referred to in the trade as "modern first editions" or "modern firsts," you should consult guides to determining first editions such as *First Editions: A Guide to Identifications,* which describes how publishers denote first editions; general bibliographies covering many authors; and specific bibliographies on individual authors. The New York-based Antiquarian Booksellers Association of America's web site ABAA.org is another good resource. Book dealers also will provide you with invaluable information; many are willing to accompany collectors to auction previews (pre-sale exhibitions) to evaluate items and bid on their behalf for a modest fee.

If your heart is set on Faulkner's *The Sound and the Fury,* for example, you will not only want the first edition, but the first "state" and first "issue" of that book. According to *Book Collecting 2000* by Allen and Patricia Ahearn, states occur when changes such as the insertion of an errata page or the correction of ty-

Tennessee Williams, *A Streetcar Named Desire,* New York: New Directions, 1947, 8 vo. Original fragile lavender printed boards (hardcover binding), with dust wrapper (dust jacket) illustrated by Lustig. A very clean, bright, collectible copy of a book that shows wear with great ease. First edition, signed by the author. Auction estimate: $700–$900. Price realized: $8,050. (Courtesy Butterfields, San Francisco) "This book meets nearly all the criteria for a top-quality modern first edition," Williamson says. "Both the book and the jacket are in near perfect condition. The high price reflects not only its quality but also the fact that two buyers bid aggressively for it."

pographical errors are made during the printing or before any copies of the book have been published or gone on sale. There also may be changes in the typeface, the number of pages, or the type of binding cloth used. In some cases, an author may have made changes in the text. Such changes are known as points, and are listed in bibliographies. The first state of a book in which the original format has been preserved is most desirable. Some authors' books exist in more states than those of others. First editions of books by some 20th-century authors, such as Faulkner for example, were published in numerous states.

An issue occurs when alterations, additions, or deletions are made after some copies of the book already have been published or gone on sale. Like the first state, the first issue of a book is most desirable because it represents its earliest published form.

Limited editions (books published in limited print runs) and books signed by an author or inscribed (dedicated) in the author's handwriting for presentation are also desirable and fetch higher prices at auction. Collectors also prize the early versions of a book, printed before its publication, which include editors' proof copies and advance review copies.

"One of the most important considerations when buying a modern first edition is whether or not it still has its original dust jacket or wrapper, which is integral to the value," says Christine Von Der Linn, a book specialist at Swann. "Dust jackets were introduced in the early 20th century. They not only protect the book, but are part of its original form. The value of books twenty years old or older increases an average of 400 percent if they still have their original dust jackets, provided the jackets are in good condition."

A modern first edition without a dust jacket, such as Jack London's *Call of the Wild,* fetches from $300 to $600 at auction, while the same example with a dust jacket would bring several thousand dollars. A first edition of Fitzgerald's *The Great Gatsby* without a dust jacket sells for about $600 to $900, while a copy with a dust jacket would bring from $15,000 to $20,000 at auction. The value of a dust jacket has more to do with its rarity than its artistry. Since dust jackets were fragile and easily torn, early owners tended to discard them.

Experts say that the condition of both a book and its dust jacket is paramount for 20th-century literature.

"You don't want a book with a broken binding or split spine, or loose or discolored pages," Williamson says. "You should also avoid books with shelf-wear on the edges, bottom, or top. And the fewer chips, tears, and creases in the dust jacket, the better and more valuable the book. Slight blemishes are more acceptable, however, on rare dust jackets, which happens to be the case with Jack London's books. The same is true for books that are in short supply. Less desirable condition will not significantly diminish the value of a copy of *The Great Gatsby,* for example. The rarer the book, the more one can tolerate condition problems."

"If it's within your budget, always go for the best condition when buying modern first editions," advises Bauman. "The value of these books is not solely dependent upon their content. Take Hemingway's *For Whom the Bell Tolls,* for example. A copy in average condition is worth about $400 to $500, while a copy in extraordinary condition would generally sell for five times that price."

Although many auction houses describe condition in their books and manuscripts catalogues, you should always request a written condition report, or ask the auction specialists for more details. Catalogue descriptions also indicate the size of a book, whether 8vo (also called octavo—a small hardback size), quarto (a large hardback size), or folio (the largest size, similar in dimension to a coffee-table book). The size of a book usually does not affect its value.

"Twentieth-century literature is a good area for the beginning collector; it's not only familiar and accessible but affordable," observes Williamson. "While prices vary according to the stature of an author and the cultural and historical importance of a book, many modern titles are still available for less than $1,000."

Signed and inscribed first editions by the great 20th-century writers such as Hemingway, Fitzgerald, and Joyce have brought as much as tens of thousands of dollars at auction. Modern firsts by authors who wrote only a handful of books, such as J. D. Salinger and Fitzgerald, are among the most sought after. Still undervalued, however, are first editions by 20th-century African-American and women writers, such as Richard Wright, Eudora Welty, and Katherine Anne Porter, as well as those by poets throughout the centuries, ranging from John Donne to Walt Whitman, many of which sell for a few hundred dollars.

"You can never pay too much for a great book. And if it's the only one of its kind, who's to say what's too much?" says Dr. Matthew J. Bruccoli, collector and professor of English at the University of South Carolina, to which he donated the world's most comprehensive Fitzgerald archive, including more than two thousand books by, about, and inscribed by the author as well as more than ten thousand manuscripts, proofs, and letters. "It's no secret that being an English professor is not the royal road to wealth, yet I've always done very well when buying at auction. It's not about money. It's a game of knowledge, taste, courage, and determination. All you have to do is know more about the item you want than anyone else. Trust your own taste and literary judgment; don't rely on others. Research the publication history of the authors you like and study their markets. Consult past and present auction catalogues and price guides like *American Book Prices Current*."

As with most other areas of collecting, modern first editions are susceptible to foul play. Sometimes an author's signature and inscription are forged. You should also be on the lookout for "pirated editions"—existing books reprinted by lesser-known publishers without authorization. Auction houses may knowingly sell pirated editions as curiosities, which should be clearly indicated in the catalogue.

"The Book of the Month Club reprints books that look so much like original first editions that an inexperienced buyer could be fooled," Von Der Linn cautions. "This fact is not always spelled out in the book; there may only be a small indentation in the cover, for example, indicating that it is not a first edition."

Books are not only prized for their literary and historical cachet. They can be works of art unto themselves. Some people collect books for their beautiful leather bindings, for example, while others buy leather-bound books simply as decorative accessories for their homes.

"Generally, the finer the craftsmanship and more elaborate the gilt tooling of the binding, the higher the value, particularly those by well-known European binders such as Sangorski and Sutcliffe, and Rivière," says Willamson.

Although the art of fine bookbinding began at least as early as the Middle Ages, a great portion of bound books on the market are European travel, history, and literary titles that date from the 17th to 19th centuries. You'll find lavish, filigreed bindings on 18th-century French books, while 18th- and 19th-century British bindings are more conservatively decorated. You can buy beautifully bound 19th-century volumes by Shakespeare, Dickens, Thackeray, and other major European writers for several hundred to several thousand dollars. American books were usually not as well constructed or as elaborately bound as European books. Leather bindings are still being made today, but experts say they are becoming a lost art.

Some book collectors prefer the art of illustration and focus their efforts on old travel books illustrated with engravings and photographs; children's books incorporating the work of noted illustrators like Arthur Rackham and Maurice Sendak; or literature and art books illustrated by celebrated artists such as Matisse and Picasso. Many fine illustrated books are available at auction for less than $1,000. Books produced solely as collections of engravings (plate books) are among the most expensive on the market. John James Audubon's four-volume set *The Birds of America* (1827–1838), illustrated with exquisite color engravings, sold at Christie's in 2000 for $8.8 million, a record auction price for a printed book.

If you're interested in American history, you'll find

Billy the Kid, the New Mexican Outlaw; or the Bold Bandit of the West!
3 wood-engraved scenes and 2 portraits. 8 vo, rebound retaining the original front yellow pictorial wrapper with minor soiling and short tears at edges, Denver, 1881. Auction estimate: $10,000–$15,000. Price realized: $20,700. (Courtesy Swann Auction Galleries, New York) "This book sold above its estimate because it's rare and in fairly good condition. It is only one of three known copies, and one of the earliest biographies of Billy the Kid written just after his death," Markowitz observes. "The popular folk-hero status of Billy the Kid also enhances the value of this book."

a wide selection of printed material at auction, including early American (pre–1800) religious texts, often in the form of sermons; books about Indians, the Civil War, and the Wild West; slavery-related broadsides (posted bills); Poor Richard's Almanacs; travel narratives; maps; and much more. Prices range from one hundred dollars to tens of thousands of dollars depending on the historical significance and rarity of the item.

"Whatever area of printed Americana appeals to you, it's generally desirable to look for the earliest published forms," notes Jeremy B. Markowitz, a book specialist at Swann. "There are always exceptions, however. Sometimes later editions contain more maps and illustrations, so that would make the book more valuable. Each category, of course, has its own specific criteria. If you plan to collect Civil War material, for example, the most valuable books and pamphlets are Confederate in subject, were written during the War, and printed in the South. You'll find a lot of histories of regiments and collections of military commands. Confederate printed material is less common than Union material because the South had shortages of paper and printing machinery. If you're interested in books about Western subjects, the better examples were usually written and printed in the West."

Since there are many facsimiles or copies of popular books such as Poor Richard's Almanac (written by Benjamin Franklin), ask an auction specialist to confirm that the item you plan to bid on is indeed an original. As with all books, condition is another important consideration.

"Does the book still have its original binding, or has it been replaced with a new binding? An original binding in very good condition will add value to the book," Markowitz says. "You don't want to see a lot of scratches or scuff marks on the book. Stains, wormholes, and foxing—small brown spots on the pages—will also reduce the value. Less desirable condition is more acceptable, however, for rare books. When it comes to illustrated books, if all the maps and plates are in good condition, then other condition problems do not significantly affect their value."

Perhaps you are more interested in manuscripts, which are also widely available at auction and reasonably priced. The term "manuscripts" technically refers to all written material, including letters and other documents, but is often used to describe written material other than letters. Letters and manuscripts written or signed by noteworthy individuals such as American presidents, authors, scientists, artists, and entertainers are popular collectibles. When a letter or manuscript is entirely written in the hand of the person to whom it is attributed, it is called an autograph letter or manuscript. (The term autograph does not refer to the signature itself.) Autograph letters and manuscripts may or may not be signed and generally fetch higher prices than signed letters and manuscripts typed or written by someone else. The more historically and culturally important the person who penned or signed a document, the more valuable it is. And the more the noteworthy individual has touched a document, the more valuable it is.

The highest price ever paid for a manuscript at auction was $30.8 million for Leonardo da Vinci's

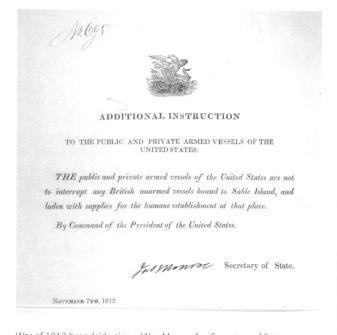

War of 1812 broadside signed "Jas Monroe" as Secretary of State, commanding public and private vessels to let unarmed British ships bound for Sable Island pass unharmed. Washington, November 7, 1812. 7$^1/_2$" x 7$^3/_4$". Auction estimate: $500–$700. Price realized: $575. (Courtesy Swann Auction Galleries, New York) A broadside is a printed announcement on a single side of a sheet of paper that was either distributed or posted on a wall. "This is a fine example of an autograph that might appeal to a beginning collector," Lowry says. "It's attractive, readable, perfect for display, and reasonably priced. Depending upon the historical importance of the content, signed documents by presidents before they actually took office are usually priced lower than documents signed by presidents while in office."

Codex Hammer, which sold at Christie's in 1994. This autograph manuscript presents the great artist-scientist's ideas on cosmology, mechanics, geology, and other scientific disciplines. While a signed autograph letter by President Abraham Lincoln referring to the Emancipation Proclamation brought $748,000 at Christie's in 1991 (an auction record for a presidential letter), less historically important autograph letters and manuscripts by Lincoln and other high-profile presidents such as Kennedy and Jefferson can be bought for less than $10,000 at auction.

And you still can find a lot of autograph material by presidents, artists, scientists, and other noteworthy figures for less than $1,000. You also can collect signatures only, many of which are priced under $200. Ask auction specialists to provide you with price lists from past sales or consult *Sander's Pricing Guide to Autographs* so that you have an idea of what you should be paying for particular items. Don't rely solely on auction-

catalogue estimates, which only approximate market value and are sometimes either intentionally conservative to attract bidders or slightly inflated to accommodate the seller's expectations.

Authenticity and content are the other important criteria to keep in mind when collecting letters and manuscripts. Because this field has been known to turn up its fair share of fakes, make sure you are buying from a reputable auction house and read the terms of guarantee in the auction catalogue before you bid. Many manuscripts were copied and sold as facsimiles, which are not the same thing as fakes. For example, there are hundreds of facsimiles of the Declaration of Independence, one of the most sought-after collectibles, but less than thirty examples of the original are known to exist. Facsimiles of the Declaration are usually printed on yellow parchment paper, but the real document was printed on high-quality white paper, according to Markowitz.

As for content, letters and manuscripts referring to important historical events are most desirable, whether it is a letter written by a Civil War soldier describing the Battle of Gettysburg or Albert Einstein's notes on his Theory of Relativity. Letters from one notable figure to another bring higher prices than letters from a notable figure to a lesser-known or historically insignificant figure. Rarity, as always, also affects value. Take Einstein, for example, whose letters and manuscripts come up frequently at auction. An Einstein autograph letter in which he refers to Nazi Germany is more rare and desirable than one of his autograph thank-you notes.

"When buying autograph letters and manuscripts at auction, you should choose something as close as possible to the moment of creation," advises George Lowry, president of Swann Galleries and an expert on autographs. "Condition is less important in this field than in most areas of collecting, particularly because there are so many one-of-a-kind items. You have to determine how likely it is that you will ever find another example of the document you want. Anything that is especially rare and has a certain romance and mystique is always desirable, whether it's a letter or manuscript by the reclusive writer J. D. Salinger, or by Amelia Earhart, or the American president William Henry Harrison, who died after only thirty days in office."

Once you've completed your background research, studied the auction catalogue, and spent time evaluating the object of your desire at the auction preview, you're ready to bid.

"Before you even raise your paddle, decide on your top bid," Von Der Linn says. "Auctions are exciting and move at a fast pace. There's a fever pitch in the room, and it's easy to just keep bidding beyond your budget. Know your limits and try to avoid 'trigger elbow.' When determining your top bid, keep in mind that the final price you'll pay includes a buyer's premium, which is a percentage of the hammer price, as well as sales tax."

"I've seen a lot of books sell at auction for more than they're worth," Bauman adds. "That's often because two or three buyers either don't have full knowledge about what they're bidding on, or they get caught up in the competition. I try not to let my ego override my judgment. It's too easy to make an expensive mistake. Buy within your budget. No one should lose sleep over a purchase. Collecting should be a pleasure."

Some collectors like Bruccoli, however, won't rest until they get what they want at auction.

"Collecting is different from buying; it's an organized, thought-out act involving a plan. It's also a fatal disease that has been known to cause many marriages to collapse. Fortunately, my wife supports my compulsion," observes Bruccoli, whose greatest auction coup was snapping up the only known complete, unmarked galleys for the original version of *The Great Gatsby* nearly thirty years ago for what he claims was a bargain price of $3,000. "For me it's always a question of how badly I want something. I had paid a dealer to bid for me on the *Gatsby* galleys at a New York auction house. But on the morning of the sale I decided to fly there myself. It's a good thing I did. Even though I had given the dealer my top bid, I didn't expect him to stop there, since he knew how badly I wanted the galleys. I sat beside him, and nudged him in the ribs to go a bid higher. If I hadn't gone to the sale myself, I would have lost out."

Matthew J. Bruccoli on the Price of Obsession and Other Tales from the Auction Front

When people ask me why I collect books and manuscripts, I have to say that I'm unabashedly sentimental. It gives me pleasure to hold something Fitzgerald held. And then there's a more rational reason, which is to preserve all these treasures and share them with others through museum loan exhibitions and donations. Why just take them home and lock them up? When I buy at auction, I always keep the late book collector Charles Feinberg's three golden rules in mind. They are: If you've never seen something, buy it, because you may never see it again. A book costs more today than it did yesterday, and it will cost even more tomorrow, so buy it. The only books you regret are the ones you don't buy.

Of course, when you're as obsessed as I am, you won't stop at just books and manuscripts. I remember when Fitzgerald's briefcase came up for auction years ago. I went only to watch the auction, because I knew I didn't have enough money at the time to buy the briefcase. As luck would have it, someone I didn't like emerged as the leading bidder. My hand went up automatically, and I started to bid. I didn't think he deserved it. I wound up buying the briefcase, and I had to run all around New York borrowing $15,000 from friends. The more I'm in this, the more I realize there are no accidents.

Market Watch
ILLUSTRATED ART AND
ARCHITECTURE BOOKS

*I*llustrated art and architecture books including artist and architect monographs, catalogues raisonnés, books about art and architectural history, and architectural pattern books are prized for their beauty. Art dealers, architects, academics, and historians were among the first to collect these books, many of which contain original works of art in the form of lithographs, etchings, and engravings.

"Art and architecture books with original artwork by well-known artists like Miró, Picasso, and Chagall are more affordable than people think," says Swann's Von Der Linn. "A lot of these books sell at auction for less than $1,000. You can buy a book, for example, about the ceiling of the Paris Opera, with an original Chagall lithograph for the frontispiece, for about $150 to $175. Prices depend on the quality of the illustration and the print run—the number of books available. The best examples have clear, crisp illustrations in vibrant colors and are in good condition with no soiling or tears. You should look for complete copies, meaning that all the illustrations are intact."

Joan Miró, an original lithograph for the art magazine *Derrière Le Miroir*, #164/165, *L'Oiseau Solarie, L'Oiseau Lunaire, Etincelles,* Paris, 1967. Auction estimate: $400–$600. Price realized: $373. (Courtesy Swann Auction Galleries, New York)

❖❖❖❖❖❖❖❖❖

RECOMMENDED MUSEUM COLLECTIONS:

* The Pierpont Morgan Library, New York, NY
* The New York Public Library, New York, NY
* The Rosenbach Museum & Library, Philadelphia, PA
* Harry Ransom Humanities Research Center, The University of Texas, Austin, TX
* The Huntington Library, San Marino, CA
* The Beinecke Rare Books and Manuscripts Library, Yale University, New Haven, CT

SALES OF BOOKS AND MANUSCRIPTS AT SELECTED AUCTION HOUSES:

* SWANN—20 to 25 sales per year
* BUTTERFIELDS—spring, fall, winter
* SOTHEBY'S—June, December
* CHRISTIE'S—May, December
* PACIFIC BOOK AUCTIONS—one sale per month

Chapter 4
CHINESE CERAMICS

Over the past decade, Chinese pottery and ceramics have been filtering out of China in great numbers, often excavated from millennia-old tombs. And many pieces are finding their way to the auction block.

Whether you're shopping for a Ming vase, a Tang horse, or a Han sculpture, you'll want to be armed with as much information as possible before you cast your first bid.

Dealers agree that condition is one of the most important criteria when it comes to buying Chinese ceramics.

"Once you find a piece you like, ask for a detailed condition report from the auction house," says New York City dealer Eric Zetterquist, who specializes in Chinese pottery and ceramics from as early as 3000 B.C. up through the Ming Dynasty (1368–1643). "Many people don't even know these reports are available. Condition can sometimes mean the difference between $1,000 and $50,000."

You should also ask the auction-house experts to explain anything that is unclear about the condition of a ceramic as it is described in the catalogue. A good time to do this is at the auction preview, a presale exhibition of the lots to be sold that usually lasts from several days to a week.

"A hairline crack in a piece of Ming porcelain can be devastating to its value, while such a crack in a 2,000-year-old Han vase is almost negligible," Zetterquist says. "And don't panic if you find a 7th- to 10th-century Tang horse with a broken, reattached leg, which is common on these old pieces."

Catalogue descriptions can indeed be cryptic. So read carefully.

"A catalogue entry that reads 'a Ming blue-and-white covered meiping' is different from one that reads 'a Ming blue-and-white meiping and *a* cover,'" says Chinese-art dealer James Lally of New York City. "The latter entry indicates that the cover does not necessarily belong to the jar and that it could have come from another source. Similarly, an entry that states 'a blue-glazed horse, Tang Dynasty' is not the same as 'a blue-glazed horse, Tang style,' which means that the precise date is unknown."

Dating also affects the value of Chinese pottery and ceramics. For pieces from the Tang Dynasty (618–906) and earlier, ask to see a thermoluminescence certificate. This radioactive test is an important indicator of authenticity.

You'll find that most ceramics bear "reign marks" of about six Chinese characters that refer to specific dates during an emperor's reign.

"If you decide to bid on a Ming vase, you should know exactly when during the three centuries of the Ming Dynasty that vase was made," Lally says. "Is it early, middle, or late Ming? Prices for wares from these periods vary according to the supply and demand in the market at that time."

When it comes to quality, the astute collector should be asking What is the texture of the porcelain? Is it smooth or rough? Is the cobalt color on a Ming vase what it should be? Is there a noticeable style and flow to the painting? In the case of a Tang horse or Kangxi sculpture (1662–1722), are they well-proportioned? Does the piece give me pleasure?

"All these factors determine how you're going to bid," says Allan Chait of New York City's Ralph M. Chait Galleries. "And the best way to prepare yourself is to read, research, and look. Visit museums to study objects similar to what you want to buy. Go to the presale exhibitions and handle the pieces. And seek out a reputable dealer for advice. Having good taste isn't enough."

Some collectors will ask a dealer to bid for them at auction, particularly if they want to remain anonymous. For this service, dealers charge 5 to 10 percent of the hammer price of the piece acquired. There is no charge if you don't buy anything.

"Dealers function as a bit of an insurance policy for an auction purchase," says Lally. "Find someone with whom you hit it off personally. His or her job is to make sure that you buy something of value that will make you happy in the long run."

There's a difference between collecting and accumulating, according to Zetterquist. "A collection is a work of art itself. It should form one meaningful statement. When you're bidding at auction, you should start out with a goal in mind. Know how high you're willing to go to avoid spending twice as much as you should. Practice self-restraint, and don't get caught up in the excitement of bidding."

You can find a poor, average, good, or great ceramic from any period of Chinese history, and it helps to know what distinguishes them. The best-quality pieces have glazes that show good color, are accurately dated and in good condition (a minimum of chips, cracks, repairs), and are aesthetically beautiful.

If you are not necessarily seeking perfection, there are plenty of fine, imperfect examples that are just as beautiful as the best pieces, but at more reasonable prices.

"While you might spend $100,000 to $150,000 for a perfect, 15th-century blue-and-white Ming vase or dish, you may prefer to spend about $15,000 to $20,000 for a similar piece with a hairline crack repaired with epoxy, which may suit your purposes just fine," Lally advises. "Of course you won't get as much of a discount on rare pieces with cracks, such as a dish with a double-phoenix pattern versus the more standard lotus-scroll pattern."

The rarity of a particular ceramic is another factor that determines value and affects bidding. Before setting your top price, you will want to know whether the Ming dish you want is an ordinary shape with an unusual pattern or design, or whether it has a common pattern that happens to be found on only a few dishes. Perhaps it is a 12-inch dish from the end of the 15th century, which is rarer than a more common 15-inch dish. Or if it's a Tang horse you're after, you should know that walking horses are rarer than standing horses.

"Tang horses can be estimated at anywhere from $6,000 to $100,000 in the auction catalogue," Chait says. "But these estimates are simply guideposts for those who are not familiar with the material. The real price is determined by the bidders. And the more armed you are with knowledge prior to the sale, the better purchase you'll make."

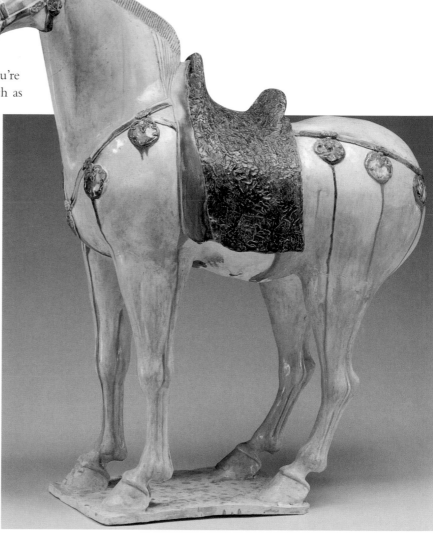

Large and rare sancai-glazed caparisoned horse, Tang Dynasty, height 31½". Auction estimate: $90,000–$120,000. Price realized: $178,000. (Courtesy Sotheby's, New York) This Tang horse is described rare in the catalogue because it is unusually tall. Glazed horses are scarcer than unglazed horses, but that does not mean that they are more desirable, for the carving on an unglazed horse is often sharper in detail. The word sancai refers to the three-color glazes typical of Tang horses: green, yellow, and brown. Sculptural quality and proportion are also important in determining the value of a Tang horse. Minor repairs are common to these sculptures and do not significantly alter their value. Since the horses have been buried for many centuries, a Tang horse without repairs is a horse in question, according to New York dealer Allan Chait.

However, don't assume that you'll come up with fixed criteria that will always serve you well at auction.

"The market changes with the whims of fashion and taste, and so does the criteria of connoisseurship," says Lally. "A bidder is like a marksman in front of a moving target."

So buyer beware, especially of fakes. Chinese ceramics are a favorite terrain of highly skilled con men in China.

"The most common ones are partial fakes, where only part of the piece has been restored," says Zetterquist. "Or someone might glaze a piece that's supposed to be unglazed, with the hope of making it more valuable. The thermoluminescence test is important in identifying fakes. Just make sure that the whole object has been tested, since an original, old base could be attached to a fake sculpture."

A piece needn't have been recently reproduced to be deemed a fake.

"Some Ming fakes are 200 years old," Lally says. "You might find 18th-century copies of a 15th-century vase. The type of cobalt coloring usually gives it away. Later copies show a more mechanical, stippled and dotted application of color."

Assuming that you have identified the object of your desire and ruled out the possibility of a fake, your goal is then to become the highest bidder at the lowest possible price. With that end in mind, it's best to keep a low profile before and during the auction.

"If the auctioneer and other collectors sense your enthusiasm for a particular piece, you'll set off a bidding war that could drive up the price unnecessarily," Lally cautions.

Bidding isn't a game; it's a serious, risky business.

"Anyone can raise their arm," says Chait. "But the trick is to know when to raise it. Timing is crucial. You have to get a sense of the flow of the auction and observe the auctioneer's style. With practice, you'll know just when and how you want to bid on that Ming vase."

Ming Dynasty vs. Ming-style: Differences in the quality of color, glaze, clay, and pattern distinguish true Ming porcelain from later Ming-style copies, such as this example. Auction estimate: $5,000–$7,000. Price realized: $9,775. (Courtesy Sotheby's, New York)

RECOMMENDED MUSEUM COLLECTIONS:

• The Metropolitan Museum of Art, New York, NY
• Museum of Fine Arts, Boston, MA
• Asian Art Museum of San Francisco, CA
• Cleveland Museum of Art
• The Art Institute of Chicago

SALES OF CHINESE CERAMICS AT SELECTED AUCTION HOUSES:

• SOTHEBY'S—March, September
• CHRISTIE'S—March, September

Chronology of Dynastic China

NEOLITHIC	10th–early 1st millenium B.C.		Xuande	A.D. 1426–1435
SHANG DYNASTY	16th century–c. 1050 B.C.		Zhengtong	A.D. 1436–1449
ZHOU DYNASTY	c. 1050–221 B.C.		Jingtai	A.D. 1450–1456
QIN DYNASTY	221–206 B.C.		Tianshun	A.D. 1457–1464
HAN DYNASTY	206 B.C.–A.D. 220		Chenghua	A.D. 1465–1487
THREE KINGDOMS	A.D. 200–265		Hongzhi	A.D. 1488–1505
JIN DYNASTY	A.D. 265–420		Zhengde	A.D. 1506–1521
SOUTHERN AND			Jiajing	A.D. 1522–1566
NORTHERN DYNASTIES	A.D. 420–589		Longqing	A.D. 1567–1572
SUI DYNASTY	A.D. 581–618		Wanli	A.D. 1573–1619
TANG DYNASTY	A.D.618–907		Taichang	A.D. 1620
FIVE DYNASTIES	A.D. 907–960		Tianqi	A.D. 1621–1627
LIAO DYNASTY	A.D. 907–1125		Chongzhen	A.D. 1628–1644
SONG DYNASTY	A.D. 960–1279		QING DYNASTY	A.D. 1644–1911
Northern Song	A.D. 960–1127		Shunzhi	A.D. 1644–1661
Southern Song	A.D. 1127–1279		Kangxi	A.D. 1662–1722
XIXIA DYNASTY	A.D. 1038–1227		Yongzheng	A.D. 1723–1735
JIN DYNASTY	A.D. 1115–1234		Qianlong	A.D. 1736–1795
YUAN DYNASTY	A.D. 1279–1368		Jiaqing	A.D. 1796–1820
MING DYNASTY	A.D. 1368–1644		Daoguang	A.D. 1821–1850
Hongwu	A.D. 1368–1398		Xianfeng	A.D. 1851–1861
Jianwen	A.D. 1399–1402		Tongzhi	A.D. 1862–1874
Yongle	A.D. 1403–1424		Guangxu	A.D. 1875–1908
Hongxi	A.D. 1425		Xuantong	A.D. 1909–1911

Allan Chait on "Sleepers"

❧

I remember a time 35 years ago when my dad, Ralph, saw a late-17th-century Kangxi vase at an auction preview that he'd read about in a book and that he knew was valuable, although the auction house hadn't identified it as such. He happened to mention to a collector friend that he had his eye on a "sleeper," but didn't reveal which one it was. The collector then took a series of experts to the preview to find the sleeper, without success. My father had instructed me to go to the sale, buy the vase, and bring it back right away. The same collector later bought it from him at a considerably higher price. That vase is now in a museum. So it's possible to profit in the long run when you're armed with a little bit of knowledge at auction.

Market Watch
SOUTHEAST ASIAN CERAMICS

Southeast Asian ceramics represent one of the best collecting opportunities now, particularly 14th- to 15th-century Thai ceramics and 15th- to 16th-century Vietnamese ceramics, according to Zetterquist, one of the few dealers in this field.

Celadon bowls, Si Satchanalai kilns, Thailand, 14th–15th century, 10" and 8¹⁄₂" in diameter. $5,000 and $3,800. Photograph by Maggie Nimkin. (Courtesy Zetterquist Galleries, New York)

"These pieces are not only beautiful and gaining international recognition, they are very collectible pricewise," says Zetterquist. "You can buy a 15th-century Thai celadon ware in perfect condition for as little as $2,000, compared to a Chinese ceramic with a similar pedigree that would easily cost five times that."

While Southeast Asian ceramics are heavily influenced by Chinese ceramics, both the Thais and the Vietnamese had their own interpretations.

"These pieces are very much original works of art," Zetterquist says. "With Thai ceramics, you tend to see a lot of celadon (light green) glazes. The Vietnamese often made underglaze cobalt-blue ceramics with creamy-colored backgrounds. They are generally more colorful than Thai wares. Both types of ceramics incorporate stylized floral and wildlife motifs."

Because of the recent economic development of Southeast Asian countries like Thailand and Vietnam, these ceramics are attracting more attention from the West.

"A lot of their popularity has to do with being able to collect the highest quality pieces for much less money than you'd spend on Chinese, Japanese, or Korean ceramics," Zetterquist adds. "Any time you can buy at the top of a market for less than $10,000, within the art world as a whole, that's an enormous opportunity."

Chapter 5
CHINESE FURNITURE

Chinese hardwood furniture from the late Ming (1550–1644) and early Qing (1644–1750) dynasties has seen a dramatic surge of interest over the last ten years. Prized for its masterful construction, simple design, and richly grained woods, this elegant furniture, long the domain of a small group of collectors, attracted worldwide attention in 1996 when Christie's sold the collection of California's Museum of Classical Chinese Furniture for $11.2 million, the highest total ever for Chinese furniture at auction.

"While there is a limited supply of the finest classical Chinese furniture, it's still possible to purchase masterpieces at reasonable prices well below the millions brought by the best American and European furniture," says New York dealer Marcus Flacks of MD Flacks Ltd. "That represents excellent value, considering that Chinese furniture was the best ever made in terms of its design and wood quality, and sophisticated mortise-and-tenon joinery, which requires great skill. But this furniture lacks the name recognition, because it wasn't signed."

Christie's, Sotheby's, and Butterfields auction the widest selection of Chinese furniture. Most of what has survived is from the late Ming and early Qing periods, when furnituremaking in China was at its height. Among the many classic forms, you'll find cabinets, daybeds, altar tables, painting tables, stools, yokeback chairs (also known as scholar's chairs, because the yoke or top brace resembles a scholar's hat), and horseshoeback chairs, both armless and armed.

Whichever form you desire, you should first of all consider whether the piece is aesthetically pleasing in design and proportion. Chinese furniture is usually designed in geometric shapes, with different types of aprons and stretchers. There are both minimal and heavily carved, ornate pieces.

"The minimal Ming pieces have been particularly popular with Western buyers," says Theow H. Tow, Christie's international director of Chinese Works of Art. "They have a clean, modern look that complements contemporary art and interiors."

There is often a lot of restoration on Chinese furniture because of its age. At the presale exhibition, you should ask a specialist to point out any alterations to the original shape or size of the piece you'd like to buy.

"The majority of Chinese furniture has such balance and proportion. If a particular piece looks wrong to the eye, chances are that something is wrong with it," Flacks notes.

If the restoration is the main element, the central panel of a table, for example, or a chair has a replaced back splat or yoke, then you shouldn't bid on that object. However, the aprons beneath the seats of chairs and the footrests are replaced 90 percent of the time and are considered acceptable.

Caned seats with water stains (a good sign that a chair is old) are also acceptable. And it's not essential that the seats be original; many have been destroyed from years of use. Horseshoeback chairs often have brass braces. These repairs strengthen the structure and even enhance the quality.

You will want to avoid "marriages" in which two old pieces of furniture have been made into a whole new piece. So beware of the Ming bookcase that was formerly a canopy bed. Since catalogue descriptions don't always list the extent of restoration, ask the auction specialist for a written condition report.

"The skeletal structure should be totally original," says New York dealer Leon Wender of China 2000 Fine Art, who specializes in Chinese furniture and paintings. "Check to see that the wood color and grain are uniform. The arms and legs and other structural pieces should look like they came from one tree not added at a later date. Be aware that table legs are sometimes cut down from their original size. Inspect the piece you want to buy with a magnifying glass and a flashlight. And don't be afraid to ask the auction specialist a lot of questions. It also helps to have done your own background research before you start bidding."

Tow recommends looking behind and under furniture for traces of lacquer, which show that a piece is

A huanghuali horseshoeback armchair, quanyi, early 17th century, height 40", width 24½", depth 19". Auction estimate: $18,000–$25,000. Price realized: $12,650. (Courtesy Christie's, New York) Armchairs with curved rests (top rail) in which the back of the chair flows down to form the arms in a graceful curve, were called *quanyi* by Beijing cabinetmakers. Westerners have dubbed them horseshoeback armchairs. This form is one of four types of Ming and early Qing chairs. "Like many horseshoeback chairs, the top rail of this one is made of five separate pieces of wood," says Tow. "This chair is a good example of its kind. It has nice carving, and is in decent condition. It sold below its estimate, because the unlikely event of a hurricane on the day of the sale kept a lot of people at home."

old. The original makers often lacquered these areas to protect the wood. You'll also want to be familiar with the type of wood used. The best-quality Chinese furniture—and most expensive—is made of either the purple sandalwood *zitan* or the yellow rosewood *huanghuali,* revered for its rich graining and color (which can range from blond to reddish in tone). Furniture made of these woods was collected and used by wealthy Chinese.

"Huanghuali and zitan pieces are very popular with both Chinese and Western collectors, so they are often expensive and harder to find," says Tow. "As a result, interest has shifted to more affordable, alternative woods like ironwood and elm."

High-quality pieces made of rare woods like huanghuali and zitan sell at auction for up to $500,000, whereas many wonderful pieces in alternative woods can be found for under $15,000. You can buy a fine pair of elmwood horseshoeback chairs, for example, for $4,500 to $7,500, or a walnut altar table for $7,500 to $10,000; their huanghuali counterparts would would cost from five to ten times more. Single chairs and square tables (which are more difficult to use) bring lower prices.

"If you can afford it, go for the best woods. Otherwise you're better off buying a great example in a lesser wood than buying an average example in huanghuali or zitan," Wender advises.

As with all furniture, the condition of its surface patina affects the quality.

"Over the years, many old pieces were stripped with sandpaper or bleach with the idea that clean, shiny furniture was more desirable," says Flacks. "But that erases the history. It's more important to have the original patina, which makes the surface richer and more complex, and gives it a depth of color."

While most of the Chinese furniture on the market was made from the 16th to the 18th centuries, it is difficult to determine exact dates because the makers are unknown.

"Don't always take the date listed in the catalogue at face value," Wender says. "The furniture could be newer than stated."

When the catalogue describes a piece as "Ming-style," it means that it was made sometime after the Ming period. Likewise, the vague term "Asian hardwood" indicates that the exact wood is unknown.

Based on careful research and consultations with scholars and conservators, most auction houses guarantee the information in their catalogues. Be sure to read the terms of guarantee or warranty listed in the front or back pages. In Christie's catalogues, for example, the information which appears in uppercase type for each lot guarantees its authenticity.

Another advantage to buying at auction is the possibility of making some great discoveries.

"Some lots may not be as thoroughly researched as others, due to the auction houses' large volume of merchandise and constant deadline pressure," Wender notes. "Prospective buyers have more time to research certain objects, so they may find that a certain horseshoeback chair or altar table is acutally more valuable than the estimate indicates."

Dealers suggest that you spend ample time inspecting property at the auction houses' exhibitions (also called previews or viewings), which run for several days before the sale. If you're serious about collecting Chinese furniture, you can also arrange to have a dealer preview certain pieces before the exhibition, while they are still in the auction warehouse.

When it comes to bidding, the best strategy is to outresearch the competition and establish a limit in your mind, according to Wender.

"And don't start bidding too soon. Initially, it's better to gauge the demand, so you know who you're bidding against," he says.

"Use the catalogue estimates as a guideline and ask the auction experts what price they think a particular piece of furniture will bring," Flacks adds. "Most of the high-quality pieces tend to sell above their estimates. Also be aware of the buyer's premiums which are added to the hammer price. Novice collectors may want to pay a dealer to bid on their behalf. It gives them the advantage of his expertise and knocks his potential clients out of the bidding process."

Altar table, 16th century, elm, height 34³/₄", depth 17", length 51¹/₄". $10,000. (Courtesy China 2000 Fine Art, New York)

❧❧❧❧❧❧❧❧❧

RECOMMENDED MUSEUM COLLECTIONS:

- Minneapolis Institute of Arts
- The Metropolitan Museum of Art, New York, NY
- Museum of Fine Arts, Boston, MA
- Cleveland Museum of Art
- Nelson-Atkins Museum of Art, Kansas City, KS

CHINESE FURNITURE SALES AT SELECTED AUCTION HOUSES:

- CHRISTIE'S—March, September
- SOTHEBY'S—March, September
- BUTTERFIELDS—May, October

Market Watch
CHINESE SCHOLAR'S OBJECTS

*O*ne of the best buys among Chinese antiques are scholar's objects made during the golden age of Chinese furniture, from the late Ming to early Qing dynasties. At that time the Chinese literati, a class of scholar-officials, wielded great power as the moral and cultural leaders of society. They lived simply in country retreats, often in the mountains overlooking streams, where they built what have become known as scholar's studios. These studios were filled with accessories required to practice painting and calligraphy.

Group of Chinese scholar's objects. From left to right are a small square chess table, huanghuali ($25,000), holding two seal boxes, burlwood (left) and zitan (right); painting chest (on floor), in which scrolls were stored, huanghuali ($18,000); side table, huanghuali ($60,000), holding a small chest (left) and picnic box (right), both huanghuali, and a melon-shaped seal-paste box, which held the red ink used to make artist's seals, boxwood. Small objects range in price from $2,000 to $12,000. (Courtesy MD FLacks Ltd., New York)

"Throughout Chinese history, painting and calligraphy have been considered the most important art forms," says Flacks. "Practicing them was part of a cultured person's life, and scholar's objects like brush pots, small cabinets, scroll pots, and boxes were part of that ritual."

Scholar's objects were made from the same precious woods found in Chinese furniture. Scroll pots, which held rolled-up scrolls and paintings, were often made out of hollowed-out tree roots.

"These small objects are of the highest quality and very reasonably priced," Flacks adds. "They are an excellent introduction to collecting Chinese furniture. At auction, it's one area where you can really win."

You can buy scholar's objects at auction for as little as $500 to $800. The best examples of brush pots, cabinets, boxes, and scholar's rocks bring from $1,500 to $15,000.

Chapter 6
CONTEMPORARY ART

"Why do I collect Contemporary art? Because it's dynamic, immediate, and fun to live with. It invites you to be part of the cultural process as it's happening, and it's often more affordable than art of comparable quality from earlier periods," says Robert Lehrman of Washington, D.C., who has built a world-class collection of Contemporary art by Joseph Cornell, Gerhard Richter, Agnes Martin, Susan Rothenberg, Eric Fischl, and others, and serves as chairman of the board of Washington's Hirshhorn Museum.

Having recovered from the speculation and inflated prices of the 1980s that spurred the art market recession of the early 1990s, the market for Contemporary art is stronger than ever, fueled by a robust national economy, a growing number of collectors, and an increasingly global, media-saturated culture that teases the eye with a nonstop flow of visual imagery.

But don't despair. The multimillion-dollar Willem de Koonings and Jackson Pollocks that inevitably grab headlines are the exceptions. You don't have to be a millionaire to buy contemporary art at auction. In fact, you'll find many fine quality works by promising, emerging artists for $5,000 to $10,000, whether paintings, sculpture, photographs, drawings, mixed media, videos, or digital and installation art. You just have to know the territory. And that means visiting museums, galleries, art fairs, and auctions, and immersing yourself in artist's monographs, past and present auction catalogues, exhibition catalogues, and art magazines such as *Artnews, ArtForum, Art in America,* and *Parkett.*

The timeline for what constitutes Contemporary art is a matter of debate and varies from one auction house to another. Christie's, for example, organizes sales of Contemporary art mostly made by living artists from 1965 onward. Contemporary-art sales at Sotheby's, however, also include works by Abstract Expressionists such as Jackson Pollock, Willem de Kooning, and Marc Rothko (who made their mark in the late 1940s and the 1950s) as well as the Pop artists

who followed, including Roy Lichtenstein and Andy Warhol. Along with noteworthy successors such as Frank Stella, Jasper Johns, and Robert Rauschenberg, who are still working, these artists are often referred to as Postwar or Contemporary masters.

Christie's and Sotheby's hold Contemporary art sales in May and November, just before or after their major Impressionist and Modern art auctions. Their evening sales of Contemporary art offer major higher-priced works, and the day sales that follow offer a wide variety of works that are more modestly priced. On the West Coast, Butterfields sells Contemporary art along with Modern art (usually defined as art made during the first half of the 20th century) and Latin American art in twice-yearly 20th-century art auctions.

"We've decided to focus more on the best works by younger artists, which are more affordable to a broader base of buyers than the multimillion-dollar works by blue-chip artists like Pollock and Johns that formerly dominated our evening sales of Contemporary art. Those works are now offered in our Postwar art sales," says Philippe Segalot, Christie's international head of Contemporary art.

Since the middle of the 20th century, Contemporary art has passed through certain phases or periods loosely defined as Abstract Expressionism; Pop art, which came into its own in the 1960s; Minimalism, expressed by such noted artists as Agnes Martin, Robert Ryman, and Donald Judd during the 1970s; and Neo-Expressionism, a style associated with the 1980s works of artists Julian Schnabel and Eric Fischl. Other important artists such as Cindy Sherman, Bruce Nauman, and Robert Gober have explored issues dealing with the human body, self, and identity.

Insiders agree that what most characterizes the art of the present moment is the lack of an overriding theme or direction. Artists are working in a variety of styles and media including everyday objects, textiles, wax, wood, plaster, metal, fiberglass, lighting, video, photography; and the list goes on.

Johnathan Borofsky (b. 1932), *Duck Dream Painting with Chattering Man at 2,847,789*, painted wood, aluminum, bondo and electrical motor sculpture and acrylic and charcoal on canvas with tape and recorder (3 parts) height of man 82¹/₂", paintings: 136" x 99". Auction estimate: $20,000–$25,000. Price realized: $11,500. (Courtesy Butterfields, San Francisco) Although this work came from the collection of one of America's noted Contemporary-art collectors, the late Laila Twigg-Smith of Honolulu, it sold below its low estimate primarily because of its large size.

"Despite all the new media, the ancient traditions of painting and sculpture are still with us," observes New York dealer Joseph Helman. "Artists today are extending those traditions. Jeff Koons's work, for example, is a combination of sculpture and tableau. Robert Rauschenberg and Frank Stella work in a collage format that is a direct outgrowth of painting."

The ever-broadening definition of Contemporary art is evidenced in Christie's recent Contemporary art sales, which have featured contemporary design with such pieces as a futuristic, industrialized chaise by Australian artist Marc Newson and an acrylic chair by Shiro Kuramata.

The dissolving boundaries between media, between art and ideas, and between artist and audience are precisely what makes Contemporary art often difficult to categorize, evaluate, and even comprehend. As with any type of art, its appeal is subjective, and perhaps even more so, because for the most part it lacks an established historical track record by which to measure its value. We have the luxury of years of scholarship and criticism to aid us in our quest for the "perfect" Roman sculpture or Impressionist painting, for example. And a longer auction history helps us to more astutely gauge the current market for those works and determine what we are willing to spend.

Although beauty is, of course, always in the eye of the beholder, you must navigate the dynamic, unpredictable waters of the Contemporary art market with a keen confidence in your own taste and judgment. As always, the advice of good dealers, museum curators, and auction experts will significantly sharpen your understanding and aesthetic awareness of the art of our time, whether you are planning to collect or simply to redecorate your home.

"Information is the difference between collecting and shopping," says Helman. "If you want to start collecting, you have to look at a lot of art. Decide what you like, and focus on certain artists. Ask yourself why you want to buy a particular work of art. Is it aesthetically pleasing, historically important? Does it move you emotionally, challenge you intellectually? Don't be afraid to take risks. Saying 'I know what I like' also means you like what you know, and that can inhibit your growth. If you're really open, great art will expand your eye and your taste. Don't get locked into preconceived notions about what art should be."

When buying Contemporary art at auction, you should use the same criteria of connoisseurship that you would for fine art of other periods, with some variations.

"Authenticity is not as important an issue for Contemporary art as it is for earlier art because most of these artists are living or represented by galleries, so their work is easily authenticated," notes Segalot.

Andy Warhol, however, is one exception. His silkscreen paintings, which were often produced in series and executed by a team of artists in his famous New York City studio, The Factory, must be authenticated by the Andy Warhol Foundation.

The aesthetic quality and historical importance of a work must be judged within the context of the artist's oeuvre (entire body of work).

"Certain periods of an artist's work are more desirable or popular than others. Generally, it's the iconic images, the works that catapulted an artist to recognition, created controversy, or were particularly innovative that are the most sought after," says Michael Maloney, director of 20th-century art at Butterfields. "Warhol's early Pop images of Marilyn, Mao, and the Campbell's Soup cans bring higher prices than his later 'Endangered Species' series, for example."

Likewise, Robert Rauschenberg's revolutionary "combine" works from the late 1950s, which incorporate a host of found objects and are more sought after than his later works. Collectors will also pay a premium for Cindy Sherman's "Untitled Film Stills," a series of photographs from the late 1970s in which Sherman acted out various Hollywood movie roles and which established her reputation. Her more recent "history" portraits are also in demand, as are Julian Schnabel's innovative "plate" paintings from the 1980s and Jeff Koons's porcelain sculptures from the late 1980s, which were inspired by stuffed toys, greeting cards, and pornography.

Even though much of what constitutes Contemporary art has been created relatively recently, you always should inquire about the condition of the piece you plan to bid on. Imperfections, restorations, and repairs most likely will reduce the value of an artwork. Most established auction houses will provide written condition reports for the objects in their sales.

"The extent to which condition affects the value of a work varies with each artist," says Chicago dealer Richard Gray, who also has a gallery in New York. "For example, minor flaws in the pigments of Jackson Pollock's paintings are not so important, whereas Mark Rothko's work is very condition sensitive; so much of its aesthetic quality depends on its visual impact. If a Rothko painting is bleached out or abraded, you won't have the full aesthetic experience. The same is true with Minimalist works by artists like Brice Marden and Robert Ryman, for which the precision and fidelity of the image is crucial to its success. Of course, if the picture is rare and important, condition will have less impact on value."

"If you're planning to buy a painting, you wouldn't want to see cracking or paint loss on the surface," Maloney adds. "While restorations are not as prevalent on Contemporary paintings as on older paintings, it's a good idea to ask the auction specialist at the preview to show you the work in question under ultraviolet light, since restorations may affect the value. Works on paper such as drawings, prints, and watercolors are fragile and more susceptible to condition problems. Paint loss and bleaching from sunlight will usually diminish their value. And since artists today are working in so many experimental materials, there is the issue of longevity. How long will that work made of rubber last? Rubber tends to dry out and chip over time. What is it going to look like in 30 years?"

The size and scale of a work also can affect its value.

"Installation art is very difficult to move, display, and store, as are extremely large sculptures and paint-

Cindy Sherman (b. 1954), Untitled, color coupler print, 20" x 16", signed in ink on reverse "Cindy Sherman 16/125 1990–91." Auction estimate: $2,000–$3,000. Price realized: $3,760. (Courtesy Christie's, New York/Courtesy the artist and Metro Pictures) "This photograph is a strong image printed in a large edition, which makes it more affordable," Segalot says. Generally speaking, contemporary photographs are made in small editions comprising five to ten units.

ings," says Gray. "Since few people can accommodate them in their homes, large works often sell for less than works of standard size by a particular artist. For example, an immense Rauschenberg painting is not nearly as expensive as one would think. Just because it may be five times the size of one of his smaller works, it will not necessarily be five times the cost."

Conversely, you will also find small works by well-known artists that are often more affordable than many of their typical larger-scale pieces, all criteria being equal.

As in every collecting field, provenance (ownership history) and exhibition and publication history may enhance the value of Contemporary art, particularly if a work was once owned by a noted collector or dealer or was part of an important museum exhibition, perhaps a retrospective of a particular artist or an international survey of Contemporary art, such as the Biennial organized by New York's Whitney Museum of American Art. Publication in art magazines and books also adds to a work's cachet. When traceable, this information is usually listed in most auction catalogues along with the description of an artwork.

You should also consider the rarity of the Contemporary art that you plan to bid on. For example, if you want to buy a classic Jackson Pollock "drip" painting from the 1940s, and you know that most are in museums or private collections and rarely come on the market, then be prepared to pay a premium when an example becomes available. Ask auction experts, a dealer, or your local museum curator about the market availability of works that interest you and prices they have fetched at auction in the past.

"The rarity of certain works also depends upon the artist's production. Charles Ray, for example, produces only a few works per year, so they are likely to command high prices," Segalot observes. "Works by well-known Contemporary artists who die prematurely are also obviously limited in number, so collec-

Robert Motherwell (1915–1991) Untitled, signed and dated: RM 1967, acrylic on paper 23 1/2" x 18". Auction estimate: $20,000–$40,000. Price realized: $33,350. (Courtesy Butterfields, San Francisco)

tors will pay more for them. Felix Gonzalez-Torres, who died in the early 1990s, falls into this category. And while the quality of an individual work of art is more important than the period in which it was made, the sheer weight of history sometimes enhances its value. Works by known artists who were prominent during a specific art historical period such as Minimalism or Neo-Expressionism can become more valuable as time passes. However, it is interesting to note that the best art by Jeff Koons, which has brought close to $2 million at auction, sells for more than minor works by Monet."

It is often difficult to determine precise values at any given moment for works by Contemporary artists because so many of them are still producing art and therefore continuously increasing the supply of their works. And since they don't have a long history or constituency, there is a less established market for their work.

"Value is an indirect measure of the size of an artist's constituency—the individuals who own their work, deal in it, write about it, or exhibit it," says Gray. "For Contemporary artists, this constituency is still establishing itself. The fact that an artist like Frank Stella continues to make art keeps his more current work at a relatively accessible price level—about $65,000 to $300,000—which is less than you'd pay for works by Modern masters such as Picasso or Brancusi. And this is true for other high-profile Contemporary artists like Susan Rothenberg and Bruce Nauman. Keep in mind, however, that early work by noted artists, whether or not they are still producing, will become more rare over time and continue to rise in value."

If you're in the market for a work by Warhol, David Hockney, Sigmar Polke, or Jean-Michel Basquiat, you can expect to pay from $100,000 to more than $1 million, depending on the criteria noted above. Works on canvas by postwar masters such as Robert Motherwell and Sam Francis can be bought for $50,000 to $250,000, while their works on paper bring from $20,000 to $50,000. Many quality works in a variety of media by young, emerging artists sell for less than $10,000.

"For the beginning collector, works on paper are a great way to enter the market," says Maloney. "You can buy good examples by Contemporary masters for about one-third the cost of their paintings, sculpture, or mixed-media works. Many collectors are attracted to works on paper because they are the best window into an artist's working process."

Prints by well-known Contemporary artists are a

particularly good value since they are sold in editions, unlike drawings and watercolors, which are one-of-a-kind works. (See separate Works on Paper chapter). Photographs have become one of the fastest-growing areas of the Contemporary art market, and their prices have approached those brought by paintings and sculpture.

"Contemporary photographs have been recognized as an important art form only within the past five years," notes Segalot. "While you can still buy quality photos by artists like Cindy Sherman, Richard Prince, and Thomas Struth for $10,000 to $30,000, some photos by these artists have sold at auction for more than $200,000."

At auction houses such as Christie's, Sotheby's, and Butterfields, Contemporary photographs are included in Contemporary art sales, whereas 19th- and early-20th-century photographs are auctioned in separate photographs sales.

"Whatever type of Contemporary art appeals to you, buy it because you love it, not just for the name recognition or because you think you'll be able to sell it at a higher price later," Lehrman advises. "And always try to view the work in person at the auction preview before you bid on it. Auction houses offer a great opportunity to view a lot of art at once. Don't rely only upon the photographs in the auction catalogues. There is no substitute for an immediate, first-hand experience of a work of art."

Of course, you always should learn as much as possible about your object of desire and the artist's body of work in general before you raise your paddle to bid.

"Do your homework. Talk to dealers, curators, and auction experts. Request condition reports. Know the market value of works by the artists that interest you. Determine a fixed idea about the value, both aesthetically and economically, of the piece you plan to bid on," counsels Gray. "And don't get carried away by your emotions while bidding, or you'll pay too much. You need both expertise and discipline when buying at auction. If you notice a lot of interest in a particular work, and you don't have to have it at all costs, then be willing to let it go. Also remember that auctions do not automatically guarantee fair market value, although the houses themselves cite this as one of the benefits of buying at auction. Prices are contingent on so many different factors—whether it's two big egos engaged in a bidding war, or a blizzard on the day of the sale that results in a scanty showing of bidders, which means less competition to drive up the prices."

"A lot of our buyers bid by telephone, either because they can't attend in person or they find that it allows them to be more rational and disciplined while bidding," Maloney says. "It's possible to get caught up in the saleroom drama and spend more than you had planned when you're bidding in person."

Many well-known dealers and collectors prefer anonymity. They either bid by telephone or appoint someone else to bid for them. If they are seen bidding at auction, the item they want often becomes more desirable to others in the room, which spurs more competition and higher prices.

"If I'm buying at auction, and I really want to get a specific work of art, as close as possible to the price I'm willing to pay, I find that it's more strategic for me to bid by telephone," Helman notes.

Some collectors prefer to bid through dealers representing them in the saleroom. In some cases, these transactions may be executed via cellular telephone, which is different from typical "telephone bidding," in which an auction representative present at the sale simply takes your bids over the phone but does not advise you how to bid.

"I usually pay a dealer a small fee to bid for me in the saleroom while I talk to him on the phone during the sale," Lehrman says. "That way I'm not as likely to get swept away by auction fever. He can also advise me. In the heat of the moment, he may say, 'that's too much to spend, let it go,' which gives me some added perspective."

"Try to refrain from buying anything at auction for a time, while you're visiting galleries, museums, and attending auctions," Helman advises. "And question everything. Auction houses promote certain artists that they think will sell well. The estimates listed in the catalogues are not always the most accurate indication of a work's value. Remember that auction houses represent the seller. Reserves and estimates are negotiated and will reflect the agreement between two sellers."

Collectors stress the importance of building relationships with auction experts, who will be better able to advise you if they know your interests and your budget.

"Auction experts can give you a tremendous amount of additional information about the work that interests you, beyond what's listed in the catalogue," Lehrman says. "Ask them if similar works have sold recently at auction and for what prices. Once you've developed a rapport with someone, he or she can also alert you in advance about works coming up in the future that may interest you."

SELECTED MUSEUM COLLECTIONS:

- Whitney Museum of American Art, New York, NY
- Museum of Modern Art, New York, NY
- San Francisco Museum of Modern Art
- Museum of Contemporary Art, Los Angeles, CA
- The Art Institute of Chicago
- Walker Art Center, Minneapolis, MN

SALES OF CONTEMPORARY ART AT SELECTED AUCTION HOUSES:

- CHRISTIE'S—May, November
- SOTHEBY'S—May, November
- BUTTERFIELDS—April, October
- PHILLIPS—May, November

Robert Lehrman on Timing, Preparation, and Payoff

I remember one auction several years ago when a great painting by Richard Diebenkorn came up, and I really wanted it. Everyone knew that a picture of this quality by Diebenkorn rarely comes on the market, so there was a lot of interest. The fact that the artist had recently died made it even more coveted. While I was looking at the Diebenkorn, at the auction preview, I also happened to notice that Warhol's *Sixteen Jackies*—a large black-and-white silk screen comprising sixteen images of Jackie Kennedy—was also being auctioned, and I was struck by its power. But I still wanted the Diebenkorn. I gave my top price, over the phone, to the dealer who was bidding for me in the saleroom, but I wound up being an underbidder. The painting had sold far above its high estimate. I knew beforehand that I would try to buy the Warhol if I didn't get the Diebenkorn. And since I didn't buy the Diebenkorn, I had funds available. I knew when the Warhol was coming up and gave my top price again to the dealer who was bidding for me. I told him to ask me during the bidding if I wanted to go one bid over my top price. But there was a glitch in our communication, and he bid higher without asking me. I got the painting, but worried that I had paid too much for it, even though I was secure in my knowledge that it was an important work. The next day, I realized how lucky I was, when the underbidder offered to buy it from me for a profit. I wasn't willing to part with it.

Market Watch
CONTEMPORARY MULTIPLES

"Multiples" are works made in editions. They include everything from photographs and prints to sculpture and mixed-media objects. Each multiple is signed and numbered by the artist. Although some auction houses offer Contemporary prints in separate sales devoted to prints of all periods (see Works on Paper chapter), others such as Christie's and Butterfields offer Contemporary prints and other multiples in their Contemporary art sales.

"Buying a multiple by a major artist is a good way to start collecting Contemporary art," says Segalot. "You can find very good examples at auction for just a few thousand dollars, whether it's a photograph by Cindy Sherman, a print by Robert Gober, or an object by Damien Hirst."

Chapter 7
EUROPEAN CERAMICS

Ceramics, one of the world's oldest art forms and encompassing both pottery and porcelain, have been prized by collectors for centuries for their aesthetic beauty and practical uses. Western civilization has been producing ceramics since the time of the ancient Greeks and Romans, but these earth-and-fire creations reached a peak of refinement with European porcelain in the early 18th century, one thousand years after the Chinese invented it.

Porcelain produced during the 18th century by the royal factories at Meissen in Germany and Sèvres in France, as well as that made by such British manufacturers as Worcester, Chelsea, and Coalport, are among the finest ceramics the world has ever seen. Services and individual teapots, plates, cups and saucers, and soup tureens, among other forms, by these noted makers are readily available at auction. Stonewares made by the influential 18th-century British factory Wedgwood also turn up frequently at auction. Auction houses such as Christie's and Skinner hold sales devoted entirely to European ceramics of various periods. Antique European ceramics are also offered in European furniture and decorations sales at these houses and others.

"Antique European ceramics are an excellent buy today, when you consider that you can find many wonderful pieces for less than $1,000. New pieces by famous porcelain makers such as Meissen and Sèvres are often more expensive and generally not of the same high quality as the older examples," says Jody Wilkie, head of European ceramics and glass at Christie's. "Another reason antique ceramics are appealing is that, with care, they will continue to look the same as they did when they were first made. The decoration doesn't change once it's fired, whereas the paint on an Old Master painting, for example, is unstable and alters over time. Antique ceramics are also easy to collect; not only is there such a wide variety from which to choose, they take up less space than furniture. When it comes to decorating, they are more versatile in interiors than people think. Good design is good design. A brightly colored Sèvres dessert service, for example, can be a major statement in a modern monochromatic room with glass tables."

The Meissen factory in Saxony, Germany, established in 1710 under the patronage of August the Strong, was the first European factory to produce white porcelain and is still in business today. The majority of Meissen porcelain at auction are sculptural figures made during the 19th and early-20th centuries, most of which replicate 18th-century models. Meissen figures represent everything from mythological and commedia dell'arte characters, such as Harlequin, to animals and portraits of royalty and aristocrats. Meissen also produced tablewares decorated with Chinese- and Japanese-inspired motifs as well as European flowers and genre scenes. Eighteenth-century Meissen figures and tablewares are rare on the market and bring the highest prices.

"One of the most important criteria to consider when buying Meissen figures is the quality of the modeling and painting," says Stuart G. Slavid, director of ceramics, European decorative arts and silver at Skinner. "Figures modeled by Meissen's most famous 18th-century sculptors, such as Johann Joachim Kändler, while rare, are the most sought after. Kändler also designed exquisite tableware for Meissen, including the famous Swan Service of more than two thousand pieces depicting modeled swans. Meissen produced many later copies of Kändler's Rococo designs, which sell for much less. Even a figure by an anonymous 18th-century sculptor can bring as much as ten times more than a later example."

Nineteenth- and early-20th-century Meissen figures are made of a whiter, crisper porcelain and are painted with a broader spectrum of colors than earlier figures. The type of factory mark stamped on or incised in the porcelain also helps to distinguish early Meissen figures from later examples. Factory marks, which are found on most European ceramics, are useful indicators of authenticity.

Meissen porcelain allegorical figure (left), Germany, late-19th/early-20th century, the female figure modeled holding a script, inscribed no. 369, crossed-swords mark, height 16¹/₂". Auction estimate: $2,300–$3,000. Price realized: $1,610. (Courtesy Skinner, Boston)

Meissen porcelain allegorical figure (center), Germany, late-19th/early-20th century, the female figure modeled holding a scepter, inscribed no. 369, crossed-swords mark, height 16¹/₄". Auction estimate: $2,000–$3,000. Price realized: $1,725. (Courtesy Skinner, Boston)

Meissen porcelain allegorical figure (right), Germany, late-19th/early-20th century, the female figure modeled playing a musical instrument, inscribed no. 369, crossed-swords mark, height 16¹/₂". Auction estimate: $2,000–$3,000. Price realized: $1,840. (Courtesy Skinner, Boston)

"These Meissen figures of typical allegorical subjects are rather large, so the prices achieved were less competitive than they might have been had the figures been smaller and therefore more easily displayed in a china cabinet," Slavid notes.

"The Meissen mark is represented by blue crossed swords. It is often found on the backs of 18th-century figures and underneath later figures," Wilkie says. "Nineteenth-century figures usually have both a factory mark and a model number. Some 18th-century figures may not be marked. But once you start recognizing the texture and color of Meissen porcelain, you will be able to distinguish it from porcelain by other makers. Meissen porcelain is a pure shade of white and has been purified to the degree that you rarely see little air pockets or bubbles on the surface. Bear in mind that during the 19th century a lot of porcelain factories in Germany were copying Meissen products, but they could not compete in quality. Their marks were very similar in appearance with minor alterations. They wanted to trick people into believing that their wares were Meissen. The style of the Meissen mark itself changes over the years, so be sure to familiarize yourself with the porcelain marks of various factories before you bid."

"You should always look at the aesthetic quality of the Meissen figure first, not the mark. Marks are the easiest part to forge. It's much harder to forge quality," Slavid advises. "The best way to start collecting European ceramics is to buy some books first. So many collectors overlook the wonderful variety of reference books that are available on the subject, many of which are excellent guides to the marks of different factories. Auction catalogues from past sales are another valuable source of information. They contain excellent photographs, detailed descriptions, and price information. Every good collector has a great personal library."

Size also affects the value of Meissen figures. Large figural groups, which are often elaborately modeled and painted, usually bring higher prices than individual figures. The average height of a Meissen figure is between three and nine inches. Figures that are exceptionally tall—say, eighteen inches or higher—can be a good value, since many collectors find their size prohibitive for display in their china cabinets.

Ceramics are especially susceptible to condition flaws that can compromise their value.

"Ceramics collectors used to be more discriminating about condition than they are today, because so many of the finest pieces are becoming harder to find," says Slavid. "Simple breaks and chips that have been professionally restored are more acceptable now. But a Meissen figure that has been largely reconstructed is still not desirable. Chips on the arms, legs, and face of a figure are less acceptable than chips on the applied leaves and flowers at the base of a Meissen figure. The more rare the figure, the more forgiving you should be about condition."

As with all antiques, Meissen figures that have remained as close as possible to their original state are the most valuable and sought after.

"While any type of restoration will compromise the value of a Meissen figure, a piece with a reglued original arm, for example, is preferable to a piece with a new arm. Uneven color in a particular area often indicates that paint has been applied to cover a crack or a glue seam. The newer color will be a slightly different shade than the original because it oxidizes over time," Wilkie counsels. "Sometimes colors can be overfired during the original production, which results in popped air bubbles. Figures can also display ash specks known as kiln speckling that results from either the mineral content of the clay or dirt in the kiln. You would not want to bid on a Meissen figure that suffers from too many of these flaws. That said, bubbles and speckling on the face of a figure are less desirable than bubbles and speckling at the base of a figure."

Also beware of 18th-century Meissen porcelain that has been decorated at a later date. These figures or tablewares may be described in auction catalogues as "later decorated." It is preferable to buy pieces that have been fired and decorated during the same time period.

You can buy individual antique Meissen figures at auction for $300 to $20,000; figural groups can be bought for $1,200 to $50,000. Life-size, white animal sculptures by the sculptors Kirchner and Kandler have brought prices in the hundreds of thousands at auction.

Since its inception in 1738, the porcelain factory that began in Vincennes and later moved to Sèvres in France under the patronage of Louis XV has produced some of the world's finest porcelain. In the 18th century it was prestigious for kings to have their own porcelain factories, which competed in making beautiful objects. The Sèvres factory still produces porcelain vases and tablewares, which have traditionally reflected the design currents of the period in which they were made. Most of the finest antique Sèvres porcelain on the market is in the curvilinear Rococo style of the mid-18th century and the subsequent neoclassical style, which incorporates ancient Greek and Roman motifs.

Unlike Meissen, which produced hard-paste porcelain in the tradition of the Chinese, Sèvres first produced soft-paste porcelain because it hadn't discovered the right hard-paste clay until the third quarter of the 18th century. Soft-paste porcelain, whose glazes have a greater translucency and depth of color than hard-paste porcelain, nevertheles became the factory's hallmark and most sought-after wares. Even after the discovery of hard-paste, Sèvres continued to make soft-paste porcelain into the 19th century. Sèvres porcelain is characterized by beautiful ground colors, including bleu celeste (a pale turquoise color), dark blue, yellow, green, and pink; painted reserves featuring flowers, birds, and genre scenes inspired by 18th-century paintings; and gilding.

Whether or not you decide to bid on a Sèvres vase or plate, you should evaluate your object of desire for its aesthetic quality, authenticity, condition, rarity, and provenance.

"The extent and quality of the decoration, whether painted, gilded, or both, are important factors in determining the value of Sèvres porcelain," Wilkie notes. "Pieces with simple stock patterns, such as a scattering of flowers on a white ground, are most common. Pieces with richly colored grounds, gilding, and more complex decoration, such as reserves depicting Chinese motifs or elaborate landscapes and mythological scenes, bring higher prices. Similarly, tablewares with overall geometric patterns are more costly than pieces with geometric borders. An unusual shape, such as a shell-shaped flowerpot known as a *cuvette mahon,* can also enhance value. Remember that certain colors and styles were popular during certain periods. If you see a design that was first introduced in 1755, for example, but which has been repeated on a plate produced in 1780, the latter plate is not as desirable as a plate from the period in which the design originated."

Like Meissen porcelain, 18th-century wares by Sèvres's great artists such as the sculptors Jean-Claude Duplessis and Louis-Simon Boizot, who was noted for biscuit (white, unglazed) figures, and the painters Jean-Louis Morin and Charles-Nicolas Dodin, bring higher prices than wares by less accomplished Sèvres artisans. The recently identified Sèvres painter Louis Denis Armand L'Aine, known as "the Crescent Painter" because he signed his pieces with a small crescent moon, worked for the factory for more than forty years and excelled at painting birds.

"In the 18th century, the best Sèvres artisans were as highly regarded as fine artists and produced the factory's most beautiful wares. One of the great things about collecting Sèvres porcelain is that it is very easy to document, because the factory kept detailed records. Most pieces are marked with interlaced *Ls* (for Louis) and usually have painter's, potter's, and gilder's marks. And they are dated according to an alphabetical system," says Leon Dalva of New York's Dalva Brothers, dealers specializing in 18th-century French furniture and works of art. "Porcelain made during the earliest years, when the factory was located in Vincennes, is marked with the letters *A* to *D*. When the factory moved to Sèvres, in 1753, the dating continued with the letter *E*."

A considerable amount of Sèvres porcelain was commissioned by royalty and wealthy individuals.

"Those with important provenances, such as the

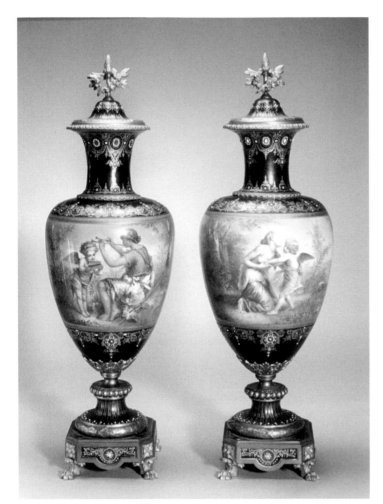

Important pair of Sèvres porcelain vases and covers, France, 19th century, gilt-metal mounted, cobalt ground with scrolled gilt foliage and enameled, jeweled borders, handpainted central panels with classical subjects, artist signed M. Demonceaux. Auction estimate: $30,000–$50,000. Price realized: $32,200. (Courtesy Skinner, Boston) "These Sèvres vases achieved a significant price due to their large size, fine-quality metalwork and painting, and the fact that they were signed. Pairs of Sèvres vases with this desirable formula rarely show up on the market," Slavid says.

auction than intact large services, which are rare. While Sèvres wares can be displayed as works of art in their own right, they can also be used. Many collectors search for pieces with the same pattern, to complete a dinner service. Since some Sèvres patterns have been continuously produced over the years, a "married" service with a common pattern, comprising pieces with the same pattern from different firings, is often not as valuable as a service comprising pieces with the same pattern that were fired at the same time. The very elaborate sets were not repeated.

Although traditional Sèvres collectors tend to prefer 18th-century soft-paste examples, Sèvres 18th- and 19th-century hard-paste wares are gaining more attention.

"Early-19th-century Sèvres is fabulous; it's a whole new aesthetic with neoclassical motifs and Eyptian images inspired by Napoleon's campaigns in Egypt," says Wilkie. "Because this porcelain is hard-paste, the colors take on a different hue. Sèvres has always made an effort to keep pace with the times, continuously adapting new designs while at the same time reissuing old patterns. There were Art Nouveau and Art Deco Sèvres porcelain, and there are today's contemporary designs, whereas most of Meissen's current designs are still based on their 18th-century models. A new dinner plate by Sèvres that is printed with an 18th-century pattern, however, does not have the same 'soul' as an old hand-painted plate. In terms of overall quality and affordability, you're better off buying an antique porcelain dinner service by Sèvres or other European factories rather than a new service, even though you may not find an even number of every shape, and the pieces may be a little worn. The only service that is 100 percent handmade and produced on a commercial scale today is by the Danish company Royal Copenhagen, whose Flora Danica wares, which are based on an 18th-century design, are more costly than a lot of beautiful antique porcelain."

While most Sèvres porcelain is marked, the factory sold a large amount of plain white porcelain during the early-19th century that was anonymously decorated. These pieces, which were decorated with Sèvres patterns, sometimes years after the porcelain was originally produced, are referred to as "later-

great services made for Louis XVI and Marie Antoinette, for example, are the most sought after and costly, and often find their way into museums," Dalva says. "Of course, the factory also made plates for everyday services and vases that weren't important decorative objects requiring exceptional skills. The elaborate decorative vases were produced in small numbers and bring some of the highest prices. That's not to say that cups and saucers are always less valuable. Some of the high-quality, early Vincennes examples, whose decoration and colors are more subdued, can sell for as much as a good vase."

Individual Sèvres cups, saucers, soup tureens, plates, and other forms turn up more frequently at

decorated Sèvres" and should be indicated as such in auction catalogues. You may also see "Sèvres-style" pieces, which were fantastical interpretations of original Sèvres but not of the same high quality and therefore less valuable. As in every collecting field, it is advisable to seek the counsel of a trusted auction specialist or dealer before you place your first bid. Of course, even the experts can be fooled, and you may discover that a later-decorated piece has been miscatalogued as the real thing or vice versa.

"Sèvres-style pieces, which weren't made at the Sèvres factory, weren't intended as forgeries but probably more as an homage to the originals. The later-decorated pieces were often intended as forgeries and usually don't have the same subtlety and sophistication of decoration as genuine Sèvres porcelain," Dalva observes. "But as long as you are aware of what you're buying, there is no harm in paying less for Sèvres-style or later-decorated Sèvres porcelain if that is what appeals to you. You should also be cautious of Sèvres pieces whose decoration has been removed with acid and repainted with more colors and more complex decoration in order to increase their value. These forgeries could have occurred as much as one hundred years later. It's always a good idea to seek outside advice before buying at auction."

As with other types of porcelain, the condition of the Sèvres vase or plate on which you plan to bid also helps to determine its desirability and value.

"Of course you always want to buy something with as little damage as possible. The more rare the piece, the less important condition becomes. If only a small number of a certain type of vase were made for Louis XV, for example, and there is only one on the market, you should not let a few scratches or chips prevent you from buying it if you have the funds to do so," Dalva says. "If you're bidding on a $200 plate, however, or on a piece that you will likely see again on the market, then hold out for near perfect condition."

You can buy good-quality, single Sèvres plates, cups, saucers, and other tablewares at auction for $500 or less. A serving dish, made for the first Louis XV service, with exquisite painting and gilding on a bleu-celeste ground, for example, can bring tens of thousands of dollars. Sèvres vases sell for $30,000 to hundreds of thousands, depending upon their rarity, provenance, and the other criteria already mentioned. A pair of Sèvres ewers brought close to $1 million at an English country auction in 1999.

If your taste in porcelain is more English than Continental, you will find at auction a wide selection of antique English ceramics by well-known factories such as Chelsea and Bow of London, Worcester, Coalport, Spode, and Wedgwood, among others. Chelsea and Bow were noted for their 18th-century tablewares and figures inspired by Japanese Kakiemon and Chinese blue-and-white and famille rose porcelains. Rivals Worcester, Spode, and Coalport produced porcelain of varying shapes decorated with Chinese and Japanese patterns as well as Rococo flowers and birds. Wedgwood is best known for its colored stoneware called jasperware (because it resembles jasper), which is decorated with classical motifs in relief.

"Each factory had its own porcelain recipe that resulted in products of varying weight, color, and texture in both soft and hard paste. Worcester, for example, mixed a type of soapstone into its clay, which gives it a greenish appearance, whereas Bow used a denser paste that makes its wares heavier in weight than those of some other factories," Wilkie notes. "The English also invented bone china, a highly resistant, translucent porcelain made with crushed bones. While most 19th-century English ceramics are marked, the best way to distinguish the highly sought-after 18th-century porcelain is by the materials and firing techniques used. Unlike the royal factories at Sèvres and Meissen, English ceramics factories were small, independently owned businesses that were very competitive and often copied each other's designs. So you really can't differentiate English porcelain by its decoration alone."

Given such a broad variation of product, experts recommend that novice collectors of English ceramics begin by focusing on one type of ware. As with any collecting category, you should consult pertinent reference books; visit museums, galleries, and auction previews to compare various examples; and ask the advice of curators, dealers, and auction specialists before buying at auction.

Perhaps you are in search of the perfect Worcester teapot for your next dinner party. The Worcester factory, founded in 1751 in the city of Worcester, is the oldest surviving porcelain factory in England.

"Worcester made large quantities of great soft-paste porcelain teaware that is very popular with collectors. When deciding which Worcester teapot to buy, you should first of all inspect the quality, complexity, and rarity of its decoration," says Jill Fenichell of New York's Fenichell-Basmajian Antiques, which specializes in European ceramics and glass. "Worcester is particularly noted for its beautiful, 18th-century hand-painted wares, which often display Rococo reserves or cartouches depicting a fusion of Eastern and Western design motifs, such as Chinese-style foliage and colorful English landscapes, bouquets, and fanciful birds. Unlike Meissen and Wedgwood, Worcester changed its designs over the years. The neoclassical style became prevalent toward the end of the 18th century. The most popular Worcester porcelains include blue-and-white English interpretations of 17th-century Japanese Kakiemon porcelain and those bearing Chinese-inpired blue or yellow fish-scale patterns, some of which have reserve decorations. Pieces with ground colors are also sought after; various shades of blue are the most common, while yellow, pink, and green are rare."

Worcester porcelain was also decorated with transfer prints of 18th-century genre scenes, including lovers on swings, haywagons, and tea parties. Hand-painted wares usually bring higher prices than transfer-printed wares, with the exception of rare transfer prints such as "Milkmaid at the Gate." Generally, the earliest, most colorful, and highly decorated teapots are the most sought after. Pieces with rare design-and-color combinations, such as a 1758 "yellow-scale" teapot with a reserve floral decoration, or unusual shapes, such as rectangular and paneled teapots, are also desirable and bring high prices.

There are many different ways to collect Worcester porcelain. Some collectors focus on 18th-century pieces, while others prefer 19th-century wares, which tend to have more gilding and fanciful handles, knops, and spouts modeled in animal and plant shapes. Some collectors prefer "blue-scale" patterns; others collect only transfer-printed wares. Whether you are decorating or collecting, remember that provenance, as always, also helps to determine value.

"While 18th-century Worcester porcelain is consistently high-quality, as with any European porcelain it can be even more desirable if it comes from an important private collection. That kind of pedigree can increase its value by as much as 25 percent," Slavid observes.

Since English porcelain factories often copied one another's designs, it is often difficult for a novice collector to distinguish an original Worcester teapot without the help of an expert. Additionally, Worcester marks changed over the years as ownership changed. From 1751 through 1765, for example, a workman's mark took the form of a series of blue strokes on the base of a teapot or other wares. After 1765, the mark was a small crescent moon. You will also see interpretations of Chinese seal marks on Worcester porcelain. In addition to consulting an expert, whether an auction specialist or dealer, you should consult reference books to familiarize yourself with the marks of various factories before buying English and other European ceramics at auction.

"The factory mark is usually a good guide for authenticating English ceramics, but it is not an absolute. Some wares were not marked at all; and the marks on some lesser wares were intentionally rubbed off by retailers hoping to fool people into thinking they were better pieces by the better factories," Fenichell advises. "Also, during the 19th century, a company in Paris called Samson was renowned for making good-quality reproductions of Sèvres, Meissen, and the best English porcelain. But they were usually hard-paste copies decorated with overglaze enamels, whereas Worcester porcelain is soft-paste with underglaze enameling. If the porcelain body of the teapot has a yellow-green hue when you hold it up to the light, then it is more likely to be original."

Then there is the problem of fakes.

Worcester porcelain "Waiting Chinaman" teapot and cover (left), England, 18th century, the globular form underglaze-blue decorated, floral finial, open crescent mark, (slight nick to spout, chips to finial, line under base), height 5⅝". Auction estimate: $600–$800. Price realized: $862.50. (Courtesy Skinner, Boston) Teapots are among the most collectible English porcelain wares. This example is distinctive for its "Waiting Chinaman" decoration, which is more sought after than typical floral decoration. The condition flaws on this teapot held down its value.

Porcelain by well-known English makers was not immune to forgers hoping to profit from the factories' commercial success.

"Fakes, which are made with the intention to deceive, are different from copies or reproductions, which are marketed as such," Slavid says. "While some fakes are very good approximations of the real things, they are not of the same superior quality. The aesthetic quality, not the mark, is the best indicator of authenticty."

When it comes to condition, you should apply the same criteria to your Worcester teapot as to other types of porcelain.

"The teapot should be usable. Large cracks, stapled parts, and reglued areas on the body of a teapot will reduce its value considerably. In the 19th century and up through the 20th century it was common to fix plates and other porcelain wares by reattaching broken pieces with a strip of metal that is cut and soldered to look like a staple. Tiny cracks or chips will not reduce the value as much—particularly on 18th-century teapots—even though they still compromise the integrity of the porcelain," Fenichell explains. "The teapot will suffer in value if it does not have its original cover. The spouts and knops (or finials on teapot covers) are often chipped, which is an acceptable condition flaw as long as the cover is original to the teapot. Beware of wood, pewter, and silver handles that have been substituted for broken porcelain handles. In all cases, make sure that you inspect the piece with your hands as well as your eyes. And hold it up to the light. Remember that you are allowed to handle objects during the auction preview. You want your porcelain to look bright and lustrous, not tired from excessive wear and tear."

Other condition flaws common to porcelain that can reduce value include the flaking and rubbing-off of gilding and paint. While it is possible to have porcelain repainted and regilded, the new colors will not match the original antique colors. A Worcester teapot may show some gilt rubbing, but because it was created to withstand heat, it rarely shows flaking. English porcelain also can suffer from crazing and browning, whereby glazes crack into numerous small "spiderweb" lines that eventually turn brown from years of accumulated dirt.

Restorations also affect the value of English porcelain. "Restorations such as a newly modeled spout or handle or a patched crack are less acceptable on porcelain than on pottery and more detrimental to its value," Slavid says. "Some restorations are less invasive than others, however. A restored spout tip, for ex-

ample, would not reduce the value of a teapot as much as restoration to its body."

"When checking for restoration, hold the teapot up to the light. You should be able to see light through the porcelain. If you can't see through a certain area, then it may have been patched or filled with a synthetic material made of plaster and glue and then refired," Fenichell adds. "Of course, you may decide to buy a particularly rare or desirable piece that needs some restoration. Generally, I would fix chips and cracks on pieces that I'm going to be displaying more than using."

Auction specialists can recommend conservators. As with all antiques being sold at auction, prior to the sale you should also request a written condition report for the pieces that interest you. Most auction houses do not describe condition in their catalogues.

You can buy a quality 18th-century Worcester porcelain teapot for $500 to $12,000. Worcester plates sell from about $300 for a transfer-printed plate up to $10,000 to $20,000 for an armorial plate that is intensely patterned, hand painted, and made for the Prince of Wales, for example. Worcester cups and saucers bring from $400, for an example with a blue-and-white transfer print of a pine cone pattern, up to about $9,000 for an example with a yellow-scale pattern and floral reserve. Elaborate hand-painted plates with blue-scale patterns and fancy bird reserves sell for from $1,500 to $2,500. Blue-and-white Worcester wares from the early 1750s bring from $4,000 to $12,000. Eighteenth-century porcelain tablewares by other noted English factories bring similar prices, depending upon the criteria of connoisseurship previously discussed. As with most types of ceramic tablewares, you are most likely to find individual pieces from various services. Collectors will pay a premium for complete services, which are rare.

Whether you are in the market for a Sèvres plate or a Worcester teapot, remember that antique porcelain tablewares were meant to be used. Although fragile in appearance, they are sturdy and well made. So don't be afraid to empty your breakfront and treat your dinner guests to a visual feast. Of course, you will want to ensure that they remain in admirably good condition.

"Clean your ceramics with soap and water, but don't scrub them or put them in the dishwasher, which can abrade the glaze and eventually wear down the enamel. Don't set plates on radiators or stoves or put them into the oven. The heat will cause them to brown," Fenichell says. "And if you want to guard against breakage, buy some glue tack at the stationery store and affix it to your shelves. My friend's ceramics stayed intact even during an earthquake!"

Now that you have done your homework, you're ready to bid. But first, a few helpful tips.

"Don't just bid from the catalogue. Come to the auction previews when you can. Study the objects. Touch them. Fall in love with them. And talk to the specialists and build relationships that will serve you in the future," Slavid counsels.

"Make notes on the piece that interests you at the auction preview, and ask us questions. Don't feel as though you're bothering us. We're very interested in meeting new buyers and collectors," Wilkie adds. "And telling us what types of art and antiques appeal to you helps us keep abreast of the vagaries in the market."

Experts also do not recommend that you buy art and antiques for investment.

"Art should not be viewed as a liquid commodity. It has an emotional appeal. Collectors and dealers react viscerally to it. If you buy what you love and buy the best you can afford, you are likely to put together an admirable collection," Dalva says. "You have to be very astute when buying at auction. Remember that auction houses are in the business to sell, and some items are promoted more than others, particularly if they belonged to someone famous. Just because an object was in the collection of the Duke and Duchess of Windsor, for example, does not necessarily mean it's of the highest quality, and may or may not deserve the price it brings. Also keep in mind that auction estimates can sometimes be either too high or too low, either to satisfy the sellers or attract buyers. They are not always accurate indicators of value."

As for bidding, the word of the wise is to decide on your top bid price in advance and stick to it, or allow yourself the leeway to go one bid above your top price.

"It's easy to get carried away with your emotions in the heat of the moment. Use your heart to decide which object you love, and use your head while bidding. Remember that many similar pieces are likely to show up again at auction, so you will have another chance," Fenichell advises. "And don't forget to factor the buyer's commission and applicable sales taxes into your top bid price, which could increase it by as much as 20 percent."

You should also not let the bidding activity cloud your judgment. Sometimes desirable objects sell for less than anticipated. Conversely, some bidders may be prepared to pay anything to get what they want.

"I remember sitting next to a woman at an auction who kept elbowing her husband in the ribs because she needed a pair of vases for a specific spot in her home. She eventually got them for about three times what they were worth, and her husband had some sore ribs," Dalva says.

❖❖❖❖❖❖❖❖❖

RECOMMENDED MUSEUM COLLECTIONS:

- The Metropolitan Museum of Art, New York, NY

- Museum of Fine Arts, Boston

- Nelson-Atkins Museum of Art, Kansas City, KS

- Los Angeles County Museum of Art

- Birmingham Museum of Art, AL (Wedgwood)

- Philadelphia Museum of Art

- Wadsworth Atheneum, Hartford, CT

SALES OF EUROPEAN CERAMICS AT SELECTED AUCTION HOUSES:

- CHRISTIE'S—January, April/May, October/November (included in English and French furniture sales)

- SOTHEBY'S—January, April, October (included in English and Continental furniture sales)

- SKINNER—July, December (English ceramics sales); January, April, July, October (Continental ceramics included in English and Continental furniture sales)

Market Watch
ANTIQUE WEDGWOOD JASPERWARE

Some of the world's most recognizable ceramics are the colored stoneware vases, plates, bowls, and other forms known as jasperware that the British potter Josiah Wedgwood began producing at his Staffordshire factory in the 1760s. While these wares are still being made today, there is a plentiful supply of antique jasperware available at auction, at prices often lower than those of new examples. Jasperware is one of the many varieties of Wedgwood pottery, which includes creamware, majolica, and black basalt ware. Jasperware is distinguished by its hand-applied relief decoration incorporating classical motifs inspired by ancient Greek and Roman art. Subjects include figural scenes and portrait medallions of historical figures such as Roman emperors, English royalty, and poets. The stoneware bodies were made in various shades of blue, green, yellow, and other colors, dark blue being the most common.

"Wedgwood pottery, and jasperware particularly, has always been popular with collectors who appreciate its elegance and sculptural quality," Slavid says. "Some people collect jasperware from various time periods; others collect a specific color or enjoy studying the classical history of the decoration. And some people buy it solely for decorative purposes. Over the years the company introduced new forms, and continues to make copies of earlier examples. While new jasperware often sells for higher prices than antique jasperware, the older pieces are better crafted. The most important criterion is the quality of the sculptural decoration. Eighteenth-century jasperware has the best-quality decoration, and its pottery body feels like silk, whereas 20th-century wares are more granular to the touch."

Wedgwood pale-blue jasper dip tea canister and cover (top left), England, late-18th century, applied white classical relief of children above an engine-turned band, impressed lower case mark (chips and hairlines to foot rim), height 5³⁄₈". Auction estimate: $200–$400. Price realized: $431.25. (Courtesy Skinner, Boston)

Two Wedgwood solid-blue jasper items (center left), England, late-18th century, a covered sugar bowl with applied white classical relief, engine-turned foot and cover, height 4¹⁄₄"; and a stand with applied white acanthus and stiff leaf border, diameter 5¹⁄₄"; impressed marks. Auction estimate: $400–$600. Price realized $1,092.50. (Courtesy Skinner, Boston)

Jasperware prices also depend upon the rarity, type, and combinations of color and decoration. Since crimson is rarer than other colors, a crimson piece made in the early 1920s, for example, is likely to bring more than an earlier dark blue piece. Three-color wares are less common than two-color wares and bring higher prices. "Dice" patterns and the less common "strapware," or basketweave, patterns also add value. Most jasperware is ornamental and not meant to be used.

"Antique jasperware is easy to collect because most of it is marked. The marks changed over the years, which helps you to determine the age of a piece," Slavid says. "There are also a lot of reference books on Wedgwood and numerous Wedgwood societies that you can join to learn about collecting. For its overall quality and craftsmanship, 18th- and early-19th-century jasperware represents great value when you consider that many of these period pieces can be bought for less than $500 and will continue to increase in value with the passing of time."

Chapter 8
EUROPEAN FURNITURE

The explosion over the past two decades of museum exhibitions, publications, lectures, courses, fairs, and study tours on the decorative arts continues to feed Americans' growing appetite for antiques. And the proliferation of "shelter" magazines has both nurtured and mirrored an active interest in home decorating and design. As a result, more and more antiques enthusiasts and collectors, both established and new, are bidding at auctions, once the domain of dealers. And they are mixing a wide range of styles and periods to create interiors that reflect a unique personal aesthetic.

Whether you are in the market for a George III bookcase, a Louis XVI sofa, a French provincial armoire, a Biedermeier chair, or an Italian Renaissance credenza, you will find a diverse selection of antique European furniture at auction, at prices that are often lower than those of newly made furniture.

"The market for European furniture has never been stronger," says Karen Cangelosi, a European-furniture specialist at Phillips, de Pury & Luxembourg, which holds each year three sales of furniture and decorations in New York and four sales of more modestly priced furniture at its St. Louis affiliate, Phillips-Selkirk. "The trend is towards less elaborate furniture that blends well with an informal lifestyle. Whichever European furniture style or period interests you, my advice is always to buy the best you can afford. If you plan to collect, you will eventually want to 'trade up' or upgrade your collection as you learn more about what you're buying. Everyone usually makes some mistakes in the beginning, but that's part of the learning process."

Antique English furniture has long been popular with collectors, who value its classical lines, rich woods, and high-quality craftsmanship. Eighteenth-century furniture made during the Queen Anne (1700–1720), Georgian (1714–1805), and Regency (1805–1820) periods has traditionally been the most sought after. Queen Anne furniture, which shows up less frequently on the market, is usually made of wal-nut and characterized by simple, graceful forms and cabriole legs. By contrast, furniture made during the reign of George I (1714–1727) and George II (1727–1760) is crafted mostly of mahogany and is heavy and architectural in design. The mahogany furniture made during the reign of George III (1760–1805), which coincided with the Chippendale period (1760–1775), displays carved details and more elaborate designs inspired by the Gothic-Revival, French, and chinoiserie styles adapted by the great English cabinetmaker Thomas Chippendale.

Other noted 18th-century English furniture designers included the Adam brothers, noted for their exquisite architectural designs, and Thomas Sheraton and George Hepplewhite, whose austere, refined furniture dominated the last two decades of the 18th century. The Regency furniture that followed (named for the period during which George III's son the Prince Regent ruled) is characterized by flamboyant Egyptian-, Greek- and Gothic-Revival styles and chinoiserie decoration.

Although the best examples from these periods have brought well over one million dollars at auction, you still can find good examples that won't break your bank, whether you are beginning a collection or looking for the perfect accent for your new home.

"Eighteenth-century English furniture is beautifully constructed and available on the market, whereas the supply of fine 18th-century American furniture is more limited," observes Mark Jacoby, owner of Phillip Colleck, a gallery in New York that specializes in antique English furniture. "The majority of 18th-century English furniture was made for the emerging merchant classes during the reigns of George II and III. At that time, America was a smaller country with fewer cabinetmakers. When compared with American furniture, antique English furniture is still undervalued for its quality. The elegant, classical design of Georgian furniture adapts to a variety of interiors. And the scale and proportions of many of these pieces are well suited to modern-day rooms."

Perhaps you want to bid on a George III mahogany bookcase-cabinet or secretary-bookcase (sometimes called a bureau-bookcase). As with all antique furniture, you will want to evaluate its quality of design and craftsmanship, authenticity, condition, and rarity. You will not be able to make an accurate judgment from the auction catalogue photograph alone. You should attend the auction preview (presale exhibition) to inspect closely the pieces that interest you. Auction specialists will gladly answer your questions and provide market information, such as prices for which similar pieces have sold at recent auctions.

"You should first of all look at the overall design of the piece," says Andrea Blunck Frost, director of English and Continental Furniture and Decorations at the auction house Doyle New York, which displays its decorative-arts offerings in attractive room settings during auction previews. "Does it have elegant, harmonious proportions, or does it look heavy and oversized? Does it have plain bracket feet or carved feet? Is the cornice plain or molded? Does it have inlay or fretwork? How much detail does it display? All these factors will affect its value."

While antique English furniture is not as elaborately ornamented as antique French furniture, pieces with more intricate carving tend to fetch higher prices. And, unlike French furniture, English furniture is rarely signed or labeled. When pieces are identified as Chippendale or Sheraton in auction catalogues, that usually means they were made during those periods and conform to the designs published in Thomas Chippendale's *The Gentleman & Cabinet Maker's Director,* or Thomas Sheraton's *The Cabinet-Maker and Upholsterer's Drawing-Book.* Only in rare cases does the original bill of sale for a piece of furniture still exist and therefore help to trace the it to a specific designer. Such a piece, of course, would be highly sought after by collectors.

You will also want to evaluate the quality of the wood and craftsmanship of the bookcase on which you plan to bid.

"Most Georgian furniture was very finely crafted of solid mahogany and mahogany veneers," Jacoby notes. "The best examples have beautifully matched veneers and consistent graining. Bookcases with unusual wood patterns are less common and more valuable. And those that have retained their original brass handles are more desirable than those with replaced hardware. Some pieces are more carefully constructed than others. You should look for precise dovetailing, meaning joinery that is flush and finely cut."

A bookcase with its original surface or patina is always more desirable and valuable than a refinished piece. Centuries of wax and dust accumulation create a surface with a rich, mellow hue that indicates age.

"The surface is a good indicator of the authenticity of a piece. If a bookcase looks too perfect, then it has probably been refinished," Cangelosi advises. "Old surfaces often have rings and dark markings that are the result of years of use. Since wood oxidizes as it ages, wood aged naturally will appear darker than newer wood. You will want to make sure that the color of the wood is the same on each part of the bookcase and that the graining matches. A lot of pieces have been cut down and reassembled later. A 'married' bookcase or a table with an old bottom and a new top, for example, would only be half as valuable as an original 18th-century example."

George III mahogany bookcase cabinet, late-18th century, height 8'1", width 49½", later broken scroll pediment carved with leafage and fretwork. Auction estimate: $6,000–$8,000. Price realized: $27,600. (Courtesy Doyle New York) "This bookcase has very nice proportions, beautiful, rich-colored mahogany, and needed little restoration," says Frost. "Competition between two bidders drove the price significantly above its estimate. They didn't seem to mind that the pediment had been replaced at a later date, which is not unusual with these old pieces."

"While collectors of English furniture are just as demanding as American-furniture collectors, most American-furniture collectors prize original, untouched surfaces. English-furniture collectors, however, generally would not reject pieces with surfaces that have been cleaned," Jacoby notes.

As with any work of art or antique, the condition of the bookcase that interests you is an important criteria of connoisseurship. Since auction catalogues rarely list detailed condition information, be sure to request a written condition report prior to the sale from the appropriate auction specialists. And remember that most auction houses do not guarantee the condition of their offerings. Everything is sold "as is." Damage that may occur to furniture during handling prior to the auction or at the auction preview will not be indicated in the catalogue, so you will want to inspect the bookcase carefully.

"I'll be honest with potential buyers if they ask whether the top and bottom are original to a piece, or if there have been any repairs or replacements, to my knowledge, which may reduce the value," says Frost. "Many pieces of antique furniture that are sold at auction, because they are so old and have been used, require at least minimal restorations such as cleaning, replacing a veneer, rewaxing or revarnishing, or adjusting doors, drawers, and hinges. If the mahogany bookcase you want to buy has turned dark from cigar smoke, for example, a restorer may be able to bring it back to its original dark brown color, which could enhance its value. We can recommend restoration experts, some of whom are present at our previews to offer estimates. Of course, you will have to calculate this added cost into your top bid price."

Some buyers bring their own decorators and restorers to previews. You may also want to take photographs of the pieces that interest you, so that you will have a better idea of how they will look in your home. Specialists at some auction houses such as Doyle New York can take Polaroid snapshots for you at the preview as well.

"Ideally, you want to buy a piece that is as close to its original state as possible, which means it should have very little restoration," says Jacoby. "You shouldn't lower your standards because you may be decorating rather than collecting. Unlike with American furniture, a restoration such as replaced feet will not significantly reduce the value of antique English furniture. With a bookcase, for example, it's more important that the cornice and mullions—the wood strips that separate the glass panels on the doors—are original. Some Georgian bookcases have delicate fretwork at the top or plinths that once supported sculpted busts and porcelain vases. Bookcases that have retained these architectural superstructures are sought after. Keep in mind that originally many of these bookcases were very large—some breakfront bookcases measured 14 feet high by 20 feet wide—and were often cut down or shortened to accommodate various interiors. Make sure that the color and patina of the wood matches on all parts, and that the hinges are correctly placed. Sometimes mirrors were added to the solid wood doors of a bookcase. An

original mirrored bookcase would usually have a small candle slide for the purpose of holding candles whose flames are reflected by the mirrors. In any case, you don't want to pay top dollar for a piece that has been altered or restored."

The cold, damp climate of English country houses, where this furniture has stood for so long, can create problems when pieces are brought to this country. Our much drier, warmer climate in many parts of the country can cause antiques to warp or crack. Jacoby recommends keeping a bowl of water inside case furniture so that the wood can absorb needed moisture. Periodic waxing also will help the wood to retain its natural glow.

When deciding which George III bookcase you'd like to bid on, read the auction catalogue carefully. An authentic George III bookcase from the period is not the same as a bookcase in the George III style that was made later. In Doyle's catalogues, for example, a lot described as a *George III Mahogany Secretary Bookcase, late 18th century,* means that the piece is, in the auction house's best judgment, "of the period indicated with no major alterations or restorations." The same lot so identified, but without an accompanying date, means that "the piece, while basically of the period, has been substantially altered or restored." A lot identified as a *George III Style Mahogany Secretary Bookcase* means that "the piece is an intentional copy or reproduction of an earlier work or style of works." Period pieces carry higher estimates, generally are more sought after, and bring higher prices. However, just because a piece may be 250 years old, does not mean that it is necessarily beautiful or desirable.

You can buy a period George III bookcase at auction for about $10,000 to $25,000, while bookcases in the George III style may cost $3,000 to $5,000. Period pieces with sophisticated inlay, carving, and molding bring from $25,000 to $50,000 or more. Some of the best examples have sold for over one million dollars. Other forms, such as Georgian dining tables of the period, can be bought at auction for $35,000 and up; side tables bring from $5,000 to $10,000. You can buy a pair of period Georgian chairs for about $10,000 to $15,000, while single chairs, which are less sought after than sets, sell for $6,000 or less. Period Georgian mirrors bring from $15,000 and up.

Some auction houses, such as Doyle New York, also hold frequent general furniture and decorations sales, which feature mainly 19th-century reproductions of earlier styles that can be bought for less than $5,000. These sales are ideal sources of affordable furniture if you are more interested in creating a certain ambience in your home than in owning period antiques.

The 18th century not only produced some of the finest English furniture ever made but was also the pinnacle of cabinetmaking in France. While Louis XV and XVI furniture has been coveted by collectors since the French Revolution, when the French aristocracy were forced to sell many of their treasures, today's less formal lifestyles have cultivated a taste for a casual, rustic simplicity that is expressed in French provincial or country antiques, which come up frequently at auction.

The majority of French provincial armoires, buffets, tables, chairs, commodes, and other forms were made by anonymous cabinetmakers during the 18th and 19th centuries in provinces outside the major cities in France. Each province produced furniture with indigenous woods and distinctive styles that reinterpreted the Louis XV and Louis XVI court styles developed by cabinetmakers in Paris. French provincial furniture, however, is made of solid wood rather than the veneers typical of more formal court furniture. The carving and hardware on French provincial pieces also differs from province to province.

Perhaps your heart is set on a French provincial armoire. An armoire from Normandy would most likely be made either of oak or a fruitwood such as cherry or apple, since Normandy is a fruit-growing region, whereas armoires made in the south of France were often crafted of olive wood. Pine also was used because it was affordable and easily carved. Some pieces are rustic in style, while others are more sophisticated. Judging from its scale and the complexity of its design and carving you would be able to tell whether the armoire came from a château or a farmhouse. Carving sometimes takes the form of floral and garland motifs on its paneled doors, crest, and apron. The climate of its province of origin can influence its design. For example, furniture made in the northern provinces of Normandy and Brittany tends to be sturdier than that made in the more hospitable climate of southern France. "French provincial furniture can be distinguished by the shape of the feet and the carving. Furniture from Provence, for example, an area in southern France, often has pointed 'slipper' feet and shell or pierce carving on the skirts," says George Subkoff, a dealer in Westport, Connecticut. "The most desirable French provincial furniture has unusual shapes and skilled carving, and was usually made for châteaux. Pieces made of walnut and the more expensive fruitwoods, versus oak and pine, tend to bring higher prices."

Provincial Louis XV
walnut armoire, ca. 1750. Molded-arched cornice
above two scroll, floral and shell-carved doors, raised on scroll feet. Height 8'8",
width 57", depth 23". Auction estimate: $8,000–$12,000. Price realized: $8,625.
(Courtesy Doyle New York)

Since many armoires stand as high as eight or nine feet, you may want to bring a measuring tape to the auction preview to ensure that it accommodates your room dimensions. You'll also want to inspect it for woodworm damage, a result of damp storage conditions in old country houses.

"You should expect to see tiny wormholes on the surface of French provincial furniture," Cangelosi observes. "But if they're all the same size, then most likely they were added by forgers in an attempt to make a piece appear old. If you see sawdust around the holes, however, then the piece still has active woodworm, which may infest other furniture in your home. Auction specialists can recommend restorers who will be able to treat this condition."

Many French provincial armoires may also have replaced feet, which does not significantly affect their value. Since these pieces are often large and heavy, their delicate feet are vulnerable to damage over time.

A set of four (two shown) fine antique German Biedermeier figured-walnut dining chairs with scroll-shape concave tablet top rails on arched styles, the vertical splats inlaid with geometric medallions, the padded seats raised on slightly splayed legs, early-19th century. $3,283. (Courtesy Phillips-Selkirk, St. Louis)

An antique German Biedermeier walnut center table, the crossbanded finely figured circular top raised on a concave-sided tapered triangular pedestal and plinth mounted with ebonized moldings, early-19th century, height 29$\frac{1}{2}$", diameter 40". $4,370. (Courtesy Phillips-Selkirk, St. Louis)

"These pieces are typical of well-crafted Biedermeier furniture. The presence of ebony inlay and the carved chair splats add to their value. The prices realized represent a very good buy given the fine quality of this furniture," notes Cangelosi.

Large areas of replaced wood, however, would diminish the value of an armoire considerably. And like most antique furniture, pieces that have retained much or part of their original patina are more desirable than those that have been refinished.

You also would want to know that you are, indeed, buying an authentic antique. Newly fabricated pieces made of old woods and elements from more than one piece of furniture occasionally show up on the market.

"If you're looking at a chest of drawers, for example, be sure to look carefully at the inside and bottom of the drawers," advises Cangelosi. "If the piece is old, the bottoms would not be shellacked and would therefore be much darker than the rest of the piece, since wood darkens with age. The shellac would have been applied only to the exposed wood. Sometimes, however, a dark stain may be applied to give the appearance of age, but it is often difficult to discern. Ask the auction specialists present at the preview if the piece that interests you has been altered in any way from its original condition."

You can find period French-provincial furniture at auction from about $3,000 to $12,000. Generally, the older the piece, the more valuable it is, depending, as

always, on the quality of design and craftsmanship, authenticity, condition, and rarity. The best examples have sold for up to $50,000 and more.

While French and English antiques traditionally have dominated the market for European furniture in America, finely crafted furniture from other countries such as Germany, Austria, Scandinavia, and Italy also turns up at auction, often under the heading of Continental furniture.

Appreciated for its simple, clean lines and architectural style, which was partly inspired by the French Directoire and Empire styles, Biedermeier furniture made in Germany and Austria during the first half of the 19th century is among the most sought after Continental furniture. Biedermeier, which refers both to the period from 1815 to 1848 and to the decorative style associated with it, is the name of a fictional character who symbolized the German bourgeoisie of that period. Constructed using mainly veneers in light-colored woods such as walnut, maple, and various fruitwoods, Biedermeier furniture is appreciated for its comfortable elegance and modern appearance. It is sometimes decorated with gilding, ebony inlay, or black paint meant to resemble inlay—details that often enhance its value. Some pieces are more intricately carved than others, which also can enhance value.

"When evaluating a piece of Biedermeier, whether it's an armchair, sofa, secretary, or buffet, for example, you should look for harmonious proportions, fine decoration, and signs of age such as oxidized wood, which takes on a darker hue than new wood," Frost says. "Because this furniture is popular and not so old, it has been reproduced in quantity. It's not easy to distinguish a new piece from an antique. In general, period pieces tend to display more detailed craftsmanship and better proportions."

Since Biedermeier furniture is not as old as 18th-century French and English antiques, its condition is not as crucial to its value.

"You should expect a piece of Biedermeier to be polished and shiny, which is the way it was made. You're not looking for the layered patina that is so integral to the value of American and English furniture of an earlier period," Subkoff observes. "And restorations such as a reattached leg will not diminish the value of a Biedermeier piece as much as it would an English Chippendale piece, for example."

You can buy a pair of period Biedermeier chairs at auction for from $2,000 to $6,000, for pieces with more decorative detail. Large sets of chairs are less common on the market and bring higher prices than do pairs. Single side chairs can be bought for $500 and up. Expect to pay from $3,000 to $8,000 for Biedermeier pedestal tables, and from $7,000 to $50,000 or more for secretaries. Rare forms such as writing tables bring from $9,000 to $15,000.

Perhaps you're more interested in Italian Renaissance furniture, which was typically crafted of dark woods such as walnut and commissioned by the church or by wealthy families. For these pieces, you will want to evaluate the quality of the carving (whether geometric or figural), intarsia (wood inlay that is usually pictorial), and veneers (which sometimes take the form of interlacing strapwork). Generally, pieces with more elaborate decoration bring higher prices.

"As with American and English antiques, the surface patina of an Italian Renaissance piece enhances its value. You want it to look old," says Subkoff. "You also want to know if the credenza you plan to bid on has been reconstructed from a larger example. Many Italian Renaissance pieces were originally very large—some credenzas, for example, were up to twelve feet long—but have been reduced in size over the years for use in modern homes. A piece that has been cut down will, of course, lose some of its value as an antique. The true collector wants as little alteration or restoration as possible, and will pay a premium for pieces in original condition. But if you are more interested in decorating than collecting, a piece that has been altered or restored may be acceptable to you. Just be sure that you are paying a fair price for it."

You can buy Italian Renaissance credenzas and tables at auction for from $10,000 to $15,000. The best examples have brought up to several hundred thousand dollars.

Now that you've done your homework and decided on the perfect pièce de résistance for your home or collection, you're ready to bid.

"Remember that auctions can be emotional affairs. Don't buy impulsively or because you want to resell something at a profit," Subkoff advises. "It's never a good idea to buy for investment. Buy a piece because you love it and want to live with it. Chances are good that it will appreciate in value anyway."

Although the finest antiques are becoming less plentiful on the market, and their value continues to increase, you still may find some bargains.

"Some people say there's no such thing as a bargain, that you get what you pay for," Jacoby says. "But if you've done your research, and you're in the right place at the right time, something could slip through the cracks. And you may notice it before anyone else. In any case, you should always set a top price limit before you start bidding, and stick to it. And remember that if you are the successful bidder, you will be paying more than just the hammer price. You have to figure in the buyer's premium, sales tax, and restoration, shipping, and storage costs into your top bid price."

"There are going to be a few sleepers in almost every auction," notes Cangelosi. "Ask the auction specialists what the interest has been in a particular piece. If there is little interest, and you are sure that the piece is worth more than it's estimate, you may have discovered a potential good buy."

The best bidder, of course, is the educated bidder.

"Try to attend a few auctions before you bid on something," Frost counsels. "Observe the auctioneer and the process. Auctions move very quickly, so you should decide in advance how much you're willing to spend. Make sure that you are visible to the auctioneer, and let him know that you are a contender early in the bidding process. Don't think that you'll beat the competition if you jump in late and place a bid at the last minute before the hammer falls. The auctioneer may miss you, since you did not identify yourself earlier as part of the bidding group for that object. If, on the other hand, he knows that you've shown interest, he'll most likely give you another look and a few extra seconds to make a decision before the hammer falls."

"While it's not often that an accidental nod or scratch will be construed as a bid, if for some reason the auctioneer mistakenly takes a bid from you, or takes a higher bid than you had intended, it's okay to raise your hand during the auction and say, 'that was not my bid.' It's more difficult to settle disputes after the auction," says Cangelosi.

Whatever your taste in European furniture, once you bring your object of desire home, you will want to maintain its age-old beauty and display it to optimal effect.

"Avoid overcleaning antiques, which removes the patina that has built up over the years. Dusting regularly with a soft cloth and applying a good paste wax twice a year is all the maintenance you need," Cangelosi advises. "Be careful not to position the antique in direct sunlight, which will cause the wood to fade. You should also have adequate humidity in your home so that the wood doesn't dry out."

Periods of Decorative Arts

in England

Tudor	1500–1550
Elizabethan	1550–1600
Jacobean	1600–1685
William and Mary	1685–1700
Queen Anne	1700–1720
George I	1714–1727
George II	1727–1760
George III	1760–1805
Regency	1805–1820
George IV	1820–1830
William IV	1830–1840
Victorian	1840–1900
Arts and Crafts	1880–1910
Edwardian	1880–1910
Liberty	1890–1910
Modern Style	1925–1935

in France

Gothic	1300–1500
Renaissance	1500–1610
Louis XIII	1590–1660
Louis XIV	1660–1710
Regence	1700–1730
Louis XV	1730–1760
Transition	1770–1780
Louis XVI	1760–1790
Directoire	1790–1805
Empire	1805–1820
Restauration	1815–1830
Louis Philippe	1830–1848
Napoleon III (Second Empire)	1848–1870
Modern Style (Art Nouveau)	1885–1914
Arts Décoratifs (Art Deco)	1918–1939

Note: Decorative-arts periods are approximate and do not correspond exactly to political periods.
Source: Art and Antique Dealers League of America, Inc.

❖❖❖❖❖❖❖❖❖

RECOMMENDED MUSEUM COLLECTIONS:

- The Metropolitan Museum of Art, New York, NY
- The Frick Collection, New York, NY
- Brooklyn Museum, New York, NY
- The National Gallery of Art, Washington, D.C.
- The Art Institute of Chicago
- Winterthur Museum & Gardens, Wintherthur, DE

SALES OF EUROPEAN FURNITURE AT SELECTED AUCTION HOUSES

- PHILLIPS (NEW YORK)—January, June, October
- PHILLIPS-SELKIRK (ST. LOUIS)—February, May, September, December
- DOYLE NEW YORK—January, May, October; general monthly sales of furniture, decorations, and paintings.
- SOTHEBY'S—January, April, October
- CHRISTIE'S—January, March, April, May, October, December
- SKINNER—January, April, July, October

Market Watch
WEST INDIAN ANTIQUES

*F*urniture made throughout the 18th and 19th centuries by indigenous craftsmen in the West Indies on sugar-rich islands such as Barbados, St. Croix, Jamaica, Martinique, and Antigua is heating up the market. Prized by collectors and connoisseurs for their elegant design and richly grained hardwoods such as mahogany and thibet, West Indian antiques integrate European styles, ranging from Regency and Empire to early Victorian, with whimsical African interpretations expressed in carved sunburst, pineapple, and palm-frond motifs, among others. Wealthy sugar plantation owners commissioned these beautiful pieces for their luxurious great houses.

Craftsmen on islands such as Jamaica and Martinique borrowed from the English and French designs favored by their colonizers, while those from the U.S. Virgin Islands (St. Croix, St. Thomas, and St. John), colonized in part by Denmark, were inspired by neoclassical Danish furniture. The distinguishing features of West Indian furniture include parquetry and marquetry veneers in contrasting tropical woods, caning on chairs, which allows for air flow, and lathe turning, which takes the form of elaborate rope twists, vase shapes, and bobbin and melon motifs on chair legs, bedposts, and other elements.

"West-Indian furniture has begun to attract international attention," says Michael Connors, a leading expert on West-Indian antiques and author of *Furniture of the Colonial West Indies,* who sells from his collection at his downtown New York City showroom. "It's of a newly discovered period and style that few people ever knew existed. Its casual elegance appeals to a nineties audience, and it is still relatively affordable when compared to antique English and French furniture and other European and American antiques."

Many finely crafted West Indian antiques can be found at the Whim Plantation Museum Antique Furniture Auction on St. Croix in the U.S. Virgin Islands. This outdoor tented auction is held every March and is attended by designers, dealers, and antique collectors. The Whim Plantation Museum, housed in an elegant neoclassical great house on the grounds of an 18th-century sugar plantation, has one of the world's best collections of West-Indian antiques.

West Indian furniture also turns up occasionally at Christie's, Sotheby's, and Northeast Auctions in Portsmouth, New Hampshire. However, it is often identified simply as "colonial" furniture in auction catalogues, along with Indonesian, Anglo-Indian, and other colonial-tropical antiques.

The majority of West Indian furniture can be bought at auction for less than $15,000. Armoires generally bring from $7,000 to $8,000; four-poster beds fetch from $10,000 to $15,000. Cupping tables (small servers for cups and utensils) sell for from $3,000 to $5,000, while sets of chairs with hand-caned seats have sold for less than $4,000. Caned planter's chairs, with extended arms on which weary plantation owners rested their legs, bring from $3,000 to $4,000.

West Indies four-post mahogany bedstead, c. 1845, Swietenia mahogany, length 86¹/₂", height 93¹/₂", width 62¹/₂". Value: $25,000–$30,000. (Courtesy Michael Connors, Inc., New York) This four-post bedstead from St. Thomas, U.S. Virgin Islands, is a quintessential example of this particular form. The ring- and twist-turned posts, vase- and ring-turned feet, and the headboard's carved stylized palm frond and zoomorphic "S" curves are typical design features of West Indian furniture.

Chapter 9
JAPANESE ART

Long considered a connoisseur's market, Japanese art offers a broad range of collecting opportunities for both beginning and seasoned collectors alike, whether their budget is big or small. Exquisite gold-leaf folding screens, woodblock prints, lacquerware, and netsuke (small, whimsically carved sculptural objects worn by Japanese men as a clothing accessory) are among the many types of Japanese art that come up for auction.

Brightly colored woodblock prints, called *ukiyo-e,* are one of the most popular and prevalent Japanese art forms. Defined as "art of the floating (fleeting) world," ukiyo-e was a genre created from the mid-

18th to the early-20th centuries that depicts the fashionable demimonde of Japan's urban pleasure quarters, where beautiful courtesans, geisha, and Kabuki actors entertained patrons from the wealthy merchant and samurai classes.

Valued for their simplicity, elegance, and bold, linear designs, ukiyo-e prints by such masters as Katsushika Hokusai (1760–1849), Utagawa Hiroshige (1797–1858), and Kitagawa Utamaro (c. 1754–1806) were commissioned by commercial publishers and distributed in large numbers. While the Japanese have historically viewed woodblocks as a less-serious art form than scroll and screen paintings, these prints

Evening Bell at Mii Temple, Utagawa Hiroshige, color woodblock print, 9⁷/₈" x 14³/₄", c. 1834–1835. $8,000. (Courtesy Sebastian Izzard LLC Asian Art, New York) This print is a fine impression with excellent color. The quality of the impression is particularly important for Hiroshige's prints, which were very popular in their day, according to Izzard.

have been passionately collected in the West since the mid-19th century. Their compositional innovations had a considerable influence on Impressionist and Post-Impressionist art, particularly the works of van Gogh and Monet, who were major collectors. The majority of Japanese woodblock prints on the market are from the 19th and 20th centuries.

Whether you're shopping at auction houses such as Christie's, Sotheby's, or Butterfields—who offer among the best selections of ukiyo-e prints—or at a small country auction, where they surface occasionally, you'll want to examine the print carefully before casting your first bid.

"The first thing I would advise is to look at as many prints as possible, wherever you happen to live, whether at auction previews, museums, or galleries," says New York dealer Joan Mirviss, who specializes in Japanese woodblock prints, paintings, screens, and contemporary ceramics. "Get to know your local curator or a knowledgeable dealer, and seek their advice. Join a group of local print collectors. Try not to rely too heavily on books, because they won't give you an accurate sense of quality and condition. Go to as many auctions as possible and take notes on the sale prices and estimates of the prints you like. You will also get a sense of the other collectors and dealers you'll be bidding against. Don't buy anything at auction for at least a year while you're training your eye."

One of the most important criteria when judging the quality of a print is condition.

"Paper is such a fragile medium, so you are likely to find prints with repaired tears and wormholes. Sometimes faded prints will be inpainted or touched-up in areas," notes Sebastian Izzard, a Japanese-art dealer based in New York. "It's harder to find 18th-century prints in fine condition because of their age. Restorations are more acceptable if the print is by an important artist or if it depicts a rare and desirable subject. Restorations on the face of a figure, however, will reduce the value more than restorations on the corners of a print. Nineteenth-century prints should be in better condition than 18th-century prints, and 20th-century prints should be in near perfect condition. Poor condition will compromise the value of these prints more so than that of earlier prints."

Avoid prints with creases and smudgy fingerprints as well as those that have been framed and matted, which will likely show fading, glue stains, and foxing—tiny brown spots that arise when the acid in Western mats leaches into a print. Prints with trimmed margins are also undesirable. When Europeans began collecting Japanese woodblock prints in the mid-19th century, they often trimmed their margins for framing. (The typical Japanese print size is about 10 inches by 15 inches.)

"Subscribing to auction catalogues is a great way to learn about Japanese prints, but you really have to see and handle them in person," Mirviss advises. "With Japanese prints, unlike screens and paintings, condition is traditionally described in the catalogue. But you have to read carefully. If a print is described as having minor wormage, then make sure it really is minor. The best way to check for repairs, wormholes, and inpainting is to hold the print up to the light with the back facing you. Wormholes are caused by Japanese paper-eating worms and have usually been repaired on good prints. You will also see prints that have been backed with paper to hide condition problems; these are less desirable than prints that have been backed as a protective measure when bound into accordian-style albums."

Most Japanese woodblock prints were issued as individual designs, or sometimes in sets and series such as Hokusai's famous *36 Views of Mount Fuji*. Albums, which were assembled later, occasionally turn up on the market.

The quality of the impression and colors also affect the value of a Japanese woodblock print. The best examples will display sharp, clear lines and vivid colors.

"The earlier the impression, the more valuable the print," Mirviss says. "Japanese prints were a mass-market art form for which thousands of impressions were printed. There were as many as forty color blocks for each print. The first few designs were the most beautifully printed. The crispness of the impression declines after many printings. My advice to collectors is always to buy the best impression, in the best condition, of the print that appeals to you."

For example, a pristine early impression of Hiroshige's famous print of *Ohashi Bridge* from his *100 Famous Views of Edo* series has sold for more than $100,000 at auction. A poor impression of the same image, even though the print may be in excellent condition, would bring about $5,000 to $6,000. A print of Hokusai's *Great Wave,* another iconic image in Japanese art, might fetch as much as $200,000 at auction if it were an early impression in superb condition with well-preserved color, while the same image would bring $30,000 or less if it were a poor impression or its colors had faded from overexposure to the sun for several decades.

"You will be better able to evaluate the condition and authenticity of a print if you train your eye to distinguish color tones," Mirviss adds. "Since colors fade over time, the purple in an 1820s print will look different from the purple in an 1850s print, for example. Purples in late-18th-century and early-19th-century prints fade to a grayish mauve. Nineteenth-century blues and browns are stronger pigments than greens, which tend to fade to blue over time. Once you've mastered the color palette, you may be able to date a print within a certain time frame."

A lot of reproduction Japanese prints flooded the market in the late-19th century. The colors of these prints will look flat and muted when compared to the real thing. Additionally, the paper on which they were printed is stiffer and smoother than the fibrous Japanese paper typical of authentic woodblock prints.

The value and desirability of a print is also dictated by artist and subject. Prints by such masters as Hiroshige and Hokusai, both of whom specialized in landscapes, and by Utamaro, who is noted for his portraits of beautiful courtesans, are highly sought after. While a print of Hiroshige's *Ohashi Bridge* has fetched over $100,000, prints of less interesting subjects from the same series, such as a horse's behind, can be acquired for less than $3,000 (assuming pristine condition in each case) as can many of his lesser-known images.

Hokusai's *Red Fuji,* another well-known image from his *36 Views of Mount Fuji* series, has brought more than $100,000 at auction, whereas most of his landscape images sell for $6,000 to $30,000. Snow and rain scenes bring higher prices than images of sunny days; moonlit scenes bring higher prices than daytime scenes.

While the majority of Utamaro's prints sell for from $10,000 to $50,000 at auction, a truly exceptional example brought just under $500,000. An average print in good condition by less celebrated artists, such as Utagawa Kunisada and Utagawa Kuniyoshi, range in price from a few hundred dollars to $2,000. Generally less-expensive than ukiyo-e prints are 20th-century prints by such artists as Hasui Kawase and Goyo Hashiguchi, who worked in a Western-influenced style. Their prints range in price from several hundred to several thousand dollars. Be prepared to spend more for prints that display the time-consuming techniques of embossing or hand rubbing, which enhance the texture.

"For their general high quality and aesthetic refinement, Japanese woodblock prints are hugely undervalued compared to prints by Western artists like Rembrandt, Picasso, and Matisse," says Toshiyuki Hara, a Japanese-print specialist at Christie's. "It's a wonderful field for the beginning collector, who only has to spend a few thousand dollars to acquire a fine example by a great master."

Japanese screen paintings, a centuries-old art form initially commissioned by the ruling classes for palaces, castles, and temples, also come up frequently at auction. They appeal to both serious collectors and the individual who simply wants to beautify their home with a stunning decorative object. Made of paper (or sometimes silk) mounted on a wood framework, they are executed in mineral pigments mostly on gold-leaf grounds. The majority of screen paintings at auction date from the 17th to 19th centuries.

They not only functioned as folding-screen room dividers in large interiors but as prized aesthetic expressions. Some of the most opulent screens date to the Momoyama period (1573–1615), when wealthy shoguns patronized the arts. Subject matter includes everything from landscapes and cityscapes to historical battles and scenes from daily life or from literature, such as *The Tale of Genji*—often considered the world's first novel, which was written around A.D. 1000 by Lady Murasaki Shikibu, a noblewoman in the imperial court.

"Japanese screen paintings are a very complex art form, comprising many different artists, schools, and styles," says Izzard. "Kano School screens are characterized by Chinese-inspired landscapes and subject matter, for example. Rimpa School screens generally depict flowers of the four seasons and scenes from literature. Whatever your taste, you should consult with a dealer, auction expert, or curator before buying a screen at auction. They'll be able to advise you on its historical importance and condition."

While collectors pay high prices for screens attributed to certain schools and well-known painters, others may be satisfied with an anonymous, sketchily painted 19th-century screen as a decorative accent in their living room. Often hung as paintings, Japanese screen paintings, like woodblock prints, are especially susceptible to restorations because of the fragility of the paper medium.

"Avoid screens with cutout and reapplied figures, flaking paint, and inpainted areas," Izzard counsels. "Read the condition report carefully. A certain amount of restoration, such as a repaired tear, is acceptable and to be expected on old screens. Finger-markings, the darkened areas around the folds, are common and don't affect the value. Also keep in mind that screen paintings are temperature sensitive. They

Artist unknown, six-panel screen: mandarin ducks, peonies, and pines; ink, color, and gold leaf on paper, 19th century 43¼" x 105". Auction estimate: $10,000–$15,000. Price realized: $8,225. (Courtesy Christie's, New York) "This decorative screen painting incorporates seasonal birds and flowers in the tradition of Chinese scholars' paintings. It has an attractive design and composition," says Olson. "It is probably one of a pair of bird-and-flower paintings that celebrate the seasons. Single screens bring lower prices than pairs of screens. Another reason for this screen's relatively low sale price is that it is not a complex subject painted by a known artist and cannot be attributed to a specific school of screen painting."

should be kept in a humidity-controlled environment; otherwise they may buckle and warp. You should use humidifiers in the winter."

Screens damaged by water while in storage in Japan will be stained at their bottoms or cut down and remounted—factors which reduce their value. Some screens may actually be fragments of six-panel or two-panel screens, or sliding doors from Japanese temples and private homes. Screen paintings were usually made in pairs, either with two or six panels. If you want a traditional gold-leaf screen, therefore, then generally you should be suspicious of four-panel screens. (However, there are some four-panel screens from the 1920s.)

"A good way to tell whether a screen has been cut down is to look at the composition. Does it flow? Is it harmonious? Are the margins intact?" says Jeffery Cline of Kagedo Japanese Art in Seattle. "Look at a small corner of the screen and use it as a template, then scan the whole screen to check for a uniformity in color and texture. Inpainted or touched-up areas will show a difference in color. Small repaired tears or hinges, and nicely executed inpainting or reapplied gold leaf, will not affect the value significantly, particularly for earlier screens. It's a matter of what you will accept and for what price."

If you want to bid on a screen that needs repairs, then ask the auction specialists to recommend restorers and estimate the added cost. You should also ask which outside experts have authenticated the screens in the sale, especially if you're planning to begin a collection. Since greater numbers of artists began to sign their screens in the late-17th century, an authentic 18th- or 19th-century screen should have both a signature and a seal, according to Mirviss. Catalogue descriptions will often state whether a screen is signed and sealed. Pay close attention to the exact wording. In Christie's catalogues, for example, the term "signed" means that the auction house believes that the signature is that of the artist. The terminology "bears signature" means that the auction house believes that the signature *might* be that of the artist.

Among the rarest and most desirable Japanese screen paintings are Namban screens from the late-16th and early-17th centuries that depict the arrival of the Portuguese in Japan. While period screens such as these bring hundreds of thousands of dollars at auction, you can find many fine antique screen paintings in good condition from $10,000 to $50,000. Historically important examples have brought more than one million dollars at auction. Auction houses also have begun to sell more-contemporary screen paintings from the late-19th and early-20th centuries that incorporate Western-influenced techniques and styles, such as realism and perspective.

"As the supply of the best material diminishes in the more traditional areas of Japanese art, collectors are turning to 20th-century Japanese art and antiques,

A five-case lacquer inro, late Edo period, 19th century, height 3⅝". Auction estimate: $3,000–$4,000. Price realized: $3,525. (Courtesy Christie's, New York)

which were influenced by Western design trends like Art Deco and modernism," Cline notes. "Whether paintings, bronze sculpture, lacquerware, or ceramics, they offer an excellent collecting opportunity at an early stage in a new market. And they are reasonably priced compared to traditional Japanese arts and Western art of the same period."

Japanese netsuke and lacquerware, including writing boxes and inro (small compartmentalized containers used to store powdered medicines and tobacco), have been popular with collectors since the late-19th century, when they began filtering out of Japan.

"Japanese men wore netsuke and inro as decorative accessories, like tie clips and cufflinks," explains Izzard. "Different occasions required different styles. They would have donned more austere pieces when meeting a shogun, for example, and fancier pieces for a night on the town. Inro were attached to the clothing with a colorful cord held in place by the netsuke."

Experts say netsuke and inro make excellent collectibles because of their small size and wide variety. Whimsically carved from ivory, lacquer, wood, or coral, netsuke subjects range from animals or people engaged in everyday activities, such as fishing and farming, to skeletons, scholars, and erotic couplings.

The majority of netsuke on the market date from the late-18th to early-20th centuries.

"The most important criteria when buying netsuke is the quality of the carving and the design itself," says Jeffrey Olson, a Japanese-art specialist at Christie's. "After a while, you'll begin to recognize certain carving styles. Signed pieces by great carvers like Tomotada and Masatsugu Kaigyokusai bring higher prices. But you have to be able to distinguish the real thing from a fake. When Westerners began collecting netsuke in the late-19th century, forgers started to make their own netsuke and apply the signatures of famous old carvers."

Confirm the authenticity of the netsuke with an auction expert or dealer before you bid. You'll also want to inspect it for undesirable chips and cracks. Netsuke can be purchased at auction from $800 to $50,000.

For inro and other lacquer objects, condition most seriously affects value.

"You don't want to see cracks, chips, or splits in the lacquer, which is an extremely fragile medium," Olson says. "These imperfections diminish the value of the object. Lacquerware needs a certain amount of humidity. There are as many as a dozen coats of lacquer over the underlying wood. If the environment is too dry, then the wood will alternately shrink and expand, which cracks the lacquer surface. A lot of collectors keep their inro wrapped up in wooden boxes for protection until they are ready to display them."

Inro were made in a variety of shapes and small sizes, with from two to seven cases or compartments. Unusual shapes that resemble shells, bells, or Mount Fuji, for example, are often more desirable. Most inro that come up for auction date from the late-18th to early-20th centuries (Edo and Meiji periods). While many are lacquered, you will also see ceramic and carved-and-painted ivory inro. The most common type of inro shows lacquer-painted and gold decoration (in the form of gold leaf and sprinkled gold powder). Some lacquer inro is decorated with silver, which tarnishes over time, unlike gold.

"The more gold used, the more costly the inro," Olson says. "Less desirable inro will be decorated with a gold alloy that will change color over time and won't be as shiny as pure gold. Some inro were decorated with large chunks of gold leaf in a mosaic pattern to create texture, a costly technique which enhances value."

Typical inro designs include scholarly landscapes with waterfalls, narrative scenes, figures, birds, flowers, and insects. Lacquer inro decorated by well-known painters such as Shibata Zeshin and Ritsuo will bring higher prices. Lacquerware rendered to look like different surfaces such as iron, lead, and wood required more skill, and is therefore more desirable. Fine-quality inro can be purchased at auction from $1,500 to $7,000.

Also available at auction are Japanese ceramics ranging from Edo Period (1615–1858) Imari-style porcelain to contemporary tea-ceremony bowls and plates; swords and sword fittings; mid-17th- to early-19th-century scroll paintings; and 20th-century watercolors and oils on canvas.

Once you're ready to bid, remember that all sales are final and that you will probably be bidding against collectors and dealers with considerable knowledge about the field. Most dealers advise neophyte collectors to seek their advice before buying at auction. They will even bid for you for a small commission on the sale price.

"It's a good idea to form a relationship with a dealer whom you can trust, particularly in an area like Japanese art that requires a lot of specialized knowledge," Cline says. "Don't try to be an expert without assistance."

Of course, the sale price ultimately depends on what someone is willing to pay for that Hiroshige woodblock print or Kano School screen. The highest bidder, whatever his or her level of expertise, will be motivated by a variety of factors, whether it's pure love

for the object or sheer competitive drive. It's all part of the saleroom drama.

"Try not to get swept up by your emotions when bidding," Mirviss advises. "Set your limit and stick to it. If you end up paying too much, you'll learn from it."

RECOMMENDED MUSEUM COLLECTIONS:

- The Metropolitan Museum of Art, New York, NY
- The Art Institute of Chicago
- Museum of Fine Arts, Boston, MA
- Brooklyn Museum of Art, New York, NY
- The Cleveland Museum of Art
- Honolulu Academy of Arts
- Freer-Sackler Galleries, Smithsonian Institution, Washington, D.C.
- Asian Art Museum of San Francisco

SALES OF JAPANESE ART AT SELECTED AUCTION HOUSES:

- CHRISTIE'S—March, September; May, December (Los Angeles)
- SOTHEBY'S—March, September
- BUTTERFIELDS—February, June, October (General Asian Art)

Chronology of Japan

JOMON	c. 10,000 B.C.–c. 300 B.C.	MUROMACHI (Ashikaga)	1336–1573
YAYOI	c. 300 B.C.–c. A.D. 300	MOMOYAMA	1573–1615
KOFUN (Tumulus)	c. 300–c. 650	EDO (Tokugawa)	1615–1868
ASUKA (Suiko)	550–710	Early Edo	1615–1716
NARA	645–794	Kambun era	1661–1673
Early Nara (Hakuho)	645–710	Genroku era	1688–1704
Late Nara (Tempyo)	710–794	Late Edo	1716–1868
HEIAN	794–1185	MEIJI	1868–1912
Early Heian (Jogan)	794–897	TAISHO	1912–1926
Late Heian (Fujiwara)	897–1185	SHOWA	1926–1945
KAMAKURA	1185–1333	HEISEI	1989–
NAMBOKUCHO	1336–1392		

Chart supplied by Art and Antique Dealers League of America, Inc.

Market Watch
JAPANESE BASKETS

Japanese bamboo baskets designed as flower containers are attracting the attention of collectors and museums, who have begun to recognize them as a serious art form. Valued for their extraordinary craftsmanship and sculptural beauty, bamboo baskets created by Japanese artists have been an integral part of both the Japanese tea ceremony (chanoyu) and the art of flower arranging (ikebana) since the 16th century. And they are still being made today.

Flower-arranging basket woven of blond split bamboo in a hexagonal form with a round neck and mouth and loop-form handle. On the reverse is an incised signature by the artist Sansai. Taisho–Early Showa era. c. 1920–1930, height 17$\frac{1}{2}$", diameter 12$\frac{1}{4}$". $12,000. (Courtesy Kagedo Japanese Art, Seattle)

Crafted in a variety of shapes, weaves, and knots, bamboo baskets reached an artistic peak between the two World Wars, beginning in the late Meiji period, when new wealth in Japan created a greater demand for fine baskets. Many of these early-20th-century baskets were made of bamboo that was exposed to hearth smoke in traditional thatched-roof houses. Their rich red-brown patinas are especially attractive to collectors.

"The best baskets are so exquisitely and harmoniously designed that they really stand on their own as sculpture. They have an immediate visual impact, and they can be used for any number of purposes, whether you simply want to display them or put flowers in them," says Cline. "Scholarship is just beginning in this field, so baskets are still in the early stages of collecting. They're just starting to show up at auction. You can buy excellent antique baskets for about $7,500 to $20,000. Good examples with less imaginative designs can still be found for a few thousand dollars. Contemporary baskets range in price from about $2,000 to $30,000. In my opinion, Japanese baskets are a great value, considering their quality."

Signed antique baskets by well-known artists such as Hosai and Chikuunsai are highly desirable, as are important works by Living National Treasures (a title given by the Japanese government to distinguished artists); contemporary baskets designed specifically for exhibitions; and antique baskets with their original wooden storage boxes, signed and sealed by the artist.

Chapter 10
PAINTINGS

While it's the megamillion-dollar van Goghs, Monets, and Picassos that make headlines, you don't have to be a millionaire to buy paintings at auction. Whether you're in the market for an Impressionist or Modern masterpiece, or an American, Latin American, 19th-century, or Old Master painting, you'll be better prepared to buy within your budget when armed with some basic criteria of connoisseurship applicable to all types of paintings.

Avid collectors will tell you that it takes years of experience to educate your eye and hone your aesthetic judgment and market savvy to ensure that every bid is your best bid. First-time buyers should not be discouraged, however. There is no need to walk home with a lemon (not of the still-life variety) if you've done your homework.

Large auction houses like Sotheby's, Christie's, Phillips, and Butterfields have separate sales devoted to specific categories of paintings, such as Impressionist and Modern art (usually grouped together) or American paintings, which are offered at specific times throughout the year. For example, the headline-grabbing Impressionist and Modern art sales take place in May and November at Sotheby's and Christie's, where they account for the highest percentages of total sales.

In an effort to provide prospective buyers with the widest possible range of paintings in this category, Christie's, Sotheby's, and Phillips, for example, offer Impressionist and Modern art in two separate sales. Part I sales feature blue-chip paintings, while Part II sales offer more modest-priced paintings and works on paper. Smaller auction houses often group paintings of various periods into general "Fine Arts" or "Paintings" sales.

Established auction houses publish catalogues for each sale, containing images and descriptions of the lots to be offered. At the very least, lot descriptions include the name of the artist, the title of the work, as well as its date, media, and dimensions. Additional information may include extended background information about the painting and artist, provenance (history of ownership), exhibition history, and a list of books in which the painting has been published. Auction catalogues also list auction guidelines, conditions of sale, commissions charged to buyers and sellers, and explanations of catalogue terminology and bidding procedures, all of which vary from house to house.

Auction experts agree that if you plan to attend auctions frequently, it's a good idea to subscribe to the catalogues and keep track of the prices realized. Published from several weeks to a month before sales, they are handy educational tools, both marketwise and art historically.

"When you've decided which painting you want to bid on, you'll want to know the answers to some basic questions, such as how important a particular artist is from an art-historical perspective. Has his work been featured in exhibitions? How does a particular painting fit into the artist's oeuvre? What is his track record at auction? Is it in good condition?" says Howard Rutkowski, head of Impressionist and Modern art at Phillips, de Pury & Luxembourg. "Don't be afraid to ask specific questions of the auction experts who roam the floor during the preview (presale exhibition).

"Ask us to show you other sale catalogues and prices for works that are comparable in subject matter, period, and size," says David Norman, Sotheby's director of Impressionist and Modern art. "We try to estimate responsibly, but it's okay to ask Why is this painting worth five million? The current market value of a work depends on several factors. How historically important is the painting within an artist's body of work? How rare is a particular subject in terms of supply and availability on the market? How does the subject compare to that of other paintings by the artist, from other periods? A classic Monet painting of the French countryside is more valuable than a Monet painting of a snow-capped Norwegian mountain, for example, while van Gogh's mature paintings from his Arles and Saint-Rémy periods are more desirable than his early Dutch-period works."

Of course, there are always exceptions. Picasso's Cubist paintings from 1911 to 1914 are not only rare in supply, they are also considered his most revolutionary and influential works when viewed in a broader art-historical context. Yet his later Marie Thérèse works, inspired by his young mistress and model, Marie Thérèse Walter, and noted for their brilliant colors and romantic appeal, bring higher prices.

When it comes to paintings with figures, you'll want to know whether or not a specific figure was an important person in the artist's life. If so, that painting will be more valuable than a painting by the same artist that depicts an anonymous figure. Paintings with attractive figures will bring higher prices than paintings with unattractive figures. Generally speaking, portraits of women bring higher prices than portraits of men. Amadeo Modigliani's female portraits, for example, sell for twice as much as his male portraits.

Generally, large paintings are more valuable than smaller paintings of the same period and subject matter. But size doesn't override quality. For example, an aesthetically exquisite Degas pastel will be worth more than one of his larger but less refined paintings. Works on paper such as drawings, watercolors, pastels, and charcoals are sometimes less expensive than oils on canvas by the same artist and offer an excellent quality-to-cost ratio. You would spend twice as much for a Renoir oil on canvas, for example, when compared to one of his well-worked pastel portraits, which sell for about $1.5 to $2 million. In descending order of value after oils on canvas are: heavily worked pastels or gouaches (works in which watercolor paint has been made opaque by the addition of white); lightly worked pastels and watercolors; works in ink; and works in pencil or charcoal. (See separate Works on Paper chapter).

"With any artist's work, I'd rather have a fabulous drawing or small painting than a mediocre oil on canvas," says Norman. "Always go for the best quality no matter what the medium."

Condition also affects value. As with all types of art and antiques, you should request a written condition report for specific works before the sale. You may do this as soon as the catalogue is available.

"Assuming that everything will deteriorate with age, you'll want to know the extent of the restoration," Rutkowski says. "Auction-house experts are not trained restorers, so you may want to ask a professional conservator to view the painting in question, particularly if you plan to spend a lot of money on it.

Has the painting been cleaned well? Is there any inpainting or touching-up of specific areas of the work? Has it been relined?"

Inpainting is applied to areas of a canvas where the paint has flaked off, or where there has been a tear or abrasion. Rarely visible to the naked eye, inpainting is best detected under ultraviolet light. Cracks in the paint, called "craquelure," are to be expected, especially with thick paint surfaces. Cracking can sometimes lead to undesirable flaking, however, if a paint surface isn't well-adhered to a canvas. A relined (or lined) canvas is one that's been taken off the stretcher and reinforced with another canvas on the reverse. It is then restretched around the stretcher.

"Relining is a preventative measure," Norman notes. "It is usually done to correct cracking. Oil paint is very malleable, and cracks can be pressed back down. If a painting has been relined, ask the experts how well it's been done, and how much it affects the value. Some relinings have caused the original surface to be flattened and compressed, which is not desirable. An unlined painting is generally more preferable to a relined painting. But condition will be less of a determining factor if the picture you want to bid on is rare. If it's going to be hard to find another one by the same artist of similar quality and subject matter, you should bid on it aggressively. On the other hand, you shouldn't chase a painting if the condition is very compromised. The whole process is a delicate negotiation of many different factors."

The market for Impressionist and Modern paintings has rebounded after the fallout of the early 1990s, which was spurred by speculative buying and the economic crisis in Japan, where wealthy collectors dominated the field during the heady, high-stakes days of the 1980s.

"We are in a healthier, more predictable market now," Norman observes. "People are more discriminating about what they're buying, more restrained in their bidding. They're not buying paintings with the aim of reselling them quickly to make money. And they're not willing to overpay for second-tier works by major artists, so prices aren't inflated. But markets are cyclical. It's never a good idea to buy a painting as an investment. We don't advise that. Everyone I know who bought only to invest, bought the wrong paintings. Whereas those who educate themselves and collect because they truly love the paintings, tend to build excellent collections."

While a good oil on canvas by a painter like Picasso or Monet will cost you several million dollars (the auction record for a Picasso painting is $49.5 million; Monet's paintings have climbed as high as $33 million), you can find works from the Post-Impressionist and mid-century Modern periods (dated roughly from 1890 to 1920 and from 1920 to 1950) for less than $500,000.

Look for paintings by the Pointillists Paul Signac and Henry Cross; Fauvists Maurice de Vlaminck, André Derain, and Albert Marquet; and the Pont Aven followers of Paul Gauguin—Émile Bernard and Maurice Denis. Experts say you'll find some good buys among works by lesser-known, early-20th-century artists such as the German Expressionists Max Pechstein, Gabriele Munter, and Paula Modersohn-Becker; the Russian avant-garde painters Mikhail Larionov, Alexandra Exter, and Liubov Popova; Surrealists such as Max Ernst and Yves Tanguy; and the Cubists Albert Gleize and Jean Metzinger.

Some of the best buys on the market can be found among Old Masters—the art-trade term for European paintings created from 1300 to about the mid-19th century.

"You can still find world-class paintings from the pre-1870 period for several hundred thousand dollars versus the several million you'd spend for an Impressionist painting of similar quality," says New York City dealer Richard Feigen. "Good Old Master paintings by lesser-known artists can be bought for as low as tens of thousands of dollars. The speculation that inflated prices for Impressionist and Modern works in the 1980s drove a lot of collectors to Old Masters, which seemed like great bargains by comparison. So there slowly began and continues to be a trend toward buying paintings from earlier periods. But this field is not easily accessible to the average collector, and especially the neophyte buyer. It's a jungle through which you must have a guide with a very trusty machete to lead you; otherwise you could fall into traps. Find a trusted dealer or museum curator to advise you, and view the painting with them."

While the same criteria of connoisseurship for 19th- and 20th-century paintings applies to Old Master paintings, you should pay special attention to attribution and condition before making your first bid.

"The earlier the painting, the more condition problems it's likely to have, and the more difficult it is to know who actually painted it," Feigen notes.

Paul Gauguin (1848–1903), *Nature Morte,* initialed and inscribed "Au Seigneur Roy," oil on canvas, c. 1886–1888, 13" x 16". Auction estimate: $150,000–$250,000. Price realized: $167,500. (Courtesy Phillips Auctioneers, now Phillips, de Pury & Luxembourg) "This painting is an excellent example of how you can own a good quality picture by a major artist like Gauguin without breaking your bank," says Rutkowski. "It is small in size and modestly priced. It's not one of Gauguin's multimillion Tahitian paintings, the works for which he is best known." Gauguin's dedication to "Seigneur Roy" makes this painting more interesting, for the painter and engraver Louis Roy (1863–1907) assisted Gauguin in 1894 with the printing of 25 to 30 impressions of the *Noa Noa* woodcuts.

"Read the Old Master auction catalogues carefully, particularly the terminology used to denote authorship. There are often clauses stating that the auction house is not responsible for the condition or attribution of paintings. When you see a signed Picasso painting, for example, you can be reasonably sure that it's by Picasso, but when you go back three hundred years, you need a lot of scholarship to back you up to ensure that a painting has been given the proper attribution. A painting may have been painted by an artist other than the one with whom it is identified; or it may have been painted by the artist's students or his studio."

In Christie's catalogue descriptions, if a work is believed to be by Francesco Guardi, for example, his name will appear in capital letters. If the work is listed as "attributed to FRANCESCO GUARDI," then, in the auction house's opinion, it is a "work of the period of the artist which may be in whole or part the work of the artist." If it is listed as being from the "Studio" or "Workshop of FRANCESCO GUARDI," then it is believed that the work was "possibly executed under the supervision of the artist." Works by a pupil or follower of the artist are listed as "School of FRANCESCO GUARDI."

Paintings that can be attributed directly to a specific artist tend to bring higher prices. The first version of a painting is also highly desirable.

"Changes that the artist has made to the canvas while painting are called 'pentimenti,'" says Anthony Crichton-Stuart, head of Christie's Old Master paintings department. "You may be able to see, for example, traces of an arm or a leg in a position different from the depicted limbs. This is a great asset, because it shows the artist in the process of working out a composition. Since artists and studios sometimes created three to five versions of the same subject, the absence of pentimenti may indicate that the painting is a repeat of the original, either by the artist himself or his studio painters, in which case he may have added only the finishing touches."

Established auction houses consult with outside scholars and experts to supplement their research. Warranties, guarantees, and conditions of sale vary with each auction house. A "Limited Warranty" section in Christie's catalogues states: "Christie's warrants for a period of five years from the date of sale that any property described in headings printed in UPPER-CASE TYPE in this catalogue which is unqualifiedly stated to be the work of a named author or authorship, is authentic and not counterfeit. The term 'author' or 'authorship' refers to the creator of the property or to the period, culture, source or origin, as the case may be, with which the creation of such property is identified in the description of the property in this catalogue."

Old Master paintings encompass a broad range of countries, periods, and schools that have specific identifying characteristics, which may or may not affect the value of a particular painting. Italian Baroque paintings, for example, were often the product of large studio practices, in which case, single attributions are rare. While many Old Master paintings are not signed, 17th-century Dutch, French, and Flemish paintings are often signed. Seventeenth-century Flemish panel paintings also bear the panel-maker's name, along with a stamped coat of arms denoting a specific panel-makers' guild.

When buying Old Master paintings, you also have to think condition, condition, condition.

"With Old Master paintings, condition is nine-tenths of the value. By virtue of their age, every Old Master painting has some sort of condition problem," says Chrichton-Stuart. "Don't immediately be taken

The Master of the Female Half Lengths (active 1500–1550), *The Virgin and Child*, oil on panel, unframed, 14³/₁₆" x 10³/₈". Auction estimate: $60,000–$80,000. Price realized: $211,500. (Courtesy Christie's, New York) "The high price obtained for this painting defies the notion that religious subject matter is undesirable," says Chrichton-Stuart. "In this case, we don't know exactly who the artist is. He has been given the name The Master of the Female Half Lengths, because the bulk of his work comprises half-length female figures, often of the Magdalene or Virgin Mary in the act of reading. Other than a few scratches and some small areas of paint loss, the painting is as pure as the day it was painted."

in by paintings that have been recently cleaned, restored, and repainted. Perhaps a painting was over-cleaned, in which the top paint layers were rubbed away. Or maybe it was relined badly, taken off the old stretcher and put on a new one."

An Old Master painting may have accumulated layers of restoration over the centuries. Ask the auction experts to show you the painting under ultraviolet light. They will recommend restorers who can estimate the cost of further restorations, if required. A painting described in the catalogue as an "oil on unlined canvas" is rare and desirable. The more untouched the painting, the better the buy.

"You have to train your eye to look at pictures that

haven't been restored, but are still in a lovely state. Something that looks like it's uncleaned and in bad condition may actually be in what we call excellent 'country-house' condition," Chrichton-Stuart advises. "However, some problems, such as flaking or heavy craquelure, may affect the value of a painting. The presence of craquelure—the natural network of cracks that forms when the paint dries—is part of the painting's history. It can be cosmetically rectified with a thin glaze of oil. If the craquelure is heavy, you may have to reline the painting, which can be undesirable."

Many Old Master paintings were executed on wood panels. They tend to be in better condition than canvases, because the panel support is sturdier. Unlike canvases, which have often been relined, paint surfaces on panel paintings are generally in a purer state. In the process of lining or relining a canvas, the paint surface and impasto often become flattened. Panels may, however, bow at the edges—a problem that is easily solvable. You are also likely to come across painting fragments, which should be avoided. When viewed in bright light, paintings that have been reduced in size will not show pull marks (or "cusping") around the edges, where the canvas was stretched and nailed.

Whether you plan to start a collection or simply want a beautiful painting to hang above your fireplace, you will find that Old Master paintings incorporate a wide variety of subjects. There are mythological, allegorical, religious, genre, and still-life paintings. A large proportion of Old Master paintings were religious because they were commissioned by religious institutions. During their time, these works were considered most important in the hierarchy of subject matter, along with history painting. Landscapes and still lifes are in demand because they are accessible and pleasing to the eye. Allegorical and mythological paintings require some knowledge of their often complex iconographies.

"Some paintings are overpriced, especially 17th-century Dutch still lifes, those by the 18th-century Venetian-view painters like Canaletto and Guardi, and 18th-century French paintings by Watteau, Fragonard, and others. The most easily understood paintings are often not the most art-historically important, yet they are very much in demand and tend to bring higher prices than more serious paintings," says Feigen. "I recommend buying against the market, not with it. Some undervalued areas to look at are Dutch Mannerism from 1590 to 1630; 17th-century Italian painters like Reni and Guercino; Vasari and other Italian Mannerists from the last half of the 16th century;

the Rembrandt School from 1640 to 1670; English landscape and romantic painters from 1760 to 1840; and French neoclassical and romantic painters from 1790 to 1850 such as Delacroix, Gericault, and Gros."

As the most important paintings become more expensive and less available, minor artists are coming to light and attracting attention. While you may not have the budget for a Rembrandt or a Goya, it's possible to find superb paintings in good condition by such artists as Lorenzo Tiepolo (son of the 18th-century Italian painter Giambatista Tiepolo) and the early-19th-century Italian Giuseppe Bison for a few hundred thousand dollars or less. Pontormo's 16th-century *Portrait of Duke Cosimo I de' Medici,* which sold at Christie's in 1989 for $35 million, holds the auction record for an Old Master painting.

If your heart is set on an American painting, you'll find yourself in a booming market. George Bellows's 1910 *Polo Crowd,* the last of three polo scenes by the artist, broke the world record for an American painting at auction when it sold for $27.5 million at Sotheby's in 1999 to a private collector bidding by telephone.

"The market for American paintings has been on an upward swing since the mid-1990s. The economy has been strong, and a lot of Americans are attracted to paintings that are part of their historical heritage," says New York City dealer Vance Jordan, whose gallery specializes in 19th- and 20th-century American paintings and watercolors. "The best examples by the best artists, with the right subject from the right period, are worth five times more than they were ten years ago."

Most in demand are paintings by quintessential American artists such as Edward Hopper and Winslow Homer; the American Modernist Marsden Hartley; American Impressionists such as John Singer Sargent, Frederick Childe Hassam, and Maurice Prendergast; and Ashcan artists Everett Shinn and George Bellows. It would be hard to find a major example by any of these artists at auction for less than $1 million.

If name recognition is not important to you, however, there are a lot of wonderful paintings by lesser-known artists on the market for less than $200,000. You may want to investigate either the works of late-19th-century tonalist painters such as J. Francis Murphy and Alexander Wyatt, both of whom worked in muted colors, or the paintings of Charles Sprague Pearce, an admired American painter of peasants. Works by late-19th-century American expatriate painters such as the Orientalist Federick Bridgeman

Everett Shinn, *Girl on Stage*, oil on canvas, c. 1906, 10" x 12". (Courtesy Vance Jordan Fine Art Inc., New York) This painting shows a number of fine cracks, which are acceptable for Shinn, who painted with a lot of impasto (thick layers of paint). The Shinn painting also displays a wavy surface, because it was poorly relined. Vance Jordan bought this painting at Sotheby's in 1996 for $45,000; he now estimates it to be worth about $275,000.

cleaned, or improperly varnished in subsequent restorations. Some of his paintings are also unfinished. Many later paintings by the mid-century artist Arthur Carles are unfinished. For these two artists, as for most artists, finished paintings are more desirable than unfinished paintings. Prendergast, on the other hand, muted the colors on a lot of his paintings as a finishing touch. His unfinished paintings are often more appealing, because the colors are brighter.

"When viewing paintings at the auction preview, remember that some paintings will look dramatically different when cleaned by a restorer after the sale," Jordan advises. "The colors will usually be more vivid. Ask the auction expert to what extent the painting has already been cleaned. You may pass up a good buy just because the painting was dirty."

While each collector has his own particular aesthetic preferences, most follow the same rules of thumb when buying paintings at auction.

"You really have to look at a lot of art to educate your eye. Read. Go to museums and galleries. Go to auctions, even if you're not planning to buy. You can't get this kind of training at a university," says Myron Kunin, chairman and chief executive officer of the Minneapolis-based Regis Corporation, who has assembled a high-profile collection of works by American Modernists such as Marsden Hartley, Arthur Dove, Charles Sheeler, and Georgia O'Keeffe. "Once I've found a painting that pleases me aesthetically, I try to determine how important it is within the artist's body of work, and whether it's a better or lesser example by that artist. I will also look at the condition. How much of the original artist's work is there? Sometimes paintings have been overpainted by other artists. I'll ask the auction specialists to estimate how much condition will affect the price. For me, the quality of the image usually overrides the condition, unless the condition is exceptionally poor. It's rare to find a century-old painting that's in great condition."

But why buy paintings at auction, when there are plenty of reputable dealers around?

"You get a fair market price. When dealers buy at auction, they mark up the price for resale," says Thomas Dedoncker, an American-paintings specialist at Butterfields, where you can find good quality

and Julius Stewart, who painted in France, are also undervalued.

Whatever your budget, American paintings, like other sectors of the paintings market, should be evaluated with the knowledge that standards of quality, authenticity, and condition vary from artist to artist.

"Auction houses have to research and sell such a large volume of material that the catalogue information is not always comprehensive or one hundred percent accurate," says Jordan. "If you want to buy a painting by the Hudson River School artist George Inness, for example, compare it with the catalogue raisonné of his works, which is a good thing to do with any artist. Inness's paintings were often faked by others, both during his lifetime and up to the present. You'll also want to know that the Inness painting up for auction has been shown to the recognized Inness scholar Michael Quick."

Ask the auction specialists to qualify the artist's signature, one of the most obvious indicators of authenticity. Inness's signatures were easily imitated. He sometimes signed his paintings over the varnish, so his signature fluoresces as though it were a forgery.

Then there is the question of condition. A large number of Inness's paintings were flattened, over-

American paintings by lesser-known artists for as low as $2,000 to $3,000. "But then, I've seen millionaires get clobbered at auction because they wouldn't take advice and thought they knew everything. A little bit of knowledge can be dangerous. The people who make the best buys come to our sales like they're studying for an exam. They read the catalogue two or three times and look at everything in person."

For Kunin, auctions are just plain fun.

"I love the thrill of the chase. Going to an auction is like going to the race track and hoping you'll win. I also like being able to look at such a broad range of paintings at one time. I get so excited when I see something beautiful and know that I just have to have it. It's an addiction, really. Drugs don't interest me, but art does."

Experts advocate buying the best painting you can afford.

"You can never pay too much for a really great picture. Rely on the auction specialists' expertise. I'll tell you if you're looking at a bad picture," Dedoncker says. "Sure, we're in the business of selling art, but it's a matter of personal integrity to advise clients properly. If you're in this to make money, you're better off in the stock market. While we never advise buying for investment, you can buy paintings that you have a powerful emotional connection with and that also will appreciate in value."

Of course, you won't be able to build the best collection overnight, if collecting is your aim. You have to be patient through the learning curve.

"I always tell people to buy at the center of the target, meaning the norm—the types of pictures a painter is known for, not the exception," Dedoncker notes. "For example, if you want an O'Keeffe, buy one of her flower or skull-and-bones paintings, not a finicky architectural painting. If the painter is known as a California painter, don't buy something he painted in Arizona. With the California Impressionist Guy Rose, you would want one of his colorful landscapes of the Pacific Ocean, hills and flowers. I also encourage regional collecting, because over time the owners are happier. And marketwise, it's better to buy and sell close to the source. Take the painter Marsden Hartley, for example. If I lived in New Mexico, I'd probably want one of his New Mexico landscapes. If I lived in New York, I'd go for one of his northeast landscapes."

When it comes to regional art, the market for California landscapes is still in its infancy. Paintings by Rose, Raymond Yelland, Richard de Treville, and others are a good value when compared to higher-priced Hudson River School and American Modernist paintings, which have more established markets.

Another significant sector of the fine-arts market is Latin American paintings, which have steadily increased in value over the past ten years. While prices for the best paintings by modern masters of the 1930s and 1940s such as Diego Rivera, Frida Kahlo, Rufino Tamayo, and Matta have sold for several million at auction, Latin American art, in general, is undervalued when compared to other sectors of the paintings market.

"You can still find a masterpiece for around $500,000, compared to the multimillions you'd spend for an Impressionist or Modern masterpiece," says New York City dealer Mary-Anne Martin, who specializes in modern and contemporary Latin American art. "And there are a lot of affordable, good-quality Latin American paintings by lesser-known artists at auction in the $20,000 to $70,000 range. As the truly great paintings become harder to find, collectors are looking to less expensive areas like contemporary Latin American art or works on paper by the modern masters."

For example, you can find a Rivera drawing for less than $10,000; a small still-life painting by the contemporary Mexican artist Elena Climent from $11,000 to $12,000; and paintings by contemporary Cuban artists such as Guillermo Kuitca and Luis Cruz-Azaceta starting at $10,000 to $20,000. Large auction houses like Sotheby's and Christie's offer more affordable works in their Part II Latin American art sales, which take place during the day. The most important paintings are offered in Part I evening sales. (As mentioned, Impressionist and Modern paintings sales at these houses are organized in the same fashion.)

The strength or weakness of international economies at a given moment should be taken into consideration when buying Latin American art.

"If you're interested in a Colombian artist, and the Colombian economy is not doing well, then you'll have some better buying opportunities, because there won't be as much competition from Colombian collectors," Martin observes. "Similarly, when Mexicans are in the market for Mexican paintings, they drive prices up. After the failure of the Mexican economy in 1994, you could buy a Tamayo for 30 percent less than you would have two years earlier. Obviously, those periods aren't as favorable for selling your paintings."

In the Latin American-art market, like all others, self-preparation means self-preservation at auction.

"Keep in mind that you're not always looking at

the best examples at auction, where dealers and collectors sometimes unload less-saleable paintings. And don't rely too much on the catalogues. The colors aren't always accurate in the photographs, and paintings catalogues don't usually report the condition in the text," Martin adds. "When you go to the preview, ask the auction expert to take the painting off the wall so you can inspect it closely. It's a good idea to take a dealer, curator, or restorer with you. Perhaps the painting is not in good condition but can be improved with restoration. When buying a diamond, you would want a certificate from the Gemological Institute wouldn't you?"

So you've finally made your selection. Now it's time to bid.

"I've tried all the bidding systems. Sometimes I bid early or later. If I want to remain anonymous, I'll bid by phone," says Kunin. "But the problem with phone bidding is that you can't tell who's bidding, whether five people are interested or none. And you have to be wary of 'chandelier bidding,' when the auctioneer makes fictitious bids on the item to encourage interest. When you're in the room, it's easier to get a sense of this. I've also used prearranged signals when I want to keep a low profile. In that case, I'll motion to a dealer by touching my eye or crossing my arms, and he will then bid on my behalf. I usually set my price in advance, and when someone reaches it, I'll go one or two bids higher. But it doesn't really matter which bidding technique you use, it's a question of who's willing to pay the most."

Veteran bidders agree that their emotions can easily take over in the heat of the moment. The bidding process happens so fast that you often don't have time to reflect. Rational bidding is always more preferable to emotional bidding.

"It's easy to go beyond your limit. Don't get carried away by the competition and think that you've paid a fair price because there was an underbidder. Just because someone else really wanted a particular painting doesn't mean it's worth owning. That person may know less than you," Dedoncker advises. "On the other hand, don't be afraid to spend more money on a great painting by a great artist. You should have a plan, but you also have to be spontaneous. And don't be fooled by the estimates in the catalogue. They're not always an accurate indication of the value of a painting. When lots carry low estimates, fifty people may think they're going to get a bargain. But the competition is likely to drive up the price, and you may leave having paid too much."

"Attend a few auctions before you buy something. Keep a record of the prices realized and compare them to the estimates. Note which paintings didn't sell," Martin counsels. "When the auctioneer says, 'passed,' he means that a painting was bought-in—an auction term for something that fails to meet its reserve price and therefore doesn't sell. Before an auctioneer buys in a painting, he'll keep repeating the same price. Also take note of whether other bidders are raising their paddles. At some auction houses, the auctioneer is allowed to bid on behalf of the owner up to the reserve price, so you can mistakenly think there's a lot of bidding action. If I see that I'm the only one bidding then I'll slow down or stop, recognizing that I'm being moved along by the auctioneer. As for bidding signals, most people just raise their paddles. The process isn't as mysterious as it looks."

Now that you've snared the painting of your dreams (hopefully one of the best examples of its kind purchased at the lowest possible price), you will feel obligated to ensure its longevity, not only for your own viewing pleasure but also for that of all the other caretakers to whom it will one day pass.

"It's a good idea to insure your paintings, especially if they're very valuable," Norman says. "Try not to expose them to extremes of temperature. Use caution when hanging them near drafty or humid areas, over fireplaces, or near an air conditioner or an open window. The painting will contract and expand, and the paint will crack. You should also pay attention to lighting, which has an incredible impact on the way a painting looks. You may want to consult a lighting specialist about installing special spotlights and floodlights. Take advantage of natural light. A good frame will also make a painting look better. Certain colors and styles of frames complement certain paintings. For example, some paintings respond more to bright gilding, while Picasso's works often look good in dark, Spanish-style frames."

RECOMMENDED MUSEUM COLLECTIONS:

Impressionist and Modern Art:
- The Art Institute of Chicago
- The Metropolitan Museum of Art, New York, NY
- Museum of Modern Art, New York, NY
- Museum of Fine Arts, Boston, MA
- Los Angeles County Museum of Art
- Cleveland Museum of Art

Old Master Paintings:
- The Frick Collection, New York
- The J. Paul Getty Museum, Los Angeles, CA
- The Metropolitan Museum of Art, New York, NY
- Cleveland Museum of Art
- The Art Institute of Chicago
- Museum of Fine Arts, Boston, MA
- Philadelphia Museum of Art
- The National Gallery of Art, Washington, D.C.

American Paintings:
- The Metropolitan Museum of Art, New York
- Museum of Fine Arts, Boston, MA
- The National Gallery of Art, Washington, D.C.
- The National Museum of American Art, Smithsonian Institution
- The Pennsylvania Academy of the Fine Arts, Philadelphia
- Brooklyn Museum of Art, Brooklyn, NY

Latin American Art:
- Museum of Modern Art, New York, NY
- Philadelphia Museum of Art
- San Francisco Museum of Modern Art
- Los Angeles County Museum of Art
- Archer M. Huntington Art Gallery, University of Texas, Austin
- Museum of Art, Rhode Island School of Design

SALES AT SELECTED AUCTION HOUSES:

Impressionist and Modern Art:
- CHRISTIE'S—May, November
- SOTHEBY'S—May, November
- PHILLIPS—May, November

Old Master Paintings:
- CHRISTIE'S—January, May, October
- SOTHEBY'S—January, May, October

American Paintings:
- CHRISTIE'S—May, September, December
- SOTHEBY'S—May, December
- BUTTERFIELDS—June, December
- SKINNER—February, May, August, September, November

Latin American Art:
- CHRISTIE'S—May, November
- SOTHEBY'S—May, November

Mary-Anne Martin on Fakes

❧

While auction houses do their best to confirm the authenticity of their offerings with dealers and scholars, fakes creep into some sales. The more popular the field, and the more valuable an artist's work becomes, the more fakes you'll see. If something seems too good to be true, ask several experts to look at it. In the Latin American–paintings market there are a lot of fake Frida Kahlo paintings, for example. She only produced two hundred paintings, and they are documented in the catalogue raisonné of her work. Some fake Kahlos are pastiches of several of her paintings. Many fake paintings come with voluminous documentation and important-looking stamps of authenticity by quasi-art historians. A gallery in South America once showed me a drawing purportedly by Kahlo that was accompanied by a certificate with a falsification of my signature and dated 1973. But I didn't have a gallery at that time. They had even created stationery for me! So both the drawing *and* the certificate were forged. Be careful.

Market Watch
BARBIZON PAINTINGS

*P*aintings by the Pre-Impressionist, Barbizon landscape artists, such as Theodore Rousseau, Charles-Francois Daubigny, Narcisse-Virgile Diaz de la Pena, Charles Jacque, and Jules Dupre, are undervalued for their quality and art-historical importance, according to experts.

Charles-François Daubigny, *Le Tonnelier (The Barrelmaker),* oil on canvas, 1872, 45" x 66". (Courtesy Salander-O'Reilly Galleries, New York) Lawrence Salander bought this large Daubigny painting several years ago at Sotheby's for $80,000. Now worth considerably more, it had bought-in three times prior to that sale.

The village of Barbizon, located southeast of Paris at the edge of the Fontainebleau forest, had become, by the mid-19th century, a haven for these landscape artists, who shared a mystical devotion to nature. Disdainful of both their industrialized society and the orthodoxy of the academy, they were the first group of artists to leave their studios and paint directly from nature, in the open air, elevating the landscape to a recognized art form.

"Barbizon paintings are vastly underrated, when you consider their beauty and skill, and the fact that the Barbizon artists were revolutionary in their day," says Lawrence Salander of New York's Salander-O'Reilly Galleries.

"They really paved the way for the Impressionists. But in contrast to Impressionist paintings, Barbizon paintings require more looking. They're not as decorative; they have a certain depth and expressive power. You can buy a very good Barbizon painting for less than $50,000, compared to the much higher prices you'd pay for Impressionist, Modern, and Contemporary works of similar quality. With Barbizon paintings you are really getting something important. It's like buying a blue-chip stock."

Chapter 11
PHOTOGRAPHS

It has only been within the last decade that photography, which was invented in 1839, has come of age as a serious art-collecting field. Once considered secondary to painting and sculpture, nearly every major museum is now actively acquiring photographs, and many, like New York's Metropolitan Museum of Art, have set up independent departments devoted to the medium. A flood of exhibitions and books about photography have increased its visibility, while its affordable prices and accessibility as an art form have made it an especially attractive collectible.

"Photography is one of the few sectors of the art market where you can still buy beautiful examples for under $10,000," says Denise Bethel, director of Sotheby's New York photographs department. "And that's true for each of the three major collecting categories, whether 19th-century, 20th-century, or contemporary photographs."

The majority of photographs that come up for auction at major venues like Sotheby's, Christie's, Swann, and Phillips are 20th-century prints. Vintage work from the 1920s and 1930s by such masters as Man Ray, Charles Sheeler, André Kertész, Edward Steichen, Alfred Stieglitz, and Edward Weston continue to command the top prices, which have soared to hundreds of thousands of dollars.

"One of the first questions you want to ask when buying 20th-century photographs is whether or not it's a vintage, modern, or posthumous print," says Daile Kaplan, vice president and director of photographs at Swann. "Vintage prints, which were made at the time the negative was generated, are more desirable to some collectors and therefore more valuable than modern or posthumous prints, which were made many years after the negative by either the photographer himself or someone authorized by him."

Some collectors feel that a print made at the time of a negative more fully expresses a photographer's intent. Vintage prints are also desirable because they are frequently more limited in quantity, particularly those made before 1950. They were never editioned (or made in multiples), a practice that is common today

with contemporary photographers, because the market for fine-art photography was almost nonexistent during the early-20th century, when artists like Kertész and Man Ray were experimenting with the new medium.

You don't have to spend your life's savings, however, to own an image by one of these masters. Their modern prints are available at auction for less than $5,000. While each auction house has different cataloguing formats, the lot description usually states the date of a vintage photograph. If the print is modern, the catalogue description will state that it was printed later, even if the exact later year is not known.

"The paper, tonality, weight, and surface patina of a modern print will be different from that of a vintage print, but it's still the same interpretation by the same artist," Kaplan notes. "A thirties print, for example, should show signs of aging. The flip side may be soiled, for example, or have notations indicating where the image was reproduced. A seventies print will generally have a cleaner, brighter appearance, no soiling on the back or discoloration in the margin."

The ultimate value of a photograph is determined by the aesthetic quality of the image itself.

"A not-so-perfect print of a great Stieglitz image like a portrait of his wife, Georgia O'Keeffe, or a New York cityscape is more desirable than a perfect print of a mediocre image," advises New York dealer Howard Greenberg.

"When I go to an auction preview to look at photographs, I focus first on the image, its technical beauty, the density of tones, the detail in the black and white areas," says Los Angeles dealer Jan Kesner. "You'll make a better purchase if you spend time before the auction looking at a lot of photographs at museums, galleries, and auction previews."

Experts advise that you know what to expect from specific photographers by comparing their work with that of others, as well as with different examples of the same image. Ask the auction specialists to show you catalogues from previous sales, or refer to price guides such as *The Photographic Art Market* and those

André Kertész, *Satiric Dancer, Paris,* silver print, with photographer's signature, negative date, and "Paris" in pencil on verso, 1926; printed 1970s, 13¾" x 10¼". Auction estimate: $5,000–$7,000. Price realized: $5,520. (Courtesy Swann Auction Galleries, New York) The negative for this iconic image by a 20th-century master was made in 1926, but was printed in the 1970s, so it is a modern rather than a vintage print.

published by Kovels' for prices of both vintage and modern prints.

"Each photographer has a different set of standards," says Bethel. "You'll want to know their techniques, iconic images, and best periods. For example, an André Kertész image of *Satiric Dancer* or *Chez Mondrian* is more desirable than a Kertész portrait of someone from his village in Hungary, while Ansel Adams's landscapes of Yosemite and the American West are more desirable than scenery from other parts of the U.S. The premier Berenice Abbott photos are those she took of New York City in the 1930s."

Kertész, for example, made a lot of modern or nonvintage prints in the 1970s of his work from the 1920s and 1930s, while Stieglitz often made photogravures, a technique in which a photomechanical reproduction is made from a printing plate rather than a negative. Since photogravures were produced in larger numbers than silver prints (the most common type of black-and-white photographs), they are also less expensive. You can get a vintage Stieglitz photogravure for under $10,000. Stieglitz himself thought they rivaled the best original prints.

You'll also want to know whether the photograph you're planning to bid on was signed by the photographer. Photographs may be signed on the face (or "recto"), the back (or "verso"), or below the mounted photo. Sometimes they are hand-stamped with the photographer's name, particularly documentary photographs that have appeared in periodicals. For example, photographs by both W. Eugene Smith, a renowned photo-essayist for *Life* magazine during the mid-20th century, and Walker Evans, a photojournalist noted for his 1930s and 1940s views of urban and rural America, are often hand-stamped.

"Generally, a photograph with a signature or a hand-stamp is more valuable than one that is not signed or stamped," notes Kaplan. "However, when it comes to vintage prints, which represent the best material of any given photographer, the absence of a signature sometimes does not affect the value. Some of Henri Cartier Bresson's vintage prints were not signed or hand-stamped, but they still bring five-figure prices, provided that they have an important provenance. His modern prints, on the other hand, are boldly signed and sell from $3,000 to $10,000. Modern prints should be signed or stamped. If they aren't, they're less desirable."

Auction-catalogue descriptions will indicate whether or not a photograph is signed or hand-stamped, and if it has been published in books and museum-exhibition catalogues, that is another factor which enhances its value.

Rapidly increasing in value in recent years are 19th-century photographs, long considered a connoisseur's collectible because of their scarcity and complex techniques ranging from daguerreotypes (the first photographs which date to 1839) to albumen prints. There has been a growing interest in the work of 19th-century French photographers like Edouard Denis Baldus, Felix Teynard, and Gustave Le Gray, whose exquisite brown-toned landscapes sell from from $10,000 to hundreds of thousands.

Although Le Gray's *Grand Wave, Sete,* circa 1855, set an auction world record for any photograph when it sold at Sotheby's in October 1999 for $840,370, you can find 19th-century photographs by anonymous photographers for less than $100 at Swann's auctions. Larger auction houses like Christie's and Sotheby's sell photographs in all categories starting at around $2,500. Sotheby's Internet auctions offer photographs for as little as several hundred dollars.

Travel albums documenting the expeditions of 19th-century travel photographers like Frances Frith, an Englishman noted for his photographs of the Middle East, are great sources of original 19th-century photographs. Swann holds separate auctions devoted to photographic literature, where you can buy travel albums, monographs about photography, and volumes on the history of the medium from $80 to $50,000.

"Photographic books are not only very affordable, they are a wonderful way to gather information about photographs and create a foundation for your collecting interests," Kaplan says.

Other good buys are family photo albums by anonymous photographers and fashion photographs by Irving Penn, Richard Avedon, and others, which have been undervalued despite their quality.

"As good 19th- and 20th-century vintage prints become harder to find, many new collectors are turning to contemporary photographs," notes Kesner. "There is a plentiful supply, and they're very affordable."

Contemporary photographs, which encompass work made over the past twenty years, are also offered in Contemporary art auctions. While Cindy Sherman

Edward Weston, *Hands of Harold Kreutzberg,* silver print, with the photographer's signature, title, and date, in pencil, 1932, 9¹/₂" x 6¹/₂". Auction estimate: $5,000–$6,000. Price realized: $6,440. (Courtesy Swann Auction Galleries, New York) Although a vintage print by a major photographer, this photograph carried a low estimate because it is not one of the iconic images for which Weston is known. This print of a German avant-garde dancer is also not in pristine condition. "Had it been in better shape, it would have sold for double the price," says Kaplan.

Felix Beato, *Mosque near Pekin, occupied by the Commander-in-Chief and Lord Elgin. Pekin October 1860.* Albumen print, with Beato's handwritten caption, 1860, 11¹/₂" x 9³/₄". Auction estimate: $3,000–$4,000. Price realized: $8,050. (Courtesy Swann Auction Galleries, New York) Felix Beato was a well-known 19th-century photographer who traveled to exotic locales. Photographs with specific attributions tend to bring higher prices than those that are anonymous. Albumen prints are the product of a 19th-century photographic technique that incorporates egg whites and gives the photograph a brownish tone.

is one of the few Contemporary artist/photographers whose work has sold for over $100,000, you can still buy excellent examples by noted Contemporary photographers like Sandy Skoglund, Tina Barney, and William Wegman for under $10,000.

Whatever type of photograph you desire, remember to examine its condition carefully, keeping in mind that standards differ from one photographer to another.

Take Weegee, for example, a famous street photographer during the 1960s and 1970s. A lot of his prints were reproduced in magazines and newspapers, so they are often wrinkled from use. They look as if they've been stepped on," Bethel says. "But this is to be expected from his work; it's part of its beauty. On the other hand, if you're in the market for an Ansel Adams landscape, you should look for something in near-perfect condition. You would also expect Edward Weston's photographs to be in good condition."

Generally, photographs with cracks and discoloration are less desirable, as are those with crescent or half-moon marks, which indicate that the photo has been mishandled. You may walk away with a good deal, however, if you buy a photograph in less-than-desirable condition at a low price, knowing that it can be conserved. Photos that have been conserved also show up at auction. But sometimes even good conservation work fails to improve a badly damaged photo.

"At first glance, something may look like it's in good condition, but it's easy to make expensive mistakes when buying at auction if you haven't inspected the photograph closely enough," Greenberg adds. "You have to be very cautious. A lot of photographs come up at auction because dealers, museums, or collectors are unloading lesser-valued examples. On the other hand, if you do your homework and uncover some information that the auction house has overlooked, you can often buy good-quality photos at very reasonable prices."

Experts agree that you should never buy anything sight unseen.

"At the preview, ask the auction specialist to take the photograph out of the frame and out of the mat so that you can see it close up," Kesner advises. "As photographs continue to increase in value, it's important to do your homework. You have to make sure that the one you want to bid on was indeed by the photographer stated, that it was printed by him or someone under his jurisdiction, and dated properly."

New York-based photograph collector, curator, and director of photography at Ricco/Maresca Gallery, W. M. Hunt recommends subscribing to auction catalogues to enhance your knowledge of the field.

"The information in auction catalogues is a great education, because it puts everything in an historical context. But the notion of connoisseurship can sometimes slow you down," Hunt says. "The first question you should ask is, Do you love it? regardless of name recognition. If my heart beats faster when a photograph really resonates with me, I never think that I paid too much for it. Don't be intimidated by fine-art elitism. Photographs are one of the most accessible mediums. We come into contact with them every day. Be reassured by your experience. You're more of an expert than you think you are."

W. M. Hunt on Bidding Strategies

Buying photographs at auction is an "adrenalized" experience. The pursuit and discovery is very personal, intense, and wonderfully satisfying. But it's easy to get carried away in the moment by the thrill of the competition, so be careful that you don't walk home with something you don't want.

There are so many different ways to bid. Everyone has their own ritual. Some people move around the room a lot to confuse their competitors. Others prefer anonymity, so they may sit up front, closer to the auctioneer, or bid by phone, or have a dealer or someone else bid for them. You can even prearrange your signal with the auctioneer, whether you plan to nod your head or touch your nose or whatever. Like most people, I just hold up my paddle when I want to bid. Some bidders keep their paddle up continuously to let the auctioneer know they're serious. Whichever method you choose, make sure that the auctioneer can see you. You may want to be coy or aggressive in your bidding. There's no real formula. It's hard to predict before you start bidding how you're going to react. I remember once getting so "muscularized" by the experience that I stood up and stared down my competitor, and I got the photograph. Another time, a photo that I wanted didn't meet its reserve, and failed to sell. I was surprised that no one was bidding on it. I called the auction house after the sale, placed a bid, and bought it for less than the low estimate.

Market Watch
PHOTOJOURNALISM

John Vachon, *Burlington, Iowa, February, 1942* (Courtesy Howard Greenberg Gallery, New York). John Vachon, whose photographs are priced at around $1,500, worked for the Farm Securities Administration during the late 1930s and early 1940s.

*A*s the highly sought after, top-quality vintage photographs by classic mid-20th-century photographers become more rare and expensive, collectors are turning to undervalued sectors of the market such as photojournalism, which has traditionally fallen outside the realm of "fine art" photography.

"What's wonderful about the medium of photography is that great photographs come in all sizes, shapes, and forms. And in recent years, its the great picture that's become the great photograph, and that picture could be achieved in any way at any time," says Howard Greenberg, who has organized groundbreaking exhibitions of photojournalism at his SoHo gallery.

Photojournalism refers to photographs made for reproduction in magazines and newspapers. Famous photojournalists include W. Eugene Smith and Margaret Bourke-White, whose photographs appeared in *Life* magazine from the 1930s to the 1960s; Walker Evans, who worked at *Fortune* for over twenty years; Arthur Rothstein, who is noted mainly for his work with the Farm Securities Administration in the 1930s; and the mid-century French photographer Brassai. The great street photographers of the 1950s, including Weegee, Robert Frank, and Lisette Model, cross over into photojournalism.

"Photojournalism is now considered a serious art form. These photos are a social document of our time, and collectors often have a personal relationship to the images they buy, whether of lunar explorations, the civil rights movement, or life in rural America," Greenberg observes. "Traditional black-and-white photojournalism is available and accessible. A lot of these photographs are waiting to be discovered. And relative to other types of photography, prices are still very reasonable for vintage prints. You can find great examples for as low as $1,000 to $5,000."

RECOMMENDED MUSEUM COLLECTIONS:

- Museum of Modern Art, New York, NY
- The Metropolitan Museum of Art, New York, NY
- Museum of Fine Arts, Boston, MA
- The J. Paul Getty Museum, Los Angeles
- Los Angeles County Museum of Art
- The St. Louis Art Museum

PHOTOGRAPHS SALES AT SELECTED AUCTION HOUSES:

- SOTHEBY'S—April, October
- CHRISTIE'S—April, October
- SWANN—February, April, June, October, December
- PHILLIPS—April, October

Chapter 12
PRE-COLUMBIAN ART

Pre-Columbian art is one of the most undervalued fields in the marketplace. Appreciation for Pre-Columbian art has lagged behind other fields such as classical antiquities and tribal art, mainly because the relative scarcity over the years of museum exhibitions and publications in this field has limited its accessibility to the public.

Although recent exhibitions such as The Art Institute of Chicago's "Ancient West Mexico: Art of the Unknown Past," and "Shamans, Gods, and Mythic Beasts: Colombian Gold and Ceramics in Antiquity," organized by The American Federation of Arts, are shifting attention to these exquisite ancient objects, you can still buy exceptional-quality Pre-Columbian art at auction at very affordable prices.

The widest selection of Pre-Columbian art at auction can be found at Sotheby's and Butterfields twice-yearly sales, which offer everything from Mayan ceramics, West Mexican clay figurines, and Costa Rican jades to Olmec stone masks, Peruvian textiles, and South American and Central American goldwork.

The term "Pre-Columbian" refers to ancient objects indigenous to the Americas and made before the arrival of Christopher Columbus and the subsequent Spanish Conquest of the Aztec Empire in 1517. Among the best-known of the many great Pre-Columbian civilizations that inhabited Central (or Meso) America and South America during ancient times are the Olmec (1200–300 B.C.), Maya (A.D. 250–950), and Aztec (A.D. 1350–1520) of Mesoamerica and the Inca (A.D. 1350–1520) of South America.

As with other antiquities, experts say condition is of paramount importance when buying Pre-Columbian art, particularly if you have your eye on a ceramic vessel, plate, or sculpture (usually animal or human figures). Common to all Pre-Columbian cultures, ceramics appear frequently at auction.

"You'll want to know whether the ceramic has either been repaired or restored," says Stacey Goodman, head of Sotheby's Pre-Columbian Art department. "A repair like a clean break that has been rejoined does not significantly alter the structure and value of the piece, whereas restorations like a tripod vessel with a completely new leg or a plate with a rebuilt rim are less desirable."

Since this type of information rarely appears in a catalogue description, you should ask the auction house expert for a written condition report prior to the auction.

"Ceramics which have been repainted are worse than those with cracks," says New York dealer Spencer Throckmorton, a specialist in Pre-Columbian art from Meso America. "Ask the auction expert to put the piece under a black light to determine whether or not it's been repainted. If you want to inspect cracks and restorations, ask the expert to spray the ceramic with water, which will make them more noticeable."

Painted vases, cups, and plates are prized for their colorful, intricate iconography. They usually bring higher prices than the underappreciated carved pieces. Mayan ceramics show the most sophisticated painting techniques and glyphs (language signifiers). One of the most developed of all the Pre-Columbian civilizations, the Maya produced extraordinary artisans skilled in a variety of media.

Mayan ceramics painted with elaborate palace scenes, human figures, and glyphs are highly desirable. A combination of red, orange, black, and white earth pigments adorn the polychrome pieces, while codex-style Mayan ceramics are distinguished by black paint on a neutral ground.

"An extraordinary Mayan codex ceramic will bring more than a great polychrome because it's rarer," says Goodman. "But, as with all Pre-Columbian ceramics, you should always look at the quality of the entire vessel itself. How well potted is it? How masterful and detailed is the painting? The more complex, the more desirable. How vibrant are the colors?"

You can find good-quality painted or carved Mayan ceramics at auction from $2,500 to $10,000. A few of the best examples have sold for up to $100,000.

Fine Nazca (a culture that inhabited southern Peru from A.D. 300–600) polychrome ceramics are available for under $1,500, while Olmec ceramics, among the rarest on the market, sell from less than $2,000 for figurines and vessels to over $75,000 for the best effigy blackware.

Perhaps you've been smitten by a dazzling gold Chimu beaker from Peru or a Quimbaya figural pendant from Colombia. Pre-Columbian goldwork is among the most beautiful and technologically sophisticated of the ancient world. Beginning as early as 1500 B.C., different cultures developed specific styles and techniques to create utilitarian vessels as well as jewelry in the form of animal and figural pendants, necklaces, bracelets, and nose and ear ornaments. The finest gold jewelry was worn by high-status individuals and shamans, for whom gold symbolized the power of the sun.

Most of the Pre-Columbian goldwork on the market comes from Colombia and Peru in South America, and from Costa Rica and Panama in Central America. The qualities that make it so seductive—color, patina, and workmanship—are the criteria to consider before you place your first bid.

"The best pieces have a superb sculptural quality and crisp casting," says New York dealer David Bernstein, who specializes in Pre-Columbian art from South America. "A solid-cast object is better than a flat-hammered object. If you're buying a piece of jewelry to wear, it should also be sturdy and free of protrusions that are easily breakable. Small circular plugs indicating where the gold has been poured into the mold should not be too noticeable."

You'll also want to know how rare a motif is. A spread-winged bird or standing shaman motif is more common than a human figure with an animal head, for example, which would carry a higher price tag. Of course, the appeal of a motif, like the color of a gold object, is a matter of individual taste.

"There is a lot of color variation in Pre-Columbian goldwork," Goodman notes. "Some pieces are a buttery-yellow gold, while others have a pink or slightly greenish hue. The latter is true of the less valuable Tumbaga gold, which has a high copper content. A slight incrustation or patina on the surface of ancient gold adds character and does not affect value. While it tends to diminish the bright color that many collectors prefer, patina is a sign of age and history and helps to authenticate the object." Despite its density, Pre-Columbian goldwork is not immune to breakage and repairs. As with ceramics, you'll want to

Mayan polychrome tripod plate, Late Classic, c. A.D. 550–950, diameter 12". Auction estimate: $10,000–$15,000. Price realized: $20,700. (Courtesy Sotheby's, New York) The majority of Mayan ceramics are dated to the Late Classic period like this example. Many have ritual drilled holes. "Mayan legend has it that these holes, also called 'kill' holes, are necessary to release the spirit of the object," notes Goodman. "Sometimes they are filled in, but more often they are left alone. They are recognized as a natural part of an ancient object and don't affect its structural integrity or value." This fine Mayan plate is in good condition, well painted, and has a complex iconography and glyphic band. The catalogue description notes that it has been documented and exhibited, which adds to its value, as does the accompanying scholar's letter providing an analysis of the glyphic band.

inspect the condition of your beaker or pendant at the presale exhibition.

"Don't bid on something unless you've held it in your hands," says Bernstein. "Repairs can be obscured with epoxy and gold dust. Ask the auction specialists to open the case and take out the object. They're very available and accommodating."

If you're unsure about your own knowledge, you may want to ask a reputable dealer to bid for you in exchange for a small commission on the hammer price.

"Dealers know the market and often know who has expressed interest in a particular piece. So they'll be able to advise you in advance on what you should expect to spend," Bernstein adds. "Also, when dealers buy at auction, they don't have to pay state and local sales taxes. If you live out of state, they can usually ship the item to you at a lower cost than the auction

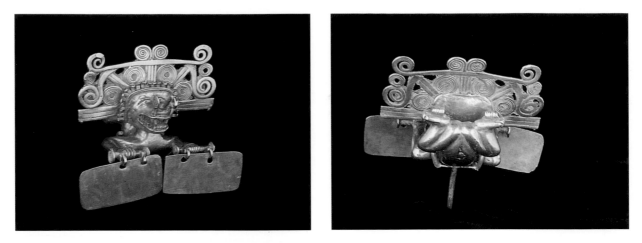

Quimbaya gold acrobat, c. A.D. 500–1000. Auction estimate: $12,000–$18,000. Price realized at Sotheby's, New York: $13,000. (Courtesy David Bernstein Fine Art, New York) "This acrobat was undervalued at its high estimate," Bernstein says. "It is superbly sculpted and well cast with fine details. The photograph in the auction catalogue did not show the beautifully molded rear body, which makes it even more desirable. It is always best to view the object in person." Quimbaya is a region in Colombia.

houses. Considering what you'd be saving, the standard 10-percent dealer commission would be significantly reduced."

If you're looking for bargains, you can't go wrong with Pre-Columbian gold jewelry. Since the value of gold increases with weight, the larger pieces will, of course, bring higher prices. You can buy a fine Pre-Columbian gold necklace at auction from $3,000 to $4,000, compared to the $5,000 you would spend on a gold necklace from Tiffany & Co. that does not have the added allure of antiquity. Good quality gold pendants range in price from $1,500 to $10,000.

Jade, a substance as hard as steel, was prized even more than gold by the Maya and Aztecs; it represented water and vegetation, lightning and rain—life itself. Costa Rican ax gods, carved from jade celts in the form of human figures or birds, sell for from $1,000 to $10,000 at auction. They were worn as protective amulets by Pre-Columbian shamans and chieftains.

Over the centuries, the whimsical design and bold beauty of Pre-Columbian jewelry have inspired artists as diverse as Renaissance goldsmiths, the late-15th-century German painter and engraver Albrecht Dürer, and contemporary sculptor Louise Nevelson.

Dealers agree that the Pre-Columbian art market in general is filled with good buys.

"It's one of the few areas where you can purchase works of excellent quality at affordable prices," says Throckmorton. "While it's a small market, wonderful things are still available. As knowledge about Pre-Columbian art increases, it will only appreciate in value. Pieces have already doubled and tripled in value over the past twenty years. Compared to contemporary art, ancient art is a great bargain, given its rarity and historical value. It also has a timeless quality that appeals to contemporary art collectors."

RECOMMENDED MUSEUM COLLECTIONS:

- The Metropolitan Museum of Art, New York, NY
- The Art Institute of Chicago
- Denver Art Museum
- Museum of Fine Arts, Houston, TX
- Dallas Museum of Art

PRE-COLUMBIAN SALES AT SELECTED AUCTION HOUSES:

- SOTHEBY'S—May, November
- BUTTERFIELDS—May, November

Market Watch
WEST MEXICAN CERAMICS

*C*eramic figures from the west coast of Mexico are heating up the Pre-Columbian art market. Created by the Colima, Jalisco, and Chinesco cultures from 200 B.C. to A.D. 200, these sculptures of animals, shamans, and everyday people were heavily collected in the 1950s and 1960s and have been finding their way back onto the market. Marilyn Monroe and Vincent Price were among their enthusiastic fans.

"West Coast figures are beautiful and affordable, and they've begun to rise in value," says Throckmorton. "You can find a fine example at auction for under $5,000, which is a very good buy. Dogs are especially popular. They are either black, red, or brown. The most desirable examples are in a standing, full-bodied position and smiling."

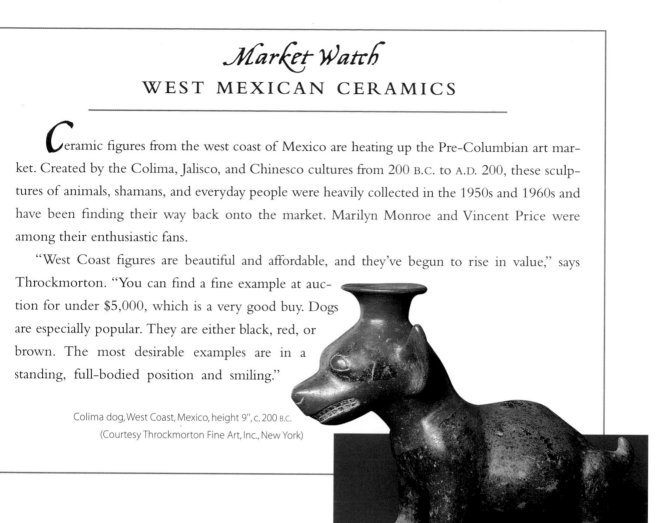

Colima dog, West Coast, Mexico, height 9", c. 200 B.C.
(Courtesy Throckmorton Fine Art, Inc., New York)

Spencer Throckmorton on Ancient Surfaces

With all antiquities, whether Pre-Columbian, Egyptian, Roman, or Cycladic, it's important to be able to distinguish an original surface. I remember buying a large pair of Egyptian bronze portraits of the god Horus at Christie's East several years ago. They were a steal at $15,000, but had attracted little interest because the patina made them look dull and unattractive. When I inspected them closely, I noticed that the original patina had been obscured by a layer of painted patina, a common restoration practice in the 19th century. The same is true for other media like stone, ceramic, and gold. After the auction, I stripped the bronzes with acetone and resold them for $100,000.

Chapter 13
RUGS AND CARPETS

Compared to antique furniture and paintings, the best of which have sold for tens of millions of dollars, antique rugs and carpets are one of the best buys at auction.

The earliest examples date to the 16th and 17th centuries, when the art reached its peak with Persian court carpets. Most of the rugs (a generic term for both rugs and carpets, which also refers specifically to sizes smaller than nine feet by six feet) and carpets (the room-size variety) on the market, however, were woven from Turkey to China, a geographic area often referred to as the Orient, during the 19th and early-20th centuries. Because rugs are made to be used, few early pieces have survived. Additionally, the new wealth created by the Industrial Revolution in the West led to an increased demand for Oriental rugs and carpets, which were noted for their superb craftsmanship.

Auction houses including Christie's, Sotheby's, Skinner, and Butterfields offer the largest selection of both European and Oriental rugs. European rugs are less prevalent. Made mainly during the last three hundred years in France and England, they include the highly prized 18th-century French rugs from the Savonnerie and Aubusson workshops.

For many, the term "Oriental rug" conjures up images of the Persian sort—large, room-size carpets ablaze with intricate floral patterns and scrolling vines in an allover design, or organized around a central medallion. There is, in fact, an extensive variety of handmade, knotted-pile and flat-woven textiles indigenous to the Orient, each type with its own distinctive weaving methods, patterns, colors, materials, and uses. The major traditional Oriental-rug-making centers are Turkey (formerly Anatolia), Iran (Persia), India, China, Central Asia, and the Caucasus (the area between the Caspian and Black Seas).

Rugs from Turkey and the Caucasus tend to be more geometric in design and blend nicely with American antiques, whereas the more curvilinear Persian and European rugs complement European antiques.

"When it comes to the marketplace, rugs fall into two separate categories—those bought by collectors, and those bought primarily for decorative or furnishing purposes," says New York City dealer F. J. Hakimian, who specializes in antique rugs from around the world, particularly late-19th-century Persian export carpets tailored to the Western taste for softer colors and less crowded designs. "Of course, these categories can overlap. Collectors don't just store their rugs or hang them on the walls for display. They also use them. And while export carpets are often used for decoration, they are still antiques that can be collected."

Auction houses are the best source for collectible Oriental rugs, which are usually older and smaller in size than their decorative counterparts. They are classified according to where and how they were made. Size is the most obvious indicator. Generally, room-size carpets were made in city workshops while many of the smaller 5×7-foot and 4×6-foot rugs were made on the smaller looms found in villages. The smallest rugs were woven by nomads on portable looms. (Older rugs were sometimes made in off sizes like 2×3 feet or 4×8 feet.)

"Oriental rugs are named for the region or city in which they were woven," says Mary Jo Otsea, head of Sotheby's rugs and carpets department. "Collectors often focus on a particular geographical area like village rugs from Turkey or the Caucasus, or tribal rugs by the Turkoman people, former nomads who occupy what is now northern Iran, Afghanistan, and southern parts of the former U.S.S.R. Collectors may also specialize in a particular time period—whether rare 17th-century or 19th-century pieces. Those who are buying rugs with the aim of furnishing an interior tend to like larger, room-size carpets like the pale-colored Turkish Ushaks, Indian Agras, or Persian Tabrizes, which were made in city workshops."

ABOVE Anatolian Yastik, last quarter 19th century, 34" x 24". Auction estimate: $800–$1,200. Price realized: $977.50. (Courtesy Skinner, Boston) "Pillow covers from Turkey (known as yastiks), and bagfaces from Persia, Turkey, and the Caucasus, are great bargains for the beginning collector," Kris says. "For as little as $300 to $600, you can buy wonderful weavings that look like miniature rugs. They have the same design, colors, and wool quality as rugs from these areas. They were made mainly in the 19th century in tribal settings or villages. Bagfaces are the fronts of utilitarian bags carried by pack animals. Turkoman bagfaces from West Turkestan are especially well made and finely woven."

BELOW Daghestan prayer rug, northeast Caucasus, last quarter of 19th century, 36" x 24". Auction estimate: $2,000–$2,500. Price realized: $2,300. (Courtesy Skinner, Boston) Prayer rugs, which serve as portable praying places for Muslims, are designed with a niche or arch that is called a mihrab. During prayer, the rug's mihrab, which is a symbolic representation of the niche found at the front of every mosque, is directed toward Mecca. Caucasian rugs with an ivory field, like this example, are rare and sought after."

Village and tribal rugs are particularly prized by collectors. Unlike the artistically controlled output of city workshops, they have a certain vitality and purity of design, often incorporating symbolic motifs that are unique to each village and passed on through generations.

Caucasian and Turkish rugs in particular are appreciated for their variety of colors and whimsical geometric designs that show the individuality of the weavers. Certain colors are highly desirable because those dyes were difficult to make. Caucasian rugs with ivory or yellow grounds, for example, and Turkish rugs with green or aubergine (purple) colors are sought after.

"Nineteenth-century Persian Heriz carpets are also in demand. They're well made with rich colors

Heriz carpet, northwest Persia, last quarter 19th century, 10'8" x 9'9". Auction estimate: $10,000–$12,000. Price realized: $11,500. (Courtesy Skinner, Boston)

Louis XV Savonnerie at Christie's in London in 1994.

In addition to pile rugs, village weavers also make kilims—pileless, flat-woven textiles in which the pattern is formed by the weft threads alone. (With rugs, the horizontal weft threads are passed over and under the vertical warp threads that are attached to a loom; knotted wool is added to the warp to create the pile of a rug.) Kilims, the majority of which come from Turkey, South Persia, and the Caucasus, predate the first pile rugs by thousands of years. Woven for domestic use as room dividers and floor and divan coverings, their designs are often bolder and more primitive than those of rugs. You can find good kilims at auction for less than $3,000.

The same basic criteria of connoisseurship applies to any type of rug that you plan to buy at auction.

"After you've determined which rugs are most aesthetically appealing to your taste, you will have some practical considerations," notes Kris. "If you plan to use the rug, you'll want a size that's compatible with a room's dimensions and architecture. The same rug will look different in different environments."

Does your room have plaster or brick walls? What is the ceiling height? Is the light natural or artificial?

"If your room has natural light, examine the carpet in a spot in the auction house where there is natural light," says Hakimian. "The type of rug design is also important when decorating. Is it condensed or open, geometric or floral and curvilinear? Remember that the rug anchors the room and unites the art and furniture."

Equally important is the question of condition. Age and use have necessitated varying degrees of restoration on the majority of rugs that come up at auction. A certain amount of repair and restoration is expected and does not significantly affect value. Repairs keep a rug from deteriorating further, while restoration involves more complicated procedures aimed at bringing a piece back to its original condition. Of course, the older the rug, the more valuable

and are more geometric in design than carpets from other parts of Iran like Tabriz and Kerman. They complement American antiques nicely," says Jo Kris, director of Oriental rugs and carpets at Skinner auction house in Massachusetts.

You can find good Caucasian, Turkish, and Persian rugs at auction for under $5,000, although the best Oriental rugs have sold for hundreds of thousands. A 16th-century Tabriz medallion carpet from northwest Persia, which brought $2.3 million at Christie's in London in 1999, holds the auction world record for any rug. The majority of fine examples, however, sell for from $10,000 for small rugs to $30,000 for larger rugs. (Prices vary according to size.) European carpets fall into the same price range, notwithstanding the record $1.8 million brought by a

it is. The challenge is finding one that has not been 75 percent restored.

"You should always try to inspect the rug in person before the sale," Kris advises. "The catalogue description may refer to 'areas of wear.' Ask the rug specialist to point out those areas. We will recommend rug dealers with facilities for repairs like stabilizations and handstitching, as well as restoration experts who do more detailed work."

You'll also see terms in the catalogue such as "repiled," which means that the original pile has fallen out and new knots were put in, or "reovercast," which means that the selvage (the side finish of a rug) has been rewrapped. "End-fraying" means that the warp ends or fringes have started to wear.

Avoid room-size carpts with dry rot, a condition that arises when stored rugs with cotton foundations become damp. (City workshop rugs are made with cotton foundations and wool pile, while village and tribal rugs are all wool.) Also beware of worn spots that have been concealed with paint, as well as synthetic dyes that make colors look either faded or garish. Cheap synthetic dyes, which were introduced in the late 19th century in Turkey and later in Persia and the Caucasus, lowered the quality of many Oriental rugs.

"Synthetic dyes reduce the value of a rug," says rug collector Samy Rabinovic, whose Newtown, Pennsylvania-based New Horizons International is the only organization that conducts rug, textile, and ceramics study trips throughout Turkey. "They cause colors to bleed and fade, whereas natural vegetable dyes, made with plants and insects, soften and mellow with age and don't change to another color. The best way to distinguish between the two is to compare the colors on the front and back of the rug to make sure they are consistent. Also, if a synthetic dye was used, the tip of the pile will be a different color from the knot base. When buying a rug, you really have to get down on your hands and knees to look closely at the colors and designs, and feel the wool. It's a very sensuous experience."

Most collectors also avoid rugs that have been chemically washed, or stripped, which fades colors to produce a worn "antique" look and destroys the foundation and the wool. The look and feel of the wool is paramount and affects the overall quality of the rug.

"The wool shouldn't be dry or coarse. It should be soft and have a nice sheen," Hakimian advises. "The finer rugs also have a finer weave and wear better. Rugs actually improve with use. Walking on a rug makes the wool softer and gives it a desirable patina. That's why an 18th-century rug looks better than one made a century later."

While many fine rugs and carpets are still being made, experts recommend investing in antiques.

"Antique rugs have a certain warmth and character. Over time, the colors mellow and fade unevenly and add depth to the design. New rugs don't have a patina; their colors are very even," says Sotheby's Otsea. "Antique rugs in every category are underpriced, when you consider their fragility and quality workmanship. And they will only increase in value."

Beyond the thrill of pursuit, there are advantages to buying rugs at auction, where you will find older examples and a wider selection than what is available from most dealers.

"Auctions are a great way to educate yourself and develop your eye," Otsea adds. "You can see and touch as many as 250 rugs and carpets in the same place at one time. And you can walk in and out without feeling obligated to buy anything."

It helps to have a plan when buying at auction, since one impulsive bid can mean the difference between an enviable buy and a costly mistake. Remember, you can't return the merchandise. Conversely, many rug dealers accept returns. They also allow you to take the rug home to "try it out" before you buy it.

"First of all, I visit museums and read books to increase my knowledge," says Rabinovic, who collects Central Anatolian rugs from his native Turkey. "Then I spend a lot of time at the previews, looking at the color, design, age, and condition of the rugs that interest me. I go back a second time and focus on three pieces. Then I decide which of those three I absolutely love. But you shouldn't think that you have to have something at all costs. You have to control your emotions while bidding, otherwise you'll start a bidding war that will drive up the price unnecessarily. You may find out later that your rug is less valuable than what you paid for it."

While rugs that are in less-than-desirable condition may deter some prospective bidders, others see them as opportunities.

"If a rug has been repaired or restored, check both the back and front to see how well it's done. If it needs to be repaired or restored, ask the auction specialists to estimate the cost, and decide whether you want to spend that extra money," Rabinovic adds. "I bought a few carpets in bad condition and restored them at a reasonable cost. It's exciting to bring an old piece back to life."

Sometimes it pays to keep your eyes open for a good rug that has been badly repaired. Others may avoid bidding on it, and you will be able to buy it at a lower price. Also ask about the rug's provenance. If it belonged to a reputable collector, it will have added cachet.

Once you've found the perfect spot in your home for your new rug, you'll want it to continue to weather the years gracefully.

"If your rug is on the floor, it should always have a mat underneath. It should also be turned periodically, and washed once every two years or more if it's in a heavy traffic area," Kris advises. "Vacuum with the pile, not against it. And antique rugs should never be dry-cleaned."

❖❖❖❖❖❖❖❖❖

RESTORATION:

- Woven Legends Restoration, Inc., 2540 Walnut Street, Denver, CO, 80205, Tel: 303-292-9865 Fax: 303-292-9801

This Oriental-carpet restoration facility or "rug hospital," located in Izmir, Turkey, offers a wide range of restoration services for fine collectible and decorative rugs, as well as for kilims, tapestries, and other textiles. Owned by the pioneering Philadelphia-based Woven Legends, the largest producer of contemporary naturally-dyed carpets made in Turkey, it's a favorite with dealers and collectors who require more extensive restorations like reweaving and repiling. For more information, contact Robert Mann in the firm's Denver office.

- The Textile Conservation Center at The American Textile History Museum, 491 Dutton Street, Lowell, MA 01854, Tel: 978-441-1198

The emphasis here is on the conservation of museum-quality textiles, including everything from antique rugs and tapestries to quilts, flags, and banners. The aim of conservation is to preserve what already exists, whereas restoration strives to bring the rug back to its original condition. Ethical and professional guidelines are set by an international group of conservators. Services are $85 per hour.

- The Textile Conservation Laboratory at The Cathedral of St. John the Divine, 1047 Amsterdam Avenue, New York, NY 10025, Tel: 212-316-7523

This highly regarded facility specializes in the conservation of a wide range of antique textiles.

- Restoration by Costikyan, 28-13 14th Street, Long Island City, NY, 11102, Tel: 718-726-1090

This well-known company handles everything from minor rug repairs to large-scale restorations.

- F. J. Hakimian, 136 East 57th Street, Suite 201, New York, NY 10022, Tel: 212-371-6900, Fax: 212-753-0277

Dealer F. J. Hakimian operates a rug repair and restoration workshop at his Manhattan gallery.

- American Institute for Conservation of Historic and Artistic Works, 1717 K Street N.W., Suite 200, Washington, D.C. 20006, Tel: 202-452-9545

The Institute provides free lists of highly skilled conservators specializing in antique rugs and many other types of art and antiques. Publications on textile care are also available.

RECOMMENDED MUSEUM COLLECTIONS:

- The Metropolitan Museum of Art, New York, NY
- The Textile Museum, Washington, D.C.
- The Art Institute of Chicago
- Museum of Fine Arts, Boston, MA
- M. H. de Young Memorial Museum, San Francisco

RUG SALES AT SELECTED AUCTION HOUSES:

- CHRISTIE'S—April, October, December
- SOTHEBY'S—February, April, October, December
- SKINNER—April, July, September, December
- BUTTERFIELDS—March, July, October

Market Watch
ART DECO RUGS

French Art Deco carpets made in the Savonnerie and Aubusson styles during the early-20th century have been attracting interest at auction.

"As more people collect early-20th-century furniture, they want carpets to match," says Hakimian. "Art Deco carpets are appealing because they have the European flair without the fuss, and are more suitable to American interiors."

The best examples were designed by Jacques-Émile Ruhlmann, Eileen Gray, Jules Leleu, and other noted French Art Deco designers. They bring higher prices than 19th-century French carpets like the mass-produced Louis XV and Louis XVI revival pieces, but are less expensive than the famous 18th-century Aubussons and Savonneries made for French royalty and nobility.

You can buy Art Deco rugs at auction from several thousand to several hundred thousand dollars. Signed pieces are the most expensive and often turn up in sales of 20th-century decorative arts. Unsigned Art Deco carpets and those by lesser known and anonymous designers are good buys. They can be found in general rug and carpet sales.

Art Deco Savonnerie carpet designed by Maurice Dufrène for Studio La Maitrise at the Galeries Lafayette, Paris, c. 1928, 12'9" x 10'2". $180,000. (Courtesy F. J. Hakimian, New York) The bold, energetic floral abstractions and vivid colors displayed in this carpet exemplify the work of early Art Deco designers like Paul Follot, Maurice Dufrène, and Clément Mère. The design scheme of black square reserves containing lush floral bouquets can be found in 18th- and 19th-century French needlework carpets. Here, the floral designs have undergone a dramatic stylization of form and color.

Chapter 14
SCULPTURE

From antiquity to the present, sculpture has been one of the most immediate, powerful forms of artistic expression in cultures around the world. Whether representational or abstract or a combination of both, it has nevertheless remained somewhat overshadowed by paintings, which tend to command the fine-arts spotlight, the headlines, and the highest auction prices. That can only mean, however, that a vast storehouse of sculptural treasures awaits your discovery, for prices that won't deplete your life savings. All you need is a well-honed eye, educated judgment, and some auction-savvy tips so that you can leave the saleroom proclaiming, "I came, I saw, I conquered," in the victorious spirit of one Roman emperor.

A Roman emperor or a Greek goddess may be just what you want—of the marble and bronze variety, of course. While the best ancient sculpture is highly sought-after by collectors, the supply of less-costly examples exceeds the demand. Fine ancient Roman and Greek sculpture can be bought at auction houses such as Christie's and Sotheby's, which hold annual antiquities sales. Pieces also show up in general furniture-and-decorations sales at other auction houses, including Butterfields in San Francisco.

"Ancient sculpture, and antiquities in general, are among the best buys on the art market. You can buy masterpieces of Greek and Roman sculpture for less than $50,000, a great value for the quality and age of these pieces, when compared to the millions of dollars you would spend on the best art of other periods, particularly Impressionist and Contemporary paintings and sculpture," says G. Max Bernheimer, head of antiquities at Christie's, New York. "An enormous amount of this sculpture has survived. Less than 50 percent of what exists is out of the ground. But the antiquities market is a small one, primarily because a lot of people aren't aware that ancient art can be collected. There is the tendency to think that it exists only in museums."

The Greeks and Romans produced sculpture in bronze, marble, and terra-cotta. Roman sculpture is more plentiful on the market than Greek sculpture, and most pieces are marble copies or interpretations of earlier Greek examples. Small-scale Greek bronzes are more plentiful than Greek marbles because bronze was favored by ancient Greek sculptors.

"The finest ancient sculptures were created by the Greeks during the Archaic period, beginning around the 6th century B.C., through the early classical period, around the mid-4th century B.C. Pieces from the late Hellenistic period of the 1st century B.C. are more available on the market, however. Greek sculpture has always been the most highly prized ancient sculpture. Its ideal beauty, refinement, and harmony of form was unsurpassed," says Dr. Jerome M. Eisenberg, owner of New York's Royal-Athena Galleries, which specializes in antiquities. "The best Roman sculpture dates from the Augustan period at the end of the 1st century B.C. through the early-1st century A.D., when the earlier, realistic portraits gave way to an idealized revival of the classical Greek works."

The majority of Greek and Roman sculpture depicts gods and goddesses from Greek and Roman mythology. Used for both decorative and religious purposes, it often graced temples. And wealthy families commissioned family busts and statues of their most-revered deities for use in household shrines. At the entrances to their homes, they would also place herms—tall pedestals terminating with the head of a particular god, such as Hermes, from whom the word "herm" was derived, according to Eisenberg.

Perhaps your heart is set on a Roman marble sculpture. You will find life-size torsos, heads, and busts of deities, as well as realistic portraits (heads in the round that are sometimes attached to busts) of specific individuals, including famous emperors such as Augustus and Hadrian. Portraits of youths and emperors, and heads of popular deities such as Apollo and Aphrodite, are among the most sought-after subjects.

As with other art and antiques, you will want to evaluate the aesthetic quality, authenticity, provenance, condition, and rarity of the Roman sculpture you plan to bid on.

"The best way to judge the quality of the carving is to look at a lot of examples at galleries, museums, and auction previews and make comparisons," Bernheimer advises. "You will, of course, find that some carving styles are more sophisticated than others. The highest-quality Roman sculpture came from urban centers, including Rome itself, Athens, and Aphrodisias in Turkey. Remember that the Roman Empire was vast. Pieces that show the undisguised use of a drill and sloppy drill holes are not as desirable, for example, as those that show little trace of drill work. Generally, the older the piece, the more desirable, all criteria being equal. For example, Roman sculpture from the early Republic, which ends in 31 B.C., and the early Imperial period—from the end of the 1st century B.C. through the 1st century A.D.—is more sought after than Roman sculpture from the 2nd century A.D. and later, which was often mass-produced."

"Collectors prefer Roman marble heads and bodies that portray youth and beauty. A body with rippling muscles, for example, is more desirable than a flabby old man. The quality of the marble is also important," notes Eisenberg. "The finest marble has a pale ivory or pure white color and a crystalline translucence. Some marbles have a blue tone. Also, you would not want to see the veins in the marble running into awkward places such as facial features."

Condition, as always, is crucial to the value of Roman marble sculpture.

"Is the sculpture missing some pieces? Are there areas of modern fill? Has the surface remained pristine, or has it been overly cleaned? All these factors affect value, so bring your magnifying glass to the auction preview," Bernheimer observes. "You can compromise a bit on condition because these pieces are so old. A Roman marble portrait that is missing a nose does not lose as much value as a Brancusi sculpture that is missing a nose, for example. Up until the early-20th century, ancient marbles were overcleaned. Today's collectors prefer ancient surfaces with encrustations, which take the form of dirt, salt, and chemical deposits, as well as ancient tree-root and plant marks. Encrustations are signs of age and authenticity, but they shouldn't be so thick that they distract from the aesthetics of the sculpture."

Ancient sculpture is likely to have repairs and restorations. Repairs incorporate elements that are original to the sculpture, while restorations often involve actual pieces of marble or a fill—a synthetic material made of marble dust or plaster that's inpainted to look like marble.

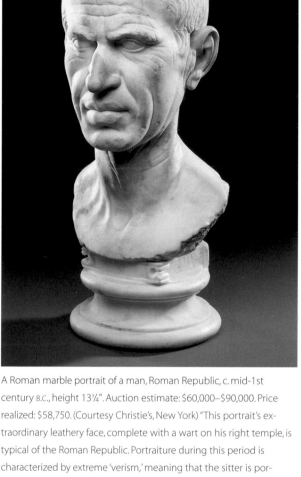

A Roman marble portrait of a man, Roman Republic, c. mid-1st century B.C., height 13¾". Auction estimate: $60,000–$90,000. Price realized: $58,750. (Courtesy Christie's, New York) "This portrait's extraordinary leathery face, complete with a wart on his right temple, is typical of the Roman Republic. Portraiture during this period is characterized by extreme 'verism,' meaning that the sitter is portrayed exactly as he appeared," Bernheimer says. "Such portraits are rare on the market. This example is also desirable for the high quality of its carving. Had its nose and ears not been restored, and had it not been overcleaned, which accounts for its smooth surface, it would have brought a higher price."

"A piece with repairs is more desirable than a piece with restorations. For example, a marble torso that has been reconstructed from numerous fragments and a lot of fill along the breaks is less desirable than a similar torso that may be fragmented but largely intact," Bernheimer notes. "The ideal torso has retained both shoulders, partial arms, and legs to about midthigh. The more repairs and restorations, the less valuable the piece. You should avoid critical breaks, chips, and cracks to facial features; these flaws are more acceptable along the edges of an ancient marble."

"Restored noses are common and do not significantly reduce the value of an ancient marble," Eisen-

Hellenistic bronze nude Poseidon, 2nd–1st century B.C., height 4⅞".
$38,500. (Courtesy Royal-Athena Galleries, New York) The sculpture's
right leg rests upon a rocky outcrop; its left arm is raised to hold a staff
or trident. The sculpture is probably based on the Isthmian Poseidon
created for Corinth by the sculptor Lysippos, and is published in the
book *Master Bronzes* by Mitten/Doeringer.

Life-size Roman marble heads and busts sell from
$25,000 to $200,000 at auction. Life-size Roman
marble torsos fetch $75,000 to several hundred thou-
sand dollars. (Fragmentary torsos bring lower prices).
Small (two to five inches) Roman marble heads can be
bought for as little as $2,000 to $5,000. Greek marble
heads have sold from $20,000 to $500,000 at auction.
Early Greek sculpure is rare and generally brings
higher prices than late Classical and Hellenistic Greek
sculpture, which is more common.

If you're in the market for a Greek bronze sculpture, you will find mainly small (from four to seven
inches high) figures of deities, Greek rulers such as
Alexander the Great, athletes, and animals. The same
criteria of connoiseurhsip applies, with some exceptions.

"Bronzes with broken parts or corroded surfaces
are not desirable. A beautiful green, blue, or reddish-
brown patina, on the other hand, can add to the value
of a Greek bronze," notes Eisenberg.

"Surface encrustations—in this case, crystalized
metal—are not as desirable on ancient bronzes as on
ancient marbles, particularly if they interfere with incised details," says Bernheimer. "The presence of
light-green powdery spots known as "bronze disease"
compromises the value and integrity of a bronze
sculpture. Auction specialists can recommend conservators who treat ancient bronzes both chemically and
mechanically to preserve the original smooth surface."

Since most ancient sculpture was made in workshops, sculptors are rarely identifiable. Small Greek
and Roman bronze sculpture can be bought for several thousand dollars. Greek bronze heads and torsos
rarely show up on the market. The majority of life-
size Roman bronze heads and torsos sell for hundreds
of thousands of dollars. The auction record for a classical antiquity is $4.5 million for a bronze head of an
athlete dating from the 1st centuy A.D. This rare Roman copy of a lost Greek original by the great sculptor Lysippos, (or by a close contemporary) sold at
Sotheby's in June 2000.

The antiquities market has shown an 8 to 10 percent increase in value every year for the past forty
years, according to Eisenberg, who notes that some of
the best buys in ancient sculpture are life-size Etruscan
terra-cotta heads, which sell for about $4,000–$8,000.
Greek and Roman terra-cotta heads sell from $10,000
to $25,000.

Because of their age, antiquities are particularly
vulnerable to issues of authenticity and provenance.
As with any area of the art market, make sure that you

berg adds. "A marble sculpture with a nose that is
mostly intact but slightly restored will be worth about
10 to 15 percent more than a marble sculpture with an
entirely new nose, however. Also, the more recent the
restoration, the less desirable the sculpture. Marble
sculpture that has been restored, cut down, chipped,
or recarved often fluoresces purple under ultraviolet
light. Marbles that have been chemically cleaned also
fluoresce a different color under ultraviolet light. A
genuine marble fluoresces ivory. Pieces that have been
cleaned with acid usually have a greasy, shiny surface
that reduces their value considerably."

Size also can be a value determinant. Roman marble torsos, for example, tend to fetch more than Roman marble heads and busts of similar quality.

are buying from a reliable source. And don't forget to read the conditions of sale and terms of guarantee in auction catalogues. Most auction houses warrant authenticity only up to a certain period of time after the sale date and do not guarantee condition. So buyer beware.

"Very few forgeries show up at major auction houses. If you harbor any doubt about the piece that interests you, ask a dealer or auction specialist whether or not its authenticity has been questioned by experts in the field," Eisenberg counsels. "In general, forgers focus on specific sculptural details rather than on the whole composition. You can also ask to view the marble sculpture under ultraviolet light. If it exhibits an ivory color, it is most likely ancient. Some pieces, although they are authentic, may be miscatalogued. So if you've done your homework, you could walk away with a great buy."

Illegal export and insufficient expertise on provenance (ownership history) are two of the biggest problems affecting the antiquities market.

"It's important to know that you have legal possession of your ancient sculpture, and that means buying from a reputable auction house or dealer," Eisenberg says. "Many countries, including Greece and Italy, prohibit the export of their antiquities. But the American government has not yet passed laws prohibiting the import of these objects. So smuggling occurs constantly. Antiquities with documented provenances are the safest buys because we know they have been acquired legally. This category includes pieces that come from known private collections or have been published and deaccessioned by museums. These pieces tend to bring higher prices than those that have a sketchy or nonexistent provenance. There's no way of proving that an antiquity has been legally exported if it doesn't have a provenance."

Other types of antiquities available at auction include Greek and Roman bronze helmets; Greek vases; Roman glass, mosaics, and painted wood portraits; Egyptian faience, sandstone, alabaster, and bronze sculpture and reliefs; Cycladic marble sculpture; and pottery, silver, and jewelry from a variety of ancient civilizations.

One of the world's greatest sculptural traditions is rooted in Africa. Sculptural objects including ceremonial figures, utilitarian implements, masks, and furniture comprise the majority of African art. Most African sculpture on the market is carved in wood and dates to the late-19th century to the mid-20th century. Since wood is a fragile material that deteriorates over time, few pieces prior to this period have survived. Several auction houses, including Sotheby's and Butterfields, have separate sales devoted to African art, which also include Oceanic art from South Pacific island countries such as Polynesia, New Caledonia, New Hebrides, and the Solomon Islands.

While experts agree that the best African sculpture is becoming more scarce and costly, there are still many fine pieces available at reasonable prices.

"The market for African art has burgeoned over the past ten years, largely due to the strong national economy, an increasing number of exhibitions and scholarly publications, and museums such as the Smithsonian's National Museum of African Art that have made this field more accessible to the general public," says Jean G. Fritts, director of African and Oceanic art at Sotheby's. "New collectors are crossing over from other collecting fields such as modern and contemporary art because they have discovered that African art has a modern aesthetic that integrates well with 20th-century art and design. After all, many of the modern European masters—Picasso, Braque, Gauguin, Brancusi, and Klee for example—were all heavily influenced by African sculpture. The fact that African sculpture is still fairly affordable is also appealing. You can buy a good piece that has age, has been used, and has a beautiful surface patina for less than $10,000."

African art, however, has not always commanded such attention.

"African art has only been accepted as a legitimate art form over the past three decades as the Western bias against third-world art faded and people began to recognize the aesthetic, emotional, and spiritual power of these objects," says New York dealer Eric Robertson. "Also, sculpture and other three-dimensional objects like ceramics, furniture, and architecture have come into their own as artistic expressions that are equally as valid as painting."

Traditionally, the most sought-after African sculpture has been turn-of-the-century ceremonial figures from West and Central Africa, particularly those by the Fang people of Gabon and the Dogon people of Mali, which are considered icons of African art and have sold for more than two million dollars. These figures were among the first African sculpture to be collected, mainly by French collectors, whose nation colonized several West and Central African countries. Whatever its country of origin, African sculpture that has been well documented, exhibited, or once belonged to an important private collection such as the Helena Rubenstein collection, or that of a famous

Three Yoruba ibeji pairs, Nigeria, early 20th century. $2,500–$6,000 a pair. (Courtesy Eric Robertson, New York) The extended heads and arms on two of the ibeji pairs are abstract sculptural features that enhance value. The cowrie shells that accompany one pair signify wealth. A shiny patina is a desirable feature that indicates use and authenticity. Carved at the direction of a ritual specialist, ibeji pairs commemorate twins who have died, and the souls of the departed twins are believed to reside in these figures.

artist such as Picasso, is most desirable. Auctions of noted single-owner collections, which often are accompanied by glossy catalogues, considerable publicity, and touring exhibitions, create quite a stir among collectors.

Sculptural carving styles vary from region to region and have been passed down through generations.

"Fang figures, for example, are typically semiabstract representations of guardian spirits. They are prized for their minimalist sculptural quality. West and Central Africa produced more sculpture than East and South Africa, whose peoples were more nomadic. Generally the older the piece, the more valuable it is," notes Robertson. "While African sculpture is still being made today, it is usually not of the same high quality as the older pieces, which are more reflective of traditional skills. Pieces that can be traced to a specific sculptor, although they are rare, also bring higher prices."

"The aesthetic quality of an African sculpture, as displayed by the sophistication of its carving, is one of the most important criteria that determines value," Fritts adds. "The best pieces emanate an emotional power that is difficult to describe in words. The more sculpture you view and compare, the better you will be able to distinguish greater from lesser examples. Also, African sculpture should show evidence of ritual or ceremonial use within a particular culture, and this is best represented by a rich, mellow patina or encrustations. You have to know how the piece was used within its culture in order to determine whether the surface is correct."

As Fang and Dogon sculpture have become less available on the market, collectors have turned to other types of African art such as figurative sculpture produced by the Yoruba tribe of Nigeria and African metal currency, which is sculptural in form.

"Nigerian objects were long overlooked, since many of the first collectors of African art were French who tended to collect art produced in their own colonies, and Nigeria was a British colony," says Robertson.

Yoruba sculpture was made of many media, including wood, ivory, metals, and clay—wood being the most common—for both ritual and utilitarian purposes. It is distinguished by its naturalistic carving and often portrays cultural heros and devotees of the deities.

"For me, Yoruba art is among the most imaginative of all African art. And it is also an excellent buy, when you consider that you might spend tens of thousands of dollars for a Yoruba masterpiece compared to the many millions you'd spend on a French Impressionist masterpiece," says retired pathologist and African-art collector Bernard Wagner of New Jersey. "Yoruba art is not only intellectually challenging, because it allows me to learn more about the differences and similarities between our cultures, but it has an authentic, humanistic quality that affects me in a very visceral way."

When buying a Yoruba sculpture, you should evaluate the quality of its carving as well as its condition and authenticity.

"While most Yoruba sculpture is naturalistic in style, those that are abstract are more rare and tend to bring higher prices. As with other types of African sculpture, a smooth surface patina is desirable; it indicates that the piece was used and therefore authentic," Robertson advises.

"Past European collectors prized smooth patinas. Now, other types of surfaces are also accepted. Some sculpture may have a smoked surface, for example, because they were placed in cooking areas," Fritts adds. "Other pieces may have encrustations from contact with sacrificial materials, such as millet, palm wine, or chicken blood, or they simply may be eroded from the natural elements."

Whatever type of African sculpture appeals to you, avoid pieces that have been heavily restored. Always ask the auction specialist what, if any, restoration a piece may have had.

"You don't want to buy a Yoruba sculpture with a replaced leg or head without knowing it," Robertson says. "Such restorations reduce its value significantly. Also, Yoruba sculpture was often painted. Some pieces may still bear traces of polychrome, which does not necessarily affect their value one way or the other."

Ibeji figures, which depict twins, are one of the most common and collectible types of Yoruba sculpture.

"The Yoruba have a very high incidence of twins. One of their customs is to carve lifelike figures that commemorate twin deaths. These ibejis are commissioned and used in specific rituals," Fritts explains. "The finest examples are old—dating to the late-19th and early-20th centuries—very finely carved, and have an encrusted, ochre-colored surface that has been smoothed down from years of use. The sculptural detail is often focused on ibeji faces and heads, which tend to be bigger than their bodies and often have an elaborate coiffure. Ibejis are small in size—from 3 to 12 inches tall. Depending upon their age and how much they were used, they may show extreme wear. Ibejis whose faces have been rubbed away, for example, or those that have suffered insect damage will lose value. Ibejis that have remained in their original pairs are usually more valuable than single ibejis."

While most African sculpture was made anonymously, there are some famous Yoruba carvers such as Olowe of Ise-Ekiti (c. 1875–1938), whose work commands a premium at auction. Olowe of Ise is noted for his elaborately carved doors and houseposts for the palaces of the kings of Yorubaland (modern Nigeria). His work has sold for hundreds of thousands of dollars.

Fine ibejis sell from $8,000 to $12,000 in pairs; a top-quality single ibeji can be bought from $5,000 to $7,000. The majority of African sculpture sells from $5,000 to $80,000, depending upon the criteria noted above. There are exceptions, of course. A Bangwa queen figure from Cameroon that sold for $3.4 million at Sotheby's in 1990 holds the record for African art at auction.

The African-art market, like others, has seen its share of fakes. You should confirm the authenticity of the sculpture you plan to bid on with a trusted dealer or auction specialist.

"Ask whether the piece has been published or exhibited, and how long it's been in a particular collection, if any. While fakes can be made to look old, they don't have the patina caused by years of wear that you find on authentic pieces," notes Fritts. "You have to compare a particular sculpture with other examples from the same period by studying museum collections and consulting exhibition catalogues and scholarly books."

"If the sculpture looks too refined or perfect, don't bid on it. Look for traces of old tool marks on the surface. Look at the proportion. Does it conform to known standards? Does it make sense aesthetically? You really have to spend time training your eye so that you can sharpen your judgment," Wagner adds.

Masks are another form of African sculpture that has long been popular with collectors. Like figurative sculpture, the majority of African masks had some type of ceremonial function. They were often used in masquerades to communicate certain lessons and proverbs. Mask styles vary according to the country and cultural group of origin. The Yoruba and Ibo of Nigeria as well as the Senufo, Baule, and Dan peoples of the Ivory Coast in West Africa produced large quantities of masks.

Dan masks, which turn up frequently at auction, are appealing to collectors for their abstract, well-sculpted faces.

"The most desirable Dan masks date to the late-19th century, have a powerful expressive quality, and have retained their original patina," Fritts observes. "Dan masks symbolize characters from tribal folklore and were used in a series of masquerades that occurred at different times of the year. There were different masks for each masquerade. It's helpful to know how the masks were used when evaluating their patinas. Certain masks have certain types of patinas. Some were blackened with natural pigments, for example, so if you see such a mask you know that it is supposed to look like this. Some have surfaces that are encrusted with dried blood and dirt. Like figurative sculpture, masks should show wear. For example, you would want a mask to show a variation in patina in certain areas that once came into contact with sweat from a performer's face. And you would want to see holes where the mask was supposed to attach to the face or to a costume. These features are not condition flaws but rather desirable marks of age and authenticity."

You can buy Dan masks at auction from $1,000 to $100,000, depending, as always, upon the criteria previously noted. Ivory Coast Senufo and Baule masks, many of which are abstract portraits of individuals, sell from $4,000 to $150,000, while Yoruba masks, which symbolize folkloric characters, can be bought from $3,000 to $50,000. Masks made by women from Sierra Leone in West Africa, which have diminutive blackened faces, sell from $2,500 to $15,000 and are especially good buys, according to Robertson.

African metal currency, a once overlooked area of African art, has been attracting more interest. Used in West and Central Africa for centuries, until the turn of the 20th century when colonial coinage replaced it, African currency was made from copper, bronze, iron, and cowrie shells in large geometric shapes such as circles, coils, and crosses and as replicas of spears, scythes, bracelets, and other utilitarian objects. Many African peoples had their own currency, which was intricately tied to social prestige and often used for dowries.

"As the best African masks and figurative sculpture are becoming harder to find, people are discovering that African metal currency is not only beautiful and readily available on the market, but very affordable. You can buy a lot of these pieces for less than $600," Robertson says. "Their minimal, abstract forms are reminiscent of modern sculpture and blend easily with all types of art and interiors."

Domestic African objects such as bowls, spoons, and furniture as well as African weapons and shields, textiles, and jewelry are also available at auction.

Whether you have been smitten by a Roman marble or a Yoruba ibeji, the same guidelines apply when aiming for the best bid.

"When buying at auction you should always seek the advice of experts you can trust, whether a dealer, collector, or an auction specialist. Visit the auction preview several times to view the pieces that interest you, and write down your questions," Robertson advises. "For a small fee, I am happy to accompany potential collectors to the auction preview to point out what's desirable and why, whether an object has been restored, whether there are similar pieces on the market, and how much you should expect to pay. Most important, you should buy what you love and not what you think has value or what may be the fashion of the moment."

"I advise beginning collectors to buy cautiously at first; you can always trade up for better pieces. And always buy the best examples you can afford," adds Eisenberg. "Start out by putting together a small library, and get to know your museum curator as well as reputable dealers in the area that interests you. You may want to spread your financial risks by buying a variety of art, unless you are an expert in a particular subject. And try to meet other collectors. But whatever type of art you decide to buy, avoid objects that have been significantly restored."

Remember that most auction houses sell objects "as is" and often do not list condition information in their catalogues. They can, however, provide detailed condition reports on request.

"You can ask for a condition report anytime before the sale. And don't be afraid to ask questions at the auction preview. The auction specialists enjoy meeting new buyers. We're there to help you. We'll tell you if a particular piece is expected to sell within its estimate, or whether it has had any restoration and to what degree," Fritts says. "We'll recommend books and museum resources such as the Goldwater Library at the Metropolitan Museum of Art, which is devoted to the arts of Africa, Oceana, and the Americas and has an extensive photo archive of works that have been on the market over the last 70 years. If we are unable to answer a question, we'll recommend scholars in the field whom you can contact. We can offer bidding advice and tell you how much interest there has been in the object you plan to bid on. Everyone has their own unique bidding strategy. I believe that you're better served by bidding in person at the sale rather than by telephone or absentee bid. It's more fun and dynamic when you're in the saleroom, and you can get a better feel for the market, what the interest is in particular pieces."

But what about the dreaded disease known as auction fever? Auction veterans always recommend setting a price limit before you start bidding and checking your emotions at the door (not the Yorubaland palace variety).

"You really have to know your field and the market value of the piece you plan to bid on," says Wagner. "I try to see as much African art as possible at museums and galleries and auction exhibitions, and I pay attention to the prices certain objects have been bringing so that I can set my top bid in advance. A lot of pieces sell for more than they're worth. I often leave absentee bids so that I don't get caught up in the saleroom drama and wind up paying too much."

⚜⚜⚜⚜⚜⚜⚜⚜⚜

RECOMMENDED MUSEUM COLLECTIONS OF ANCIENT GREEK AND ROMAN SCULPTURE:

- The Metropolitan Museum of Art, New York, NY
- The J. Paul Getty Museum, Los Angeles
- Museum of Fine Arts, Boston, MA
- Brooklyn Museum of Art, New York
- Cleveland Museum of Art
- Walters Gallery of Art, Baltimore, MD

RECOMMENDED MUSEUM COLLECTIONS OF AFRICAN SCULPTURE:

- The National Museum of African Art, Smithsonian Institution, Washington, D.C.
- The Metropolitan Museum of Art, New York, NY
- Brooklyn Museum of Art, New York
- Fowler Museum of Cultural History, U.C.L.A., Los Angeles
- Dallas Museum of Art
- The Detroit Institute of Arts
- The Art Institute of Chicago

SALES OF ANTIQUITIES AT SELECTED AUCTION HOUSES:

- CHRISTIE'S—June, December
- SOTHEBY'S—June, December

SALES OF AFRICAN ART AT SELECTED AUCTION HOUSES:

- SOTHEBY'S—May, November
- BUTTERFIELDS—May, October

Market Watch
AFRICAN FURNITURE

Most African art is sculptural, and African furniture, also referred to as tribal furniture, is no exception. Stools, neckrests, chairs, tables, and beds carved from indigenous hardwoods during the late-19th and early-20th centuries by African craftsmen from Ethiopia, Tanzania, Nigeria, Ivory Coast, Cameroon, and other African countries are one of the hottest collectibles in the African-art market. Made for either ritual or domestic use, African furniture symbolized a person's social status and wealth; the finest examples were crafted for tribal leaders.

"African furniture is prized for its elegant, sculptural carving, which can be either figurative or abstract, and its classic lines that blend easily with a variety of furniture styles. You can find excellent examples for $2,000 to $10,000 at auction, and many pieces for less than $1,000," says Fritts. "Furniture that incorporates human or animal motifs is very desirable and tends to bring the highest prices. As with other types of African sculpture, you should buy a piece that shows signs of use—a surface patina that can be either smooth or encrusted, or a different hue of wood in areas of contact. Ethiopian chairs, for example, tend to have blackened, encrusted surfaces."

While pieces showing great age and exceptional carving and patination have brought more than $25,000, you can buy an Ethiopian king's chair with abstract carving from $3,000 to $9,000 and Southern African neckrests from $500 to $25,000. Asante stools from Ghana, and Nupe stools from northern Nigeria sell for less than $1,000. Senufo beds from the Ivory Coast, which can be used as coffee tables, bring from $4,000 to $15,000.

Akan chieftain's chair, Ghana, early 20th century, height 40". $3,500. (Courtesy Collection of Eric Robertson, New York) Notable for its pleasing abstract openwork carving, this chair is an excellent example of furniture by an Akan carver. The Akan cultural group includes the Asante and Fante peoples of Ghana and the Ivory Coast in West Africa. The chair's goatskin seat and bronze elements are typical features of furniture from this region. The design of the chair is inspired by European furniture that was imported by early colonists.

Chapter 15
20TH-CENTURY DECORATIVE ARTS

Whether you're in the market for a Grueby vase, a Stickley sideboard, a Tiffany lamp, a Lalique sculpture, a Ruhlmann table, or an Eames chair, you'll find a wide range of 20th-century decorative arts at auction. As we move forward into the new millenium, and the material culture of our recent past becomes collectible history, the market for 20th-century decorative arts is stronger than ever. A whole new generation of collectors, curators, dealers, and auction specialists is cashing in on the antiques of tomorrow.

Some auction houses organize sales specifically devoted to 20th-century decorative arts, including Christie's, Sotheby's, Doyle New York, and Phillips. Others such as David Rago Auctions in Lambertville, New Jersey; Treadway/Toomey Galleries, which holds auctions in Oak Park, Illinois; and Los Angeles Modern Auctions specialize solely in 20th-century decorative arts and design.

The term "20th-century decorative arts" generally encompasses objects created by European and American designers from about 1900 to the present day and spans the art historical periods known as Arts and Crafts (1880–1915), Art Nouveau (1890–1920), Art Deco (1925–1940), and Modern (1950–present).

The decorative arts produced during the American Arts and Crafts Movement, from 1880 through the first two decades of the 20th century, have continued to attract growing numbers of collectors since the early 1970s, when museum exhibitions and publications on the subject first began to appear. Many of these collectors have created unified Arts and Crafts interiors, decorating their homes with Mission oak furniture designed by Gustav Stickley, copper table lamps by California craftsman Dirk van Erp, and Grueby and Teco pottery.

The Arts and Crafts Movement, which began in England in the late 19th century, was based upon a philosophy, advocated by the writer and designer William Morris and the art critic John Ruskin, that promoted reform in design. A reaction against both the Industrial Revolution and the taste for excessive ornamentation that characterized design in the preceding Victorian era, the movement aimed to beautify daily life with handcrafted furnishings for the home. The Arts and Crafts ideals of skilled craftsmanship, simplicity of design, individuality of expression, and the honest use of humble materials such as oak and clay (versus the more precious mahogany and glass favored in earlier periods), were translated into objects that were both beautiful and useful.

The market for American Arts and Crafts material is now at an unprecedented high, according to David Rago, of David Rago Auctions in Lambertville, New Jersey, who specializes in this field.

"The Arts and Crafts philosophy is very appealing to many people today. It's about adding soul and warmth to our busy, high-tech lives," Rago says. "Living among these beautiful, handmade objects is a rejuvenating experience. They have an almost spiritual presence that can give you a contact high. I always say, why take Prozac, when you can buy a Stickley cabinet or a Grueby vase? Arts and Crafts furniture and pottery are the team players of the decorative arts because they blend exquisitely well with all types of interiors. They have a quiet integrity and are meant to be part of a unified whole."

Arts and Crafts pottery, also called art pottery, has long commanded interest at auction. While most of the best examples are now in museums and private collections, there is still a strong market for fine pottery created during the Arts and Crafts period by such important potteries as Grueby of Boston, Newcomb College of New Orleans, and William Gates of Chicago, which was noted for its Teco ware.

"While Arts and Crafts pottery was designed as vases, bowls, tiles, and other functional objects, it was also considered art ware. Much of it tends to be green in color, an earth tone that is typical of the organic Arts and Crafts aesthetic," says Beth Cathers of New York's Cathers & Dembrosky Gallery. "Along with Shaker furniture and folk art, I believe that this art pottery is one of the most important indigenous American aesthetic expressions. Made of clay, it is literally of the earth, and this tactile quality is very immediate and appealing. As with the hand-hewn oak furniture of the period, Arts and Crafts pottery has a solidity and warmth that people find appealing. The market is very healthy now, and Arts and Crafts pottery will continue to appreciate in value. While the best pieces have brought up to $85,000, you still can buy a good but small Arts and Crafts vase for less than $5,000."

As with all art and antiques, before you bid on Arts and Crafts pottery at auction, experts recommend immersing yourself in literature on the field, visiting museums, galleries, and auction exhibitions, and studying auction catalogues. You may want to focus your efforts on one or two types of ceramics so that you can develop a specific expertise. You will discover that potteries in various regions of the United States were known for their distinctive style of Arts and Crafts ceramics.

"Boston, Chicago, and New Orleans were major Arts and Crafts ceramics centers, for example. The most outstanding Arts and Crafts potteries in these cities—Grueby, William Gates, and Newcomb College—employed a variety of craftspeople, often women, who either threw or glazed the pots by hand," Cathers explains. "These potteries were linked aesthetically because their focus was on glaze and form. They differed from potteries such as Rookwood, Weller, and Roseville of Cincinnati—another big ceramics center at that time—where the emphasis was on slip painting nature scenes and portraits on pottery blanks. There were also individual artists such as George Ohr, an eccentric fellow from Biloxi, Mississippi, who threw thin-walled pots from local clay and often decorated them with flamboyant, colorful glazes, and Adelaide Alsop Robineau of Syracuse, New York, who made beautifully carved and decorated porcelain."

Grueby ceramics were hand thrown, whereas William Gates's Teco ware was molded and more architectural in style. Grueby ceramics are characterized by thick, green glazes, some of which are evenly textured while others appear to be dripping. Teco ceramics have soft, matte-green glazes with microcrystals that create a "crushed-diamond" effect. Both wares are distinguished by their sophisticated, sculptural forms. Grueby sometimes collaborated with the noted Arts and Crafts furniture designer Gustav Stickley, who incorporated its ceramic tiles in his furniture. Pottery crafted at Newcomb College typically has bright blue glazes and incised or painted slip decoration depicting motifs from nature.

Fine and large Grueby vase (left) with applied rows of tooled leaves under a superior pulled leathery matte green glaze—a rare and successful form. Circular stamp mark. Height 7¼", diameter 10". Auction estimate: $4,500–$6,500. Price realized: $9,000. (Courtesy David Rago Auctions, Lambertville, NJ/ragoarts.com)

Fine Grueby vase (center) with floriform rim, tooled and applied broad leaves, covered in a leathery matte green glaze. Circular Faience mark. Height 7¾", diameter 4". Auction estimate: $2,600–$2,900. Price realized: $4,218.75. (Courtesy David Rago Auctions, Lambertville, NJ/ragoarts.com)

Fine and large Grueby vase (right) with tooled and applied leaves alternating with buds under a curdled matte green glaze. Grueby Faience circular stamp/AL/100. Height 10¼", diameter 8". Auction estimate: $1,250–$1,750. Price realized: $2,587.50. (Courtesy David Rago Auctions, Lambertville, NJ/ragoarts.com)

"The first vase at the left brought the highest price of the three because it is a rare form, very organic and sexy," Rago says. "The center vase is a more typical Grueby size and shape. The third piece has a lamp-base shape. Vase shapes always bring more than lamp-base shapes. The Faience marks on the second and third vases denote early Grueby examples, which tend to bring higher prices than later examples. Such pieces are distinguished by a raw, gutsy design, although they can be thick and sometimes clumsy in appearance."

"Each pottery was trying to create something different, so you have to evaluate these ceramics by their own individual standards. One of the most important criteria is the quality of the form and glaze. Does the piece have proportion and balance? Is the glaze well executed?" notes Cathers.

"A good piece of Grueby should be at least 8 to 10 inches tall and have a rich "enameled-cucumber" glaze. It should also have some decoration, whether buds, flowers, or leaves. The decoration can be either tooled, which means carved into the clay, or applied with modeled clay. Plain Grueby vases are less sought-after and bring lower prices," Rago says. "Grueby ceramics with blue, brown, oatmeal, and white glazes are less common than those with green glazes and can bring higher prices if they are of similar quality and condition. Two-color Grueby ceramics are rare and sought after. Grueby also supplied lamp bases for Tiffany & Co. If you are lucky enough to find a Grueby lamp base with its original Tiffany glass shade, you should expect to pay a premium for it."

Large Teco ceramics with organic, flowing forms and twisted handles are among the most sought-after of their kind, according to Rago. Like Grueby ceramics, Newcomb College wares are hand-thrown in the true spirit of the Arts and Crafts aesthetic. Newcomb College began as a women's college during the late-19th century with the aim of training women for employment. The majority of these ceramics, which were made by women, are hand-tooled and painted with local New Orleans flowers, animals, and other nature-inspired motifs. As with other types of Arts and Crafts ceramics, the size of a piece, the quality and complexity of its glaze, and extent of decoration all help to determine its value. Generally, large Newcomb College pieces with colorful, beautifully tooled or painted decoration are most sought after. If you're smitten by George Ohr's ceramics, which have cast their spell on many a collector, you will find that the most irregular, expressive and colorfully glazed examples tend to bring the highest prices.

Condition is also crucial to the value of Arts and Crafts ceramics, but you have to weigh it against rarity and aesthetic quality, and, in some cases, be willing to compromise a bit.

"Some chips and nicks are to be expected, but you should avoid pieces that have been heavily restored," notes Cathers. "Remember that the price should always reflect the condition. You don't want to pay a premium for something that appears to be in perfect condition when it's really not. If you're going to make

compromises, you're better off buying an important piece that has some minor condition problems rather than a secondary piece that's in pristine conditon. And I would buy one good piece rather than three mediocre pieces for the same amount."

"Cracks or chips on most types of Arts and Crafts ceramics will reduce their value by about 30 percent," Rago observes. "But the best examples from any of these potteries are rare enough that even damaged pieces will sell for substantial amounts."

You can buy Grueby, Teco, and Newcomb College ceramics at auction for as little as $1,000 for small undecorated pieces to more than $60,000 for the best examples. You can put together a collection of small beautiful Grueby and Teco pieces priced in the $2,500 to $4,500 range, according to Cathers. Expect to spend from $1,000 to about $50,000 at auction for George Ohr's ceramics.

"If you're on the lookout for some bargains, I'd suggest finding out what museum curators are collecting for themselves," Rago advises. "They have a lot of knowledge but they're definitely not overpaid. You can still find some major Arts and Crafts ceramics for less than $1,000. I would look for American Aesthetic pieces by such makers as John Bennett and Faience Manufacturing Company, which were inspired by the British Aesthetic movement of the late-19th century and are generally of superior quality. Early Rookwood ceramics from 1880 to 1890, which depict Japanese scenes, are still a good value. Since Rookwood ceramics are noted for their hand-painted decoration, condition flaws greatly reduce their value. If you're willing to compromise on condition, you can find excellent pieces of Rookwood with chips or cracks at one quarter of the price you would pay for pristine examples."

Given the fact that many experts consider Arts and Crafts to be one of the first of the modern American-furniture movements, it is not surprising that Gustav Stickley's handcrafted, clean-lined, well-constructed furniture continues to attract a faithful following, claiming among its avid collectors such celebrities as Barbra Streisand and Steven Spielberg. Influenced by William Morris, the leader of the English Arts and Crafts movement, Stickley—who also designed metalwork, lighting, and rugs—believed that a comfortable living environment was essential to a harmonious family life. Also referred to as Craftsman furniture or Mission furniture (it is reputedly similar in style to pieces found in the early California missions), the rectilinear oak sideboards, cabinets, settles, beds, dressers,

Fine and rare Gustav Stickley Morris chair with spindled sides and corbels under slanted arms, drop-in seat cushion recovered in white muslin. Height 36½", width 27½", depth 37". Unmarked. Auction estimate: $7,500–$10,000. Price realized: $8,437.50. (Courtesy David Rago Auctions, Lambertville, NJ/ragoarts.com)

Fine Gustav Stickley magazine stand (no. 72) designed by Harvey Ellis, with an overhanging rectangular top, arched apron, and sides flanking three shelves. Excellent original finish. Craftsman paper label. Auction estimate: $4,000–$6,000. Price realized: $7,875. (Courtesy David Rago Auctions, Lambertville, NJ/ragoarts.com)

"The Morris chair is an excellent example of Stickley's work, a classic Arts and Crafts form. Spindled chairs are rare on the market. The fact that this chair is unmarked does not reduce its value significantly because it still has its original finish," Rago observes. "The second piece is the best of Stickley's magazine stands, distinguished by its overhanging top and arched apron. The fact that it was designed by the noted architect Harvey Ellis enhances its value; some of Stickley's most sought-after pieces were designed by Ellis."

pieces were refinished over the years, his signature was often rubbed off in the process.

"If you're interested in Stickley furniture, the first thing I would advise is to buy a good form, a piece that is well designed and shows balance and proportion," Rago says. "As with all American furniture, original finishes are also desirable. That said, I would rather buy a good form with a new finish than a bad form with an original finish. Stickley's early, experimental furniture has ebonized finishes. The most sought-after Stickley furniture dates to this early period, from about 1901 to 1904, has a generally heavy, massive look and exposed joinery. Stickley furniture should have its original hardware and original patination. Of course, you should avoid pieces that have been cut down to suit specific size requirements or those that have suffered water damage and dry rot, factors which significantly reduce their value."

Few auction houses publish detailed condition information in their catalogues. You should request written condition reports before the auction on the pieces that interest you. Don't forget to read the terms of guarantee and conditions of sale listed in the auction catalogues, as they vary from house to house. Rago is one of the few auctioneers who guarantees the condition of the objects in his sales. Always try to examine furniture closely at the auction preview with the help of an auction specialist or a trusted dealer, who also may agree to bid for you for a small fee, often 10 percent of the hammer price. Don't be afraid to ask questions at the preview. Auction specialists are eager to meet new buyers.

While you can find original Stickley chairs at auction for as little as $500, expect to spend tens of thousands for substantial pieces and top-notch designs. The auction record for Stickley is $596,500 for an oak and wrought-iron sideboard that sold at Christie's in 1999.

Another significant segment of the 20th-century decorative-arts market is art glass, which reached its pinnacle during the Art Nouveau period in France and America from 1890 to 1920, when such renowned designers as René Lalique, Emile Gallé, Daum Frères, and Louis Comfort Tiffany created exquisite glass vases, bowls, sculpture, lamps, and objets

tables, and chairs made at Stickley's Craftsman factory in Syracuse, New York from 1898 to 1915 inspired several imitators, including his two brothers, Leopold and J.G. as well as a community of craftsmen in East Aurora, New York, known as the Roycrofters.

The L. and J. G. Stickley Company continues to produce furniture that combines designs from both Gustav's Craftsman label and the original L. and J. G. Stickley shop. These reissues (which can be costly) are sold by retailers at lower prices than the coveted Stickley originals that show up at auction. Stickley almost always signed his furniture, but because some of these

d'art inspired by organic forms and motifs from nature.

If you are a fan of the molded-glass creations of the legendary French jeweler and glassmaker René Lalique, you will be pleased to discover that his sculpture, vases, boxes, frames, car mascots, lamps, perfume bottles, clocks, and other decorative objects are available at auction. In fact, Doyle New York holds an annual auction devoted entirely to Lalique designs.

"Since you can expect an overall high aesthetic quality for Lalique glass, its value depends mostly on rarity and condition," says Eric Silver, head of 19th- and 20th-century Decorative Arts at Doyle New York. "Lalique's vases are rare, for example, and highly sought after. Generally, the larger and more colorful the object, the higher the price it brings. Lalique glass is either clear, frosted, opalescent or colored, the colored glass being the rarest and most desirable. The most prevalent design motifs are stylized animals, birds, insects, flowers, and foliage, as well as female figures and geometrics. When it comes to condition, cracks and chips and trapped air bubbles will significantly reduce the value of Lalique glass. You may see pieces that have been restored. Some vases, for example, have been ground down to eliminate chips on the rim or foot. Others that were formerly used as lamp bases display drilled holes that have been patched. These types of restorations also diminish the value."

Lalique's contemporaries, the French designers Emile Gallé and Daum Frères, produced some of the finest glass vases of all time. Gallé, the founder of the famed glassmaking colony in Nancy, France, was particularly noted for his complicated, revolutionary techniques and designs, which elevated glass to a universally accepted art form. One of his best-known techniques is overlaid glass, accomplished by the overlaying of colored glass in combination with carving, etching, and other techniques to produce a three-dimensional effect. Daum Frères is noted for its enameling and applied-glass techniques.

Both designers responded to the international Art Nouveau style and its interpretation of Japanese art, which gave rise to a distinctive decorative-arts expression called *japonisme*. Their vases are typically curvilinear, ovoid forms that are decorated with nature-inspired motifs such as birds, animals, insects, flowers and other botanical subjects, sea creatures, shells, and landscapes.

"The extent and quality of the decoration, the colors used, and condition are the most important criteria to keep in mind when buying Daum and Gallé vases," advises Nancy McClelland, international head of 20th-century Decorative Arts at Christie's. "For example, good, strong primary colors are more desirable than muddy browns and yellows. Large vases with more sophisticated and complex carving and other decorative techniques usually bring higher prices than small, plainly crafted examples. Hand-made vases are less common and more desirable than machine-made molded vases. You should also look for a signature; most of these vases were signed. And since glass is such a fragile medium, the condition of the vase is crucial to its value. Look at a lot of different examples before you bid, so that you know what these vases are supposed to look like. You should not overpay for a vase that has been ground down or restored to conceal chips and cracks. And while you are likely to see some bubbles in the glass, a vase should not have burst bubbles on the surface or in areas that detract from the decoration."

Condition is also crucial to the value of the colorful vases and lamps that made American designer Louis Comfort Tiffany (1848–1933) a household name.

"Glass collectors are very particular about condition. Ceramics collectors are a bit more accepting of minor flaws and a certain amount of restoration. Surface cracks and scratches, and chips on the lid or foot of a Tiffany vase will cause its value to plummet. Even scratches on the inside of a vase due to years of use are not desirable. And condition flaws such as broken, scratched, and damaged glass panels will significantly reduce the value of a Tiffany lamp," Silver explains.

Tiffany's trademark iridescent, organically shaped Favrile-glass vases show up frequently at auction. Large sizes, rare forms such as the floriform vase, designed to look like a flower on a stem; rare techniques such as lava (iridescent glass on a dark blue ground); cypriot (a type of iridescent glass meant to imitate ancient glass); and cameo-carved glass often bring the highest prices, assuming pristine condition.

Tiffany designed both solid-glass and leaded-glass versions of hanging lamps, as well as table lamps with bronze bases. The leaded-glass lamps are made of irregular mosaics of opalescent glass depicting either geometric or nature-inspired motifs, such as flowers and insects. The solid-glass lamps often have an iridescent finish. Elaborately decorated leaded-glass lamps, which depict everything from butterflies, dragonflies, and spiders to water lilies and magnolias, bring the highest prices and are the costliest of all the 20th-century decorative arts treasures sold at auction.

A Wisteria leaded-glass and bronze table lamp, Tiffany Studios, c. 1910, height 26", diameter of shade 18½". Auction estimate: $200,000–$300,000. Price realized: $187,000. (Courtesy Christie's, New York) "The Wisteria is often considered the quintessential Tiffany lamp model. It is a total composition, very naturalistic with an uneven border. A special feature contributing to the desirability of this lamp is that the shade was designed specifically for the base. Most Tiffany lamp shades and bases were designed separately and are interchangeable," Nancy McClelland says.

Lamps with large shades—from 20 to 30 inches in diameter—often fetch higher prices than smaller shades. Those made with complex glass techniques such as "confetti glass" (made to resemble confetti) and "drapery glass" (made to resemble drapery) also command high prices. Generally, the greater the number of colors used, the more valuable the lamp, depending upon the rarity of the pattern. Some colors, such as reds and blues, are more desirable than others, for example greens and yellows. Tiffany also produced a range of bronze bases which, depending upon their degree of workmanship, also affect the value of Tiffany lamps. Bases inlaid with glass mosaics are among the most costly.

"Authenticity is a big factor with Tiffany lamps. There are a lot of reproductions and fakes on the market that are often difficult to distinguish from the real thing. That's why it's important to buy from a reliable source," McClelland notes. "While most Tiffany lamps are signed 'Tiffany Studios' on the inside of the shade and stamped on the bottom of the base, some weren't signed. Lamps that have retained their original parts command a premium. Shades and bases of varying sizes were often switched to satisfy the aesthetic needs of various generations."

You can buy Tiffany lamps at auction for as little as $5,000 to $8,000 for a small desk lamp with minimal decoration. Lamps with geometric borders sell from about $10,000 to $50,000, while floral-decorated lamps bring from $30,000 to hundreds of thousands. The highest price ever paid for a Tiffany lamp at auction was $2.8 million for the Pink Lotus lamp (c. 1900–1910), which sold at Christie's in 1997 and holds the auction record for 20th-century decorative arts.

Expect to pay from a few hundred dollars for small Tiffany Favrile vases to as much as a quarter of a million dollars for those with rare forms. Vases by Gallé and Daum range in price from several hundred to one million dollars. Lalique vases and figures fetch from several hundred to hundreds of thousands of dollars.

Perhaps you're attracted to the sleek, elegant designs of the French Art Deco period. Collectors, interior designers, and antiques enthusiasts can't seem to satisfy their appetite for furniture made during the early decades of the 20th century by such Art Deco masters as Émile-Jacques Ruhlmann, Jean Dunand, Eileen Gray, Jean-Michel Frank, and Süe et Mare. Don't worry. These pieces are still available at auction, but you will likely pay a premium for them.

"The demand for Art Deco furniture by the most important designers has been rising steadily for the past few decades, and the top of the market is very bullish now. Prices have doubled over the last two years, helped, of course, by the strong economy," McClelland says. "But you can still find some bargains if you've done the research and know the market. Art Deco furniture has a timeless modern quality that blends well with a variety of interiors. That's why it's so appealing."

Whether you are redecorating your home or beginning a collection, you will want to inspect the Art Deco furniture you plan to bid on for its quality of design and craftsmanship, authenticity, condition, and provenance—the same criteria of connoisseurship that you would apply to all antiques. As always, you should first of all educate yourself by reading books on the subject, studying auction catalogues from previous sales, and visiting museums, galleries, and auction exhibitions, comparing your object of desire to similar examples. You should also try to build a relationship with a dealer or auction specialist who can answer your questions and advise you how to make the best bid.

"The best Art Deco furniture is distinguished by sophisticated design, harmonious proportions, and opulent materials. Exotic woods and veneers such as rosewood, amaranth, amboyna, and macassar ebony, which are prized for their beautiful grains, are more desirable than oak and mahogany, for example. Ivory and tortoiseshell inlays and the use of shagreen or *galuchat,* a type of fishskin, also enhance the value of Art Deco furniture," McClelland observes.

Both ivory and tortoiseshell are materials from endangered species. Laws against importing these materials to the United States have been in effect since the early 1970s and have become more stringent in recent years. The limited supply, therefore, of ivory- and tortoiseshell-inlaid Art Deco furniture in this country also adds to its desirability and value. On a cautionary note, if you are planning to furnish a home outside the United States, keep in mind that many other countries also restrict the import of these materials.

Since many Art Deco pieces were commissioned as one-of-a-kind luxury products by wealthy individuals, records of previous ownership (provenance) are often available and listed in the auction catalogue descriptions.

"Unlike furniture made during earlier centuries, most of the great Art Deco furniture was published and documented, so that we know who once owned a particular Eileen Gray screen or Ruhlmann cabinet," says New York dealer Anthony DeLorenzo. "If the piece happened to belong to the famous couturier Jacques Doucet, for example, it can be even more appealing to collectors who will pay for that added cachet. The number of pieces available on the market also helps to determine their value. For example, you may discover that only two pairs of a particular type of

Center table, Süe et Mare, 1925, burl amboyna, mahogany, gilded-bronze mounts, height 29", diameter 44". $35,000. (Courtesy Moderne Gallery, Philadelphia) "This is a typical example of Art Deco design. It is beautiful and elegant, made of exotic woods, and has a stylized, modern look," notes Aibel. It was shown in Paris at the 1925 Exposition Internationale des Arts Décoratifs et Industrieles Modernes, the historic exhibition that gave Art Deco its name.

chair were made, while many pairs of another type were commissioned."

And what about original finishes, which are often integral to the value of antique furniture?

"With Art Deco furniture, the look and design is dependent upon the beauty and clarity of the wood grain. Unlike antique American furniture, whose collectors prize original patinas or finishes, a refinished or restored Art Deco piece is usually more desirable than one that has lost its original color and transparency," says Robert Aibel, owner of Moderne Gallery in Philadelphia. "The value of a piece diminishes if the sun has bleached its color, or old varnishes have begun to yellow, or it has been badly scarred. Many buyers are willing to do what's necessary to bring it back to its original appearance. They want it to look as sleek as the day it was made. Although it is hard to compete with the rich luster of traditional shellac or French polish, I suggest using modern finishes that give a greater level of protection and durability, particularly if you're using the furniture. Of course, you always hope to find something that's in

A blondwood and *verre eglomisé* occasional table with bronze sabots ("shoes" that terminate the legs), French, c. 1940, height 29½", diameter 15". Auction estimate: $2,600–$3,600. Price realized: $3,055. (Courtesy Christie's, New York) This table by an anonymous maker displays the curvilinear form, light-colored wood, and decorative detail—in this case, *verre eglomisé*, a type of painted glass—that is typical of 1940s French furniture.

pristine condition, that hasn't already been restored or needs restoration, but those pieces are rare."

If the item you plan to bid on requires refinishing, you will have to figure that cost into your top bid price. Auction specialists can recommend conservators who can provide estimates.

"When it comes to restorations, keep in mind that a piece that has been refinished is not the same as one with replaced legs or large areas of replaced veneer, which would significantly reduce its value," Aibel advises. "Small repairs such as veneer patches would not affect the value as much. You should always ask about condition before bidding, especially if you're planning to spend a significant amount."

Once you've outbid the others for your prize Ruhlmann cabinet or Gray screen, you'll want to maintain its condition by keeping a consistent temperature level in your home. Excessive heat and humidity can cause inlays and veneers to crack and lift, according to McClelland. If you're living in a dry climate, however, you should have a humidity-controlled environment. And remember that excessive light will cause your furniture to fade.

Some Art Deco furniture, particularly by Gray and Dunand, is finished with natural lacquer.

"Natural lacquer is very strong, so you will find that very few of these pieces suffer from significant damage," notes DeLorenzo. "If there is damage to the surface of a table, you should not have it completely 'relacquered.' Natural lacquer doesn't exist anymore the way it was used in the 1920s and 1930s, so it would be impossible to recreate the original surface anyway. Even if you tried, the piece would no longer be a true Eileen Gray or Jean Dunand. It's okay, however, to do small touch ups, such as overlacquering a cigarette burn, which would be visible. Personally, I like to know that the table has been used. I don't mind seeing the occasional cigarette burn or glass water mark. It shows age."

"Always try to inspect the furniture that interests you, as closely as possible," Aibel adds. "It may need more repairs than you had expected. Remember that dealers and collectors often unload problem pieces at auction. Let's say a collector happened to buy a cabinet with a warped door, thinking that it could be easily repaired. Then he takes it to a conservator and discovers that, in fact, a whole new door has to be made. Such major surgery is not only more expensive but changes the entire essence of the piece. When that collector is ready to trade up, he may try to sell that piece at auction. Auction specialists do their best to catalogue objects properly, but they sometimes make mistakes. Don't rely solely on the information and photographs in the auction catalogue."

Although furniture by the top-tier Art Deco designers has sold for up to $1.87 million at auction, you can find fine coffee tables by Ruhlmann at auction from $60,000 to more than $200,000, depending upon the amount of ivory inlay and other details. Ruhlmann cabinets bring from $40,000 to more than one million dollars, while dining-room side chairs by Ruhlmann and Frank sell from $10,000 to $20,000. Frank's side tables range from $30,000 to $100,000, depending upon the materials used. Lacquer screens by Gray and Dunand fetch from $50,000 to more than one million dollars.

If these prices are slightly beyond your budget, you will be pleased to know that there were plenty of lesser-known Art Deco designers whose furniture is relatively undervalued today by comparison. Look for Art Deco pieces by such Art Nouveau designers as

Louis Neiss, Vallin Studio, Gauthier Poinsignon, and Louis Majorelle and his studio, all of whom worked in Nancy, France (a region known for both its glassmakers and cabinetmakers) but for various reasons didn't produce as much, didn't cater to as broad a clientele, or didn't receive the same name recognition as their more illustrious contemporaries.

"You could spend $40,000 on a dining table and six chairs by any of these designers versus the $70,000 you might spend on a Ruhlmann coffee table," Aibel says. "Their side chairs can be bought for about $1,000 to $2,500; great end tables sell for less than $10,000. This furniture is both beautiful and well made and costs about the same amount that you would spend on new furniture. Good-quality Art Deco furniture by anonymous makers also offers great value."

As furniture by the Art Deco masters becomes increasingly sought after and costly, collectors and buyers have also turned to its immediate successors—French furniture from the 1940s and 1950s. The neoclasically inspired French furniture of the 1940s by such artist-decorators as Jules Leleu and André Arbus, whose graceful, curvilinear designs were inspired by the earlier Directoire style; Jacques Adnet; and Gilbert Poillerat, noted for his whimsical, wrought-iron creations, was followed by the austere, functionalist French furniture of the 1950s by such architect-designers as Jean Prouvé and Charlotte Perriand, and the decorator Jean Royère, among others.

"Forties French furniture, which actually took root in the mid-thirties, has a modern, neoclassical look that was a gradual evolution from the sumptuous Art Deco style of the teens and early twenties and a reaction against the bold, Cubist-inspired designs of the late Deco period," Aibel explains. "It is sleek like Art Deco furniture, but more delicate, incorporating soft colors, curves, and decorative details such as leather, parchment, carving, and *verre eglomisé*—a type of painted glass. You don't see as much of the exotic materials that were favored during the early years of Art Deco. And some of the forties pieces, which are usually constructed of light woods, such as waxed oak and sycamore, have a less-polished finish. Fifties French furniture, on the other hand, was inspired by the modernist aesthetic of Le Corbusier and the Bauhaus that advocated industrial methods and materials, such as metal, plastic, and glass."

Experts say that while the demand has increased for forties-style French furniture by the best-known designers, prices have yet to outpace those com- manded by premium Art Deco pieces. The same criteria of connoisseurship applies, however.

Unlike Art Deco furniture, fifties French furniture, which reflected a new direction in design after the war, is made mainly of humble woods such as oak and ash, with simple varnishes. And unlike the one-of-a-kind pieces created by Art Deco and forties designers, most of Prouvé's and Perriand's furniture was industrially made in multiples for large-scale public commissions such as schools and apartment buildings. Some wear and tear, therefore, can be expected and does not significantly reduce the value of this furniture. But you probably would want to restore pieces that have been severely damaged.

"With fifties French furniture, the big questions to ask are How many were made and for which commission?" DeLorenzo says. "These are the primary factors that determine its value. For example, the architect Jean Prouvé made only seven of a certain type of lighting table for a specific commission. Their prices have increased almost tenfold over the past ten years."

One of Prouvé's most famous commissions was for Paris's Citeé Universitaire. He and Charlotte Perriand designed 40 wood-and-metal bookcases for the student dorms there at the Maison de la Tunisie. The fact that Prouvé also collaborated with the painter Sonia Delaunay on the color scheme for his "Tunisia" bookcases adds to their value. Other factors such as rare colors and dramatic designs also can enhance the value of fifties French furniture.

As with all fine art and antiques, fake Art Deco and fake forties and fifties French furniture occasionally turns up on the market. You should confirm the authenticity of your object of desire with trusted experts, whether auction specialists, dealers, or curators. There is a difference, of course, between legitimate reproductions by furniture companies, which should be designated as such in auction catalogues, and fakes, which are made to deceive and sold as originals.

"In the early 1980s, a lot of Art Deco fakes came on the market. In the early 1990s, forgers in France were copying forties furniture, which was just becoming popular among collectors," notes Aibel. "Mid-century French furniture is easier to copy than earlier furniture because the originals can be in close-to-new condition. Fakes start appearing when a particular type of furniture begins to sell well and prices increase, and they usually are of pieces by big name designers."

Authentic forties French furniture ranges in price from $10,000 to $40,000 for an oak-and-leather armchair by Arbus, for example. A wrought-iron and marble table by Poillerat fetches from $20,000 to $100,000. As with all types of antiques, furniture by lesser known or anonymous designers brings lower prices. Although the finest fifties French furniture by Prouvé, Perriand, and other noted designers has brought as much as tens of thousands of dollars, you still can buy quality tables, cabinets, and chairs for less than $20,000.

Experts agree that one of the best buys in the 20th-century market is furniture created by such iconic mid-century American designers as the husband-and-wife team Charles and Ray Eames, George Nelson, Isamu Noguchi, Harry Bertoia, and Eero Saarinen, which has been heating up the auction market under the domain of Modern Design. Many auction houses, including Doyle New York and David Rago Auctions have added separate Modern Design sales to their roster, while some, such as Los Angeles Modern Auctions (LAMA), specialize entirely in 20th-century furniture and design.

"The market for Modern Design has exploded over the past five years. A new generation of buyers and collectors has discovered that furniture made by the great American designers of the 1950s is not only beautiful, elegant, and comfortable, but historically important, whether it's an Eames molded-plywood chair or Nelson's vinyl 'marshmallow' sofa," says Peter Loughrey, founder of Los Angeles Modern Auctions, whose sales have doubled every year since 1996. "Designers of this period adapted new technologies and materials, developed during World War II, to create revolutionary forms that were highly functional, and inexpensive because they were factory-made in large quantities. Postwar furniture has an organic feel that is tactile and inviting. It's the culmination of the modern spirit, and American designers were its foremost pioneers."

So if you happened to pick up an Eames chair or storage unit, a Nelson sofa or cabinet, a Bertoia wire-backed Diamond chair, or a Saarinen molded fiberglass-and-aluminum Tulip chair ten years ago at your neighbor's garage sale or a local flea market, you have made an investment that you are not likely to regret. As the 20th century fades further into the past, modern design icons, like the centuries-old antiques that preceeded them, have begun to find their way into museums, private collections, and publications, and are increasing in value.

Although a rare 1940s molded-plywood chair by Eames and Saarinen, one of three prototypes known to have survived, sold at LAMA in 1999 for $129,000—the auction record for mid-century modern furniture—you still can buy vintage pieces from $500 to $5,000. Unlike Louis XV commodes and Chippendale tables, however, many of these modern designs have remained in production by their original manufacturers, notably Herman Miller and Knoll, who also have reissued certain pieces in response to increasing demand. Licensed designs by these manufacturers and others working with their authorization, such as the Swiss company Vitra, are usually more desirable than reproductions marketed by companies who do not have access to the designers' original specifications and therefore are likely to produce furniture of lesser quality.

While new versions of the original designs often can be bought for lower prices, are similar in quality (depending upon the manufacturer), and do not suffer the wear and tear caused by years of use, many buyers prefer the originals for their historical cachet, aged quality, and rarity.

"Good early examples of modern design are like great first-edition novels. They have specific 'points of issue' such as certain types of hardware, wire, upholstery, and factory markings that are unique and irreplaceable, that you don't see on later models. For instance, the earliest Eames molded-plywood chairs from the mid-1940s were made of thinner, more elegant plywood, and the rubber shock mounts that attach the seat and back to the frame had metal washers that gave them added stability," Loughrey observes. "A vintage Eames rosewood-and-leather lounge chair and ottoman, one of the couple's most famous and copied designs, is upholstered with top-grain leather, whereas new models are upholstered with a lower-quality leather that doesn't last as long. These new models are also made of cherry and walnut, since rosewood can't be imported anymore to the U.S. While Herman Miller continues to produce both the Eames molded-plywood chairs and leather lounge chairs, along with many other Eames designs, a lot of people enjoy the detective work of tracking down the originals. Of course, as the demand increases, these pieces are becoming harder to find. Also, some vintage designs are rare to begin with because so few were made, and others are no longer produced. All these factors contribute to their increasing value. But when you compare mid-century American furniture to earlier antiques, it is more readily available on the market and a lot more affordable. What else can you buy of such great quality that costs so little? I would

Rare and early Charles and Ray Eames "DCW" Evans Products chair. Molded plywood with mahogany veneer, aluminum, and rubber. This example exhibits all the characteristics of the very first production, c. 1946. Height 29¼", width 19½", depth 22". Auction estimate: $3,000–$4,000. Price realized: $4,600. (Courtesy Los Angeles Modern Auctions) "This is one of the Eames's earliest and best production chairs. Later examples do not have the same metal shock washers and thin plywood. Mahogany veneers are rare. You can find good later examples of this design in the more common birch, ash, and walnut veneers for about $500 to $1,000," Loughrey says.

metal, because it has steel-rod legs), and LCM (lounge chair metal) are readily available at auction. You may have noticed that copies of these classics also happen to be found in many schools and offices around the country. At the auction preview, you'll want to evaluate the chair that interests you for the type and rarity of the materials used, when and by whom it was manufactured, and its condition.

"The most sought-after Eames chairs were manufactured by the Evans company from 1945 to 1946, before Herman Miller took over production in 1950. The rare Evans pieces carry their own red label and bring some of the highest prices," says John Sollo, a modern-design specialist at David Rago Auctions. "Some chairs have a transitional label that says both Evans and Herman Miller, because Miller distributed them from 1947 to 1950; they are also more rare than those bearing only Miller labels. You also want to look at the type of wood used. The light-colored birch veneers are more costly and desirable than ash and walnut. Rosewood is the rarest and most valuable. Mahogany is also rare. Dyed and upholstered chairs are less common than the solid wood examples. The dyed chairs are usually either all red or black. Two-toned red-and-black chairs, which may have black legs, for instance, and a red seat and back, are more rare. I always say it's like buying a car; every little extra feature increases the value."

Even rarer are the Eames chairs that are upholstered in "slunk" (not skunk) skin, which is a type of calfskin. You might pay up to $30,000 for one of these examples, while the more common vintage birch chairs can be bought for less than $2,000. New models of the original Eames molded-plywood chair designs sell from $100 to $300. Vintage Eames leather-upholstered lounge chairs and ottomans sell for about $3,000 at auction; new models are priced similarly.

"Collectors will pay a premium for vintage pieces in good condition. With Eames chairs, they want the original rubber shock mounts, which are different from the shock mounts on the new models. They also want chairs with original backs, which tended to break after years of use," Loughrey says. "Condition flaws such as chips on the edges of the plywood can reduce the value of vintage chairs. Some people pre-

much rather own a design icon than spend as much if not more for new furniture."

Perhaps you're in the market for a vintage Eames molded-plywood chair, one of the landmarks of 20th-century design that evolved out of Charles and Ray Eames's experience designing molded-plywood aircraft parts and leg splints for the government during World War II. It is the culmination of their experiments with new materials and technologies, and the realization of their vision to create low-cost, well-designed furniture for the masses. Vintage Eames molded-plywood chairs, labeled DCW (dining chair wood), LCW (lounge chair wood), DCM (dining chair

George Nelson "Thin Edge" 8-drawer chest designed for Herman Miller. Rosewood-veneered plywood, aluminum, and plastic. Retains metal tag. Height 31", length 47", depth 18½". Auction estimate: $2,000–$2,500. Price realized: $3,565. (Courtesy Los Angeles Modern Auctions) "This is a prime example of Nelson's popular rosewood cabinets. 'Thin Edge' refers to a style of cabinet where the edges are one-quarter-of-an-inch thick," Loughrey notes. "Earlier examples had thicker edges. This piece had a slight stain on the upper two left drawers. It would have brought more without this condition flaw."

fer to buy chairs that have been refinished, which also reduces their value. Basically, if you plan to collect, you should look for a chair that is as close to its original condition as possible, which means that you want to see the original finish, shock mounts, and hardware intact, the rule of thumb for any design from this period."

"If you live in a sunny climate, keep in mind that the red-dyed chairs, in particular, tend to fade when exposed to too much light. You'll likely end up with a dirty-brown color instead, which, of course, will diminish the value of your purchase," Sollo adds.

If you're planning to bid on a vintage Eames rosewood-and-leather lounge chair and ottoman, you'll want to ensure that the leather isn't cracked and that the aluminum base hasn't been knicked or painted. The buttons also should be intact. Another popular Eames design is the "ESU" (Eames storage

unit), an all-purpose cabinet constructed of plywood, steel, and painted masonite.

"Collectors prefer early ESU designs to newer models, which have different screws and different-gauge metals and plywoods. ESUs painted in primary colors are also more desirable than those that are white, black, or putty-colored," notes Loughrey. "Condition flaws such as bent legs or repainted or scratched masonite panels will reduce their value. Vintage Eames ESUs in good condition from the '200' series, the most common design, sell from $3,000 to $10,000 at auction. The rarer '400' series pieces, which are taller, sell from $10,000 to $70,000. I always advise buying the best you can afford. The higher-end pieces accelerate in value more than lower-end pieces."

Perhaps a George Nelson cabinet or Marshmallow sofa has caught your eye. The cabinets and chests of drawers that Nelson designed for Herman Miller from 1948 to the late 1960s turn up frequently at auction. Their simple yet elegant designs reflect the functional aesthetic of mid-century American furniture that Nelson helped to pioneer. The rarest, most sought-after pieces were crafted of rosewood during the early years of production. Cabinets made of the blonde Primavera birch, which has an attractive, shimmering quality, are also desirable. Walnut and ash were also used.

"Color adds value to Nelson's designs. Colorful painted pieces often bring higher prices than plain wood pieces," Loughrey says. "His black cabinets with Chinese-red- and coral-toned lacquered drawers are rare and sought after, for example. Cabinets with blonde cases and black-painted drawers are also popular. His multi-colored Marshmallow sofas bring higher prices than those that are all one color, whether black or orange or green. The upholstery can also mean a difference in price. Nelson's bright-purple vinyl sofas bring higher prices than his black leather sofas, for example, probably because they are more evocative of the 1950s style."

Cabinets with rare "hairpin" legs usually bring more than those with the more common, sturdier "duck bill" legs. The Thin-Edge line of mainly rosewood dressers, which have small pointed, aluminum legs and porcelain, "hourglass" pulls, bring three to four times as much as the more common birch-case pieces. You'll also want to decide which cabinet form appeals to you. Highboys (versus lowboys) as well as bedroom furniture forms, such as dressers and night-stands, tend to bring the highest prices because these pieces satisfy certain lifestyle requirements, according to Sollo.

Condition, as always, is an important indicator of value and quality. As with other mid-century modern furniture, the best vintage Nelson cabinets still have their original finish and hardware. Vintage Nelson so-fas should have their original foam cushions. Replaced or deteriorated foam, scuffed upholstery, and cor-roded or repainted aluminum frames will diminish their value. You can buy vintage Nelson cabinets at auction for $4,000 or less. Vintage Nelson Marshmal-low sofas range in price from about $9,000 to $20,000, depending upon the criteria previously mentioned.

Among the other offerings of interest in Modern Design auctions is furniture created during the mid-20th century by pioneers of the American Craft movement such as George Nakashima, Sam Malouf, Wharton Esherick, Wendell Castle, and Paul Evans. Many of their one-of-a-kind pieces, which are appre-ciated for their fine-quality woods and organic forms, can be bought for less than $10,000 at auction.

You may have had such a good time at the auction preview, admiring 20th-century treasures, that you al-most forgot about your next task. Bidding. Fortu-nately, this aspect of the auction process does not have to be approached with the same trepidation as an emergency trip to the dentist. All you need is thor-ough knowledge of your market, some good advice, and a little practice, and, if you're lucky, you may even have some funds left over for your next root canal or, even better, your next auction purchase. Remember, the auction mantra: The more you know, the better you'll bid.

"Don't rush into buying at auction. First-time buyers should do adequate background research be-fore bidding," David Rago advises. "Read a lot about the subject and period that interest you. Go to gal-leries, museums, art fairs, and auction previews, which serve as hands-on museums. At the preview, study the objects carefully and ask permission to han-dle them. Ask questions. Sit through an auction to see how it works. You don't have to bid in order to attend most auctions. And get to know the experts—dealers, auction specialists, or restorers—most of whom will

take the time to educate a potential customer. Their advice can be invaluable. Ask other collectors and dealers about their experiences with specific auction houses. Above all, buy what you love, not for invest-ment. Financial profit should not be your primary concern when buying art, however one should always keep an eye cocked to the future."

The other auction mantra is Know your market. In the heat of the moment, there's always the danger that bidding competition may drive prices far beyond reasonable levels.

"Do some comparison shopping. Find out what dealers are selling and for what prices. Study auction catalogues from past sales so that you have a good idea of what price you should pay for the piece you plan to bid on," Aibel counsels. "Ask a dealer or auction spe-cialist, before the auction, what the interest has been in that particular piece. If there's a lot of interest, the final bid price may not be an accurate indication of that object's value. Remember that other bidders may not know the market as well as you do. Just because someone is bidding heatedly for an item doesn't mean that it's important or valuable. He may need a chest of drawers for a spot in his home and will pay what it takes to get it. If you don't get what you want, re-member that there will always be more pieces like it on the market."

Insiders also advise becoming familiar with who's bidding on what. But don't always assume that you'll have a better chance at being the top bidder when bidding against dealers. While it's sometimes true that dealers drop out of the bidding at a certain level, be-cause they have to mark pieces up for resale, they are not always buying for inventory. A dealer may, in fact, be bidding for a private collector for whom price is no object.

"Auctions are very exciting and fast moving. The best bidding strategy is to decide on your top bid in advance," notes Silver, who is also an auctioneer. "It's easy to get caught up in auction fever and spend too much. Of course, we want you to get carried away. But the less emotional you are the better bid you are likely to make."

"Have confidence in your judgment and try to buffer yourself from the noise of the auction," Cathers adds. "Be clear about how much you're will-ing to spend and hold your course. And always try to view the objects in person at the auction preview. It's very difficult to judge the quality, and particularly the condition details, of a piece from an auction-catalogue photograph or Web-site image.

RECOMMENDED MUSEUM COLLECTIONS:

- The Metropolitan Museum of Art, New York, NY
- Museum of Modern Art, New York, NY
- Cooper-Hewitt National Design Museum, New York, NY
- Los Angeles County Museum of Art
- Denver Art Museum
- Virginia Museum of Fine Arts, Richmond, VA
- The Wolfsonian Museum, Florida International University, Miami Beach, FL

SALES OF 20TH-CENTURY DECORATIVE ARTS AT SELECTED AUCTION HOUSES:

- Christie's— March, June, December
- Sotheby's—March, June, December
- Doyle New York—Belle Epoque: June, September; 20th-Century Art and Design: April, November
- David Rago Auctions—Arts and Crafts: January, May, September; Modern Design: March, May, October
- Treadway-Toomey—February, May, September, December
- Los Angeles Modern Auctions—10 auctions per year

✤✤✤✤✤✤✤✤

Anthony DeLorenzo
on the Thrill of the Chase
※

If you're planning to collect, wait until you can buy the best piece that you can afford. And don't be afraid to make mistakes. Collecting is a continual learning process. The more knowledge you gain, the better purchases you'll make. All collectors trade up for better pieces. Auctions can be a lot of fun, but they can also be dangerous to your bank account, even for us professionals. When I'm bidding at auction, it isn't always about the piece itself, even though it should be. It's about the game—winning and losing. My pulse rate instantly increases. Egos get involved. And before I know it, I've paid more than I should. I remember once at an auction years ago, I got caught up in a bidding war and was the highest bidder. Afterwards, my seven-year-old daughter tugged at my arm and said, "Daddy, you won!" Unfortunately, I had to borrow funds to pay for the piece. My best advice is to set a top price and stick with it. Don't go overboard.

Market Watch
ARTS AND CRAFTS SILVER

The Arts and Crafts aesthetic, so eagerly embraced by collectors of furniture and pottery, also found expression in silver of the period, which has gained recognition in recent years for its high-quality craftsmanship and affordable prices. Once considered too luxurious a material for the traditional Arts and Crafts interior, silver hollowware and flatware by such early-20th-century silversmiths as Arthur Stone and Katherine Pratt of Boston, the Kalo Shop and Robert Jarvie of Chicago, and Porter Blanchard and Shreve and Company of California is increasingly finding its way into private and museum collections, exhibitions, and auctions.

"Arts and Crafts silver is among the best, most affordable silver ever made in America. Even though it has begun to attract more attention, it is still a very good value when compared to Colonial American silver and late-19th-century silver by Tiffany & Company, for example, which have sold for six-figure prices," says Rosalie Berberian of ARK Antiques in New Haven, Connecticut, who specializes in Arts and Crafts silver, metalwork, and jewelry. "You can buy very good pieces by the major Arts and Crafts silversmiths for less than $5,000. Arts and Crafts silver bowls, for example, can be bought from $600 to $1,800; water pitchers sell for about $2,000 to $4,000. On the higher end, a substantial bowl with beautiful chasing by Arthur Stone, one of the best-known silversmiths of his time, brings from $6,000 to $8,000."

In the true spirit of the movement's aesthetic, Arts and Crafts silver is distinquished by simple, utilitarian forms, spare ornamentation that often incorporates nature-inspired motifs (executed in chasing, engraving, and/or repoussé), and a hand-hammered surface finish. The major silversmithing centers in America during the Arts and Crafts period were Boston, Chicago, and California, each of which produced their own unique styles.

Quality of design, size, and condition all help to determine the value of Arts and Crafts silver. "The most desirable Arts and Crafts silver has a beautiful, elegant design and shows a harmony of form, function, and decoration. Some forms, such as pitchers and candlesticks, are especially popular and tend to bring higher prices. Pieces made by the most highly regarded silversmiths, Arthur Stone of Boston and the Kalo Shop of Chicago, for example, also bring higher prices," Berberian says. "Assuming comparative good quality and condition,

Silver bowl with applied monogram, Kalo Shop, Chicago, c. 1912. $3,800–4,000. (Courtesy ARK Antiques, New Haven, CT) "This bowl is an excellent example of Arts and Crafts silver made by one of the most important silver-craft shops of the American Arts and Crafts Movement," Berberian says. "It has a handsome form and an applied monogram, a design feature that is unique to the Arts and Crafts period. Monograms on silver are usually engraved or chased. It also has a typical, but subtle, hand-hammered surface. There are numerous fine pieces of American Arts and Crafts silver by lesser-known makers that cost less. This is a top-of-the-line piece at a top-of-the-market price."

larger pieces fetch more than small pieces. You can find small trays, plates, and bowls for a few hundred dollars. As for condition, be careful of tears and breaks such as a broken spout; bumps and dents can usually be hammered out. Sometimes engraved monograms were removed, an often visible flaw that reduces the value of a piece. As with all silver, you should look for a maker's mark. Don't believe anyone who says 'This is Kalo' if it's not so marked."

Chapter 16
WORKS ON PAPER

Works on paper, a fine-arts category that traditionally encompasses drawings, watercolors, pastels, and prints, have been attracting growing interest in the marketplace, particularly from new collectors who have discovered that many excellent examples by well-known artists are available at auction for a fraction of the price they would spend on paintings of similar quality.

Artists throughout history have produced works on paper, both as studies for paintings and as individual works of art in their own right. Some auction houses, such as Swann, hold several auctions yearly devoted entirely to works on paper, while others, including Sotheby's, Christie's, and Butterfields, incorporate works on paper into broader fine-arts sales in specific categories, such as American art and Contemporary art. Christie's and Sotheby's, however, hold auctions devoted solely to Old Master drawings, as well as to prints of various periods. Christie's also organizes separate sales of Impressionist and 20th-century works on paper.

The market for Old Master drawings and prints has been particularly strong over the past several years. The colloquial art-trade term "Old Master" refers to European art that dates from circa 1400 to about the mid-19th century, as well as to the artists who created it.

"More people are buying Old Master drawings and prints because they are not only more available on the market than Old Master paintings, but they are also more affordable," says Todd Weyman, director of Works on Paper at Swann, where works on paper have become the fastest-growing and highest-grossing department. "It's a great field for the beginning collector, since you can build a strong, sizable collection without spending as much as you would for paintings of the same period. Drawings in particular have an immediacy that people connect with, and they offer a wonderful view into an artist's working process."

Whether you are in the market for an 18th-century French drawing or a 17th-century Dutch print, the same criteria of connoisseurship apply. Once you have ordered an auction catalogue, you will want to evaluate the aesthetic quality, authenticity, condition, rarity, and provenance of your potential purchase at the auction preview, an exhibition of the works being offered, which is held for several days prior to the auction and is free and open to the public.

Keep in mind that drawings (which include such diverse media as watercolor, pastel, gouache, charcoal, and pen-and-ink) are unique, one-of-a-kind works, while prints exist in multiples—numerous impressions of the same image that are produced by printmaking techniques such as woodcut, etching, engraving, and lithography. Because they exist in multiples, prints from all periods turn up at auction more frequently than drawings. For this reason, prints by a particular artist generally bring lower prices than drawings by the same artist, depending, of course, on the rarity of the print and its significance within the artist's entire body of work.

Old Masters whose drawings show up frequently at auction include the 18th-century French and Italian artists François Boucher, Jean-Antoine Watteau, Giovanni Battista Tiepolo, and Francesco Guardi, all of whom were prolific draftsmen.

Perhaps you are torn between a Boucher and a Tiepolo. You will want to evaluate the drawings' importance within the context of each artist's oeuvre, or body of work, paying specific attention to their aesthetic quality and subject matter. Since Boucher is best known for his nudes and boudoir scenes, drawings of these subjects are most desirable. He is also noted for his brilliant use of colored chalks and pastels. His color drawings therefore are more desirable and valuable than his pen-and-ink drawings. For Tiepolo, whose drawings mainly comprise watercolors and washes (which have the appearance of a light watercolor), the mythological subjects for which he is best known are more desirable than religious subjects, for example, and often bring higher prices.

"You should also consider the degree of finish of a drawing. Whether it is a slight sketch or a worked-up composition, which tends to be more valuable, as are drawings that functioned as studies for major paintings by a particular artist," says Dr. Nancy Bialler, head of Old Master drawings and prints at Sotheby's.

Condition is one of the most important value determinants for any type of work on paper.

"A tear, loss of pigment, staining, or fading will reduce the value of an Old Master drawing significantly," Weyman observes. "Old Master paintings are often retouched in areas, but this is less typical of drawings. Even so, you always have to balance condition against other factors, such as the rarity and historical importance of a drawing. Most collectors are willing to compromise on the condition of Old Master drawings, given their age and the fact that they are one-of-a-kind works that may not show up again at auction. With an artist like Boucher, for example, you want a drawing with as much pigment as possible, since chalks and pastels abrade easily. You should be even more exacting about the condition of Tiepolo's drawings, since he was so prolific."

Overexposure to light, whether natural or artificial, causes drawings to fade, which diminishes their value. That is why museums display drawings, pastels, and watercolors in dimly lit exhibition rooms. Drawings displayed in your home also should not be overexposed to light.

As with all art and antiques, provenance (ownership history) can enhance the value of both Old Master drawings and prints. Works that once belonged to noted dealers and collectors often attract interest at auction, particularly when they are part of a single-owner sale—an auction in which all offerings come from a single collection and for which a separate catalogue is usually printed. Most auctions combine property from a number of collections (some of which may be well known) as well as that from individual estates and consignments. In some auction catalogues, lots that do not come from specifically named collections are grouped under the heading "various owners." When available, further information about the provenance of each work is listed in the catalogue description, along with its exhibition and publication history, which also may add to its desirability.

As with Old Master paintings, attribution is another important consideration when evaluating Old Master drawings.

"If the drawing can be attributed to a specific artist like Rembrandt or Michelangelo, then it will be worth more than a drawing that cannot be attributed or one that is less precisely attributed, which is sometimes the case when you are dealing with centuries-old works," Bialler says. "If you've done your research, however, you may even be able to find a bargain in cases where a drawing may be incorrectly attributed or bear no attribution at all. Scholarship is ongoing in the Old Masters field, and new discoveries are constantly being made. For example, you may discover a Guido Reni drawing that has gone unnoticed or has been attributed simply to his circle or school of painters. Attribution is not as much of an issue with Old Master prints, since most prints bear an artist's signature or monogram."

When deciding which Old Master drawing to bid on, pay careful attention to the authorship terminology in the auction catalogue. In Sotheby's Old Master drawings catalogues, for example, a glossary explains that a work identified in boldface as being by **Giovanni Bellini** means that in the auction house's opinion the work is by the named artist. A drawing identified in the catalogue as **Attributed to Giovanni Bellini** means that it is probably by the artist, but there is "less certainty as to authorship," whereas a drawing identified as **Studio of Giovanni Bellini** is, in Sotheby's opinion, "a work by an unknown hand in the studio of the artist which may or may not have been executed under the artist's direction." Other definitions of authorship include **Circle of Giovanni Bellini, Style of . . . or Follower of Giovanni Bellini, Manner of Giovanni Bellini,** and **After Giovanni Bellini,** which means that Sotheby's believes the drawing to be "a copy of a known work of the artist." Generally, the further removed from the artist's own hand, the less valuable the work.

Sotheby's, however, does not guarantee the authenticity of any painting, drawing, or sculpture created prior to 1870. Be sure to read the terms of guarantee and conditions of sale listed in the auction catalogues of most established auction houses. If the catalogue does not contain this information, ask an auction-house specialist about the terms and conditions of their sales.

You can buy Old Master drawings at auction for as little as a few thousand dollars to as much as hundreds of thousands of dollars, depending upon the stature of the artist, the importance of the drawing within the artist's body of work, and its rarity on the market. Many fine drawings by Old Masters such as Tiepolo, Guardi, Canaletto, Boucher, and Watteau sell for less than $25,000, while their best drawings have brought hundreds of thousands of dollars. The highest price ever paid at auction for an Old Master drawing was $12.3 million for Michelangelo's *Study for the Risen Christ,* which sold at Christie's in London.

Perhaps your heart is set on an Old Master print. This time you are deciding between Rembrandt and Dürer, whose prints turn up frequently at auction along with a wide variety by other well-known artists, such as Goya, Piranesi, and Hogarth. Old Master prints often take the form of woodcuts, engravings, or etchings. Woodcuts, for the most part, fell out of favor by the 17th century. They were replaced by engravings, the product of a mechanical technique in which metal plates are engraved, inked, and run through a printing press. Etchings had also developed by the 17th century, the result of a sophisticated chemical technique in which copper plates are covered with resistant wax and exposed to acid to create a design.

Old Master artists were versed in a variety of printmaking techniques but tended to excel at one particular technique. While engravings and etchings are considered to be more aesthetically refined than woodcuts, which were a popular art form in their day, the value of a print is not dependent so much upon the type of printmaking technique used but rather on the availability of that type of print on the market.

"The critical question with Old Master prints is When was it printed?" Bialler notes. "Printing plates throughout the centuries were preserved and used again after the artist's death. Sometimes these plates were purchased by others. It is most desirable to buy a print that was printed in the artist's lifetime. You can distinguish these prints by the quality of the impression and the paper used. It is often hard to know, however, whether the artist who created the print actually did the printing himself, but this generally does not affect its value."

Since the majority of Old Master prints were signed—the artist inscribed his monogram or mark directly onto the wood block or metal plate—they can be attributed to a specific artist with more certainty than can drawings, most of which are not signed.

As with Old Master drawings, certain print subjects by a particular artist are more desirable than others. Dürer, a master engraver, depicted mainly religious subjects. His most sought-after prints, considered by the artist himself to be his masterpieces, are *St. Jerome in His Study, Melancholia,* and *Night, Death and the Devil,* all of which come up for auction. Rembrandt is noted for his etchings of religious subjects and self-portraits. His landscape etchings, however, are more rare and often bring higher prices. In many cases, Rembrandt's etchings were reworked by others and printed after his death. This practice continued through the mid-19th century. Rembrandt and other Old Masters often sold their printing plates to publishers and other artists. Etchings that have been reworked are not always less desirable, according to Weyman, since some collectors prefer the darker contrasts typical of these later works.

"In general, the best Old Master prints are those that were printed during the artist's lifetime, show rich ink contrasts, and were printed on paper that was used during the artist's lifetime," Weyman advises. "These old papers are identified by certain papermaker's marks, called watermarks, such as the coat of arms of Amsterdam in the case of Rembrandt's prints. The quality of the impression also affects the value of an Old Master print. An impression is a single copy of a print. The earliest impressions are the most rare and desirable and command the highest prices. They have an overall brightness and clarity that become less defined with each successive impression."

A good impression will display sharp, clean lines and will not appear to be overinked or faded. As woodblocks and engraving or etching plates wear down over time, the lines in woodcuts tend to become thicker, while the lines in engravings become worn. Later impressions also show decreased depth.

Similarly, the early states of a print are more desirable than later states. A "state" signifies a change in the print itself, whether caused by the artist's own hand or by another artist at a later date. For example, Rembrandt may have added a background to one of his prints after several impressions were already made.

As with Old Master drawings, the condition of the Old Master print you plan to bid on is another crucial consideration.

"Serious condition problems, such as folds, tears, and paper loss, can reduce the value of an Old Master print by more than half," Bialler says. "Minor flaws, such as soiling or a small crease in the corner, are more acceptable and reduce the value by about 10 to 15 percent. Many Old Master prints have trimmed margins, since collectors often mounted them in books. Trimmed margins may reduce the value slightly, but they are not a serious detriment to the print. You have to be willing to compromise on condition a bit when buying Old Master prints. Even though they are multiples, the supply is diminishing, particularly the best examples. If the condition of the print that interests you does not compromise its aesthetic quality, then you should consider bidding on it. Modern and contemporary prints should be closer to pristine condition."

You still can buy prints by Rembrandt, Dürer, Tiepolo, and other noted Old Masters for $1,000 to $5,000 at auction, compared to the millions you would spend for one of their paintings. Collectors will, however, pay a premium for the best Old Master prints. While you might pay $1,000 for a Rembrandt print that is a posthumous impression of a small religious scene or small portrait, you should be prepared to spend up to several hundred thousand dollars for a rare early impression of an important subject such as his *Three Crosses*. Dürer's prints also have brought up to several hundred thousand dollars at auction. Prints by lesser-known contemporaries of Dürer and Rembrandt, many of whom were their students, such as Hans Baldung Grien and Ferdinand Bol, can be bought for about $1,000 to $2,000.

Perhaps you're more interested in American art. As in the Old Masters market, there is a healthy demand for works on paper by noted artists including the American Impressionists Frederick Childe Hassam and John Henry Twachtman; Winslow Homer; James A. M. Whistler; and early-20th-century Modernists such as Arthur Dove, John Marin, Georgia O'Keeffe, and Stuart Davis, all of whom worked in a variety of media—whether drawing, watercolor, etching, or lithography (a printing technique based on the repellent properties of oil and water). Since the beginning of printmaking in America in the late-19th century, collectors have prized American works on paper for their immediacy, spontaneity, and accessible prices.

"Drawings and other works on paper are almost always part of an artist's oeuvre," says dealer Gerald Peters, whose galleries in Santa Fe, Dallas, and New York City specialize in American art. "They offer a more immediate artistic expression than works on canvas because they are closer to an artist's working process. And they are often less than half the price of good paintings by the same artist. It's an ideal field for the beginning collector, who can affordably put together a collection of top-quality works by well-known artists."

Whether your heart is set on an O'Keeffe watercolor or a Hassam etching, you will want to apply the same criteria of connoisseurship that you would to any work on paper.

"You should know how a specific work fits into the artist's body of work. How significant is it aesthetically and historically? With O'Keeffe, for example, you would want a watercolor from 1915 or later, when she really came into her own as an artist," Peters advises. "Marin, who worked almost exclusively in

Rembrandt van Rijn, *A Woman Reading*, etching, 1634, 4⅞" x 4". Biorklund's third state (of 3); Usticke's third state (1) (of 3); White and Boon's third state (of 3). Partial coat-of-arms-of-Amsterdam watermark. Auction estimate: $4,500–$6,500. Price realized: $9,200. (Courtesy Swann Auction Galleries, New York) "This is a strong impression of a print in good condition that does not appear often on the market," Weyman notes. "The presence of the coat-of-arms-of-Amsterdam watermark on the paper dates it to an early impression. It's unusual to see a watermark on a small print." The names that appear in the description above are authors of catalogues raisonnés of Rembrandt's prints.

watercolors, is best known for his abstracted landscapes from 1910 to 1930 that depict New York City scenes and Maine seascapes. His watercolors of New Mexico landscapes from 1929 to 1930 are also sought after. Drawings and studies for important paintings by an artist are often more valuable than their other works on paper. For example, Stuart Davis's *Eggbeaters* studies in gouache from the 1920s are highly prized because his *Eggbeaters* paintings are among his most important works."

Moving back in time, Hassam's Impressionistic etchings of New York City scenes are among his most desirable prints, and Whistler's early figural etchings from the 1860s to the early 1870s (the years consid-

Abraham Walkowitz, *Dancer*, watercolor and pen and ink on cream wove paper, c. 1900–1920. 12¹/₂" x 9¹/₈". Signed in ink, lower left. Short tear at upper right to the left of the dancer's head. Auction estimate: $1,500–$2,500. Price realized: $1,380. (Courtesy Swann Auction Galleries, New York) "This is one of the many drawings that Walkowitz did of the great dancer Isadora Duncan. The colors are intense, which is unusual for a century-old watercolor. While the watercolor is in a good state of preservation overall, the tear diminished its value," Weyman observes.

ered by many experts to be the pinnacle of his career) are also sought after, according to Weyman. The value of a print is also determined by the size of its edition. Prints from small editions (which may include from 10 to 25 impressions of the same image) usually bring higher prices than prints of similar quality from larger editions. During the late-19th century in America, artists began limiting their editions, a practice whereby they purposely issued a limited number of impressions of the same image, which gave them more control over the market for their work. Whistler, who usually limited his editions, also printed on rare 17th-century Japanese paper, another factor that can enhance the value of his prints. Amer-

ican artists also began signing their prints in the late-19th century. Prints bearing an artist's signature (versus the printed signature used by the Old Masters) are often more desirable than unsigned prints.

If you're in the market for a drawing or a watercolor, which are one-of-a-kind works, you should not expect the same pristine condition that you would from a print. But keep in mind that major condition problems, such as tears or fading from sunlight, will significantly reduce the value of any work on paper.

"Tears on the edges of a work on paper don't bother me so much. Tears that distract from the image are worse. You also want to make sure that the work has been mounted correctly. A lot of early mounts were on acidic paper, which can cause acid burns on the artwork that show up as browning," Peters observes. "With prints, you should also look at the overall quality of the impression. Early impressions are usually more clear and crisp than later impressions."

Expect to spend about $100,000 or more for top-notch watercolors and drawings by Davis and O'Keeffe, whose paintings have sold for millions. A good Marin watercolor fetches from $50,000 to hundreds of thousands, while Dove's best works on paper bring from $25,000 to $75,000. You can spend up to $50,000 for a Whistler etching or as little as $1,000 for a small etching of a generic landscape or figure by the same artist. Hassam's prints range from $1,000 to $30,000 for the Impressionistic New York City scenes for which he is best known.

Works on paper by some American artists, including William Merritt Chase, Winslow Homer, and Mary Cassatt, have soared into the millions. In the American-art market, prints by Social Realist artists such as Ben Shahn, John Sloane, and Martin Lewis, all of whom depicted gritty, urban industrial scenes, are still relatively undervalued, according to Weyman, and can be bought for a few thousand dollars at auction.

Works on paper are also a good entrée into the Impressionist and Modern art market, typically the domain of heavyweight paintings, multimillion-dollar prices, and deep pockets. But the art on paper of Picasso, Matisse, Degas, and other masters is readily available at auction for prices that won't deplete your life's savings. For example, minor examples by any of these artists, such as a simple pencil or pen-and-ink drawing can be bought at auction from $3,000 to $10,000.

Nineteenth-century French drawings of the human figure form the core of Atlanta gynecologist

Michael Schlossberg's museum-caliber art collection, a work in progress for more than thirty years.

"I'm fascinated by drawings because they are very intimate and personal and not outrageously expensive," says Schlossberg, who often lends drawings from his collection to museum exhibitions nationwide. "A painting is more of a finished product, whereas drawings bring me closer to the heart and mind of the artist and his creative process. When you train your eye over time by visiting museums, galleries, auctions, and art fairs, you discover what you like. It's often an immediate reaction for me."

"Unique works on paper—drawings, watercolors, and pastels—by notable Impressionist and Modern artists are often higher quality than oil paintings by these artists that fall in the same price range," says Meredith Harper Wiley, head of Impressionist and Twentieth-Century Works on Paper at Christie's. "Whichever artists interest you, I advise buying the best piece of art you can afford. You should always look for works that are typical of a particular artist's style and subject matter. Matisse, for example, is noted for his female figures and his highly developed sense of line, patterning, and composition. Degas, who was a highly accomplished draftsman, is best known for his dancers, equestrian scenes, and bathers. The rarity of a particular medium also affects a work's value. For example, Matisse's drawings are more plentiful than his watercolors and pastels, which generally bring higher prices. Picasso was prolific in all media."

As in other fine-arts fields, certain periods of an artist's oeuvre are more aesthetically and historically important than others. For example, Picasso's works on paper from his early "blue" and "pink" periods and his Cubist and Marie-Thérèse years all have a stronger market than his later neoclassical works; the same is true for his paintings. If your taste leans toward later masters such as Willem de Kooning and Jackson Pollock, who forged American Abstract Expressionism out of the crucible of European Cubism and Surrealism, you would want to know that de Kooning's early works on paper from the late 1940s and 1950s of female subjects are most desirable. Pollock's works on paper are rare, and the most sought-after examples were produced concurrently with his famous drip paintings.

When it comes to various types of media, watercolors and pastels by a particular artist often can fetch higher prices than drawings that don't incorporate color. Within the latter category, charcoals tend to bring more than pen-and-ink drawings, which in turn

usually bring more than pencil drawings—all criteria being equal. There are always exceptions, of course. An exquisite pencil drawing could bring more than an average pen-and-ink drawing by the same artist.

Impressionist and Modern artists created original works on paper both as studies for paintings and as works of art unto themselves. The degree of completeness and finish of a drawing, pastel, or watercolor often affects its value. Degas' highly finished pastels of ballerinas, for example, are prized by some collectors even more than his paintings. The same is true for Redon's pastels. Raoul Dufy's fully executed watercolors of regatta and racing scenes usually fetch higher prices than his watercolor sketches in which some areas are left unpainted.

Condition is of slightly more consequence to the value of Impressionist and Modern unique works on paper (as distinct from prints, which are produced in multiples) than to the Old Master works that preceded them. While flaws such as glaring tears, paper loss, and fading will significantly reduce the value of works on paper from any period, the condition of a particular work must be weighed against its age, rarity, and importance within that artist's body of work.

"You have to be realistic about condition. You shouldn't pass up a rare and important drawing by Monet or Matisse, for example, simply because it has a small tear in the margin or suffers from minor light-staining, foxing, or mount- and mat-staining," Wiley observes. "All these factors, of course, can diminish the value of a drawing, watercolor, or pastel. Although direct damage to an artist's pen- or brushwork is not desirable, you should expect some wear and tear on works that have some age."

Light-staining results from prolonged exposure to sunlight or harsh artificial light, which causes the paper to brown from oxidation. "Foxing" refers to little brown dots caused by mildew and changes in humidity or by inherent impurities in paper. Mount- and mat-staining are caused by acid in the board on which many drawings, pastels, and watercolors were mounted for presentation. The acid often causes paper to darken from oxidation. Mat-staining occurs along the edges of a work that have been covered by the mat window; mount-staining appears on the back of a work. The acid-free (or archival) board used today didn't exist during the late-19th and early-20th centuries.

"You also have to remember that unique works on paper are process-oriented creations. Certain types of soiling or buckling of the paper from the application

Edgar Degas (1834–1917), *Femme nue se coiffant,* signed "Degas" (at lower left), pastel and charcoal on tan paper laid down on board, c. 1890–1895, 14¼" x 22". Auction estimate: $100,000–$150,000. Price realized: $171,000. (Courtesy Christie's, New York) "The market for drawings is strong now, so it is not surprising that an interesting, appealing image like this one did well," says Harper Wiley. "The theme of a young woman combing her hair or having it brushed by a maid inspired Degas to produce some of his finest oils, drawings, and pastels in the final phase of his career."

Some houses, including Christie's, Sotheby's, and Swann, list more-detailed condition information in their prints catalogues. You may call the auction house or speak to an auction specialist at the preview for additional information about specific works. Curators and art dealers are also excellent resources. If you are serious about collecting, many dealers are willing to accompany you to a preview. For a small fee, they will help you evaluate the works that interest you, and even bid on your behalf.

Auction prices for unique works on paper by Picasso range from about $6,000 for a small crayon or pencil drawing to several million dollars for an important gouache or pastel. Matisse's unique works on paper bring from $9,000 for a small pencil drawing of flowers to several million for a study for one of his well-known paintings, for example. Expect to pay from $80,000 to close to $20 million for pastels by Degas, whose pure charcoal drawings without pastel heightening bring from $10,000 to $300,000. Dufy's watercolors range in price from $20,000 to several hundred thousand dollars, while de Kooning's drawings sell from $15,000 to several million dollars. Prices, of course, are always dependent upon the standard criteria. As in every field, works on paper by less-noted artists can be bought for lower prices than those by their more illustrious contemporaries. Size also can affect value; small works on paper often bring lower prices than large works of similar quality by the same artist.

Although many noted Impressionist and Modern artists were prolific draftsmen, their prints are also available at auction, often at lower prices than their unique works on paper such as drawings, watercolors, and pastels. The same criteria of connoisseurship applies to their prints, whether etchings, lithographs, woodcuts, or others. Since prints are produced in multiples, you should be more exacting about their condition. The most desirable prints will have re-

of water-based media may have occured during the artist's process, and they bring us closer to that process," Wiley adds. "A smudge created by the artist's hand, for example, is acceptable as opposed to a smudge caused by someone who may have later spilled water on the work. Works on paper can also be repaired. While repairs can diminish the value of a drawing, watercolor, or pastel, many collectors are willing to overlook them if the conservation is done well."

"When you're evaluating works on paper at the auction preview, don't be afraid to handle them and inspect them closely. We don't exhibit our works in frames," Weyman advises. "It's always a good idea to look at the back of a work in direct light so that you are able to see clearly any restorations such as repaired tears or patches, which will be less apparent on the front."

Remember to ask the auction house before the sale for a written condition report. Few auction houses list detailed condition information in their catalogues.

mained as close as possible to their original state. Remember that poor condition will compromise the value of Impressionist and Modern prints more than that of Old Master prints. Color prints usually bring higher prices than black-and-white prints by the same artist, as do prints issued in small editions of about twenty-five or fewer, versus the more typical edition size of about one to two hundred.

Expect to pay from several thousand to about $100,000 for Picasso's prints and from several thousand to $75,000 for prints by Matisse. Large color prints by masters such as Renoir, Miró, and Chagall can be bought at auction from $20,000 to $50,000, while their small etchings and lithographs of simple subjects sell for as little as $1,000 to as much as $5,000.

Contemporary prints from the mid-20th century onward by blue-chip artists such as Robert Rauschenberg, Jasper Johns, Andy Warhol, Frank Stella, David Hockney, and Helen Frankenthaler are also plentiful at auction and offer an excellent collecting opportunity. By the 1960s, more artists had begun to recognize printmaking as an important art form and to experiment with various techniques.

"Contemporary prints are an exciting field because there are so many different ways of making prints and so many visual variations. Prints have surfaces and textures that you don't see with other types of art," says Christopher Gaillard, head of Contemporary Prints at Sotheby's. "Another appeal is their affordability. You can buy the highest-quality prints by important artists for less than you would spend on a unique work such as a drawing or a painting by the same artist. And the images and techniques of printmaking can be equally as beautiful."

Before buying Contemporary prints, you should spend time viewing works by the artists that interest you at auctions, print galleries, and publishers. Print publishers—such as the well known Gemini G.E.L of Los Angeles and New York, Crown Point of San Francisco, and U.L.A.E. of West Islip, New York—invite artists to create prints, and then produce, sell, and distribute them in a combination workshop-gallery setting. Additionally, many fine-arts galleries, such as Brooke Alexander Editions and Pace Prints, both of New York, produce and sell prints by their own artists and sell other publishers' prints.

"Look at a range of work by several different artists as well as several different examples within each artist's oeuvre. If you're serious about collecting and want something that will have future value, don't buy on impulse. Take your time," says Joni Moisant Weyl, who runs Gemini G.E.L. at Joni Moisant Weyl in New York. "Initially, you should buy something that is representative of an artist's work. An artist's prints will usually follow the same aesthetic continuum as his unique works, displaying similar styles and subjects. It's a process of honing your aesthetic judgment so that you will be able to evaluate such qualities as the print's compositional balance and its relationship of form and color. You should also seek out a good adviser in the same way you would consult a professional for advice in any other field."

As with prints from other periods, the aesthetic and historical importance of the print within a specific artist's body of work, the complexity of the image, the size of the print and the print edition, and the print's rarity and condition all help to determine its value.

If you're in the market for a print by Frank Stella, for example, you will discover that his most complex and colorful prints are often most desirable, as are those from his celebrated *Protractor* and *Tropical Birds* series. Helen Frankenthaler's early prints from the late 1970s, which display her hallmark vertical, saturated strands of color, are among her most sought-after prints.

Again, condition is often more integral to the value of prints than to unique works such as drawings and paintings.

"With prints there is more of a sense that they should come out of the drawer in pristine condition," Weyl notes. "Sometimes many impressions of the same print are available on the market, so you want to make sure that the one you plan to buy is in the best-possible condition."

Condition flaws that significantly reduce the value of Contemporary prints include discolorations in the paper, staining, tears, rippling of the paper (which may be caused by improper framing), fading from overexposure to light, and creases from improper handling.

"A minor handling crease in the margin wouldn't bother me too much, but it might bother someone else," Gaillard says. "Of course, the condition criteria vary with each artist. A small tear in the margin of a print by Helen Frankenthaler would not diminish its value as much as a small tear in the margin of a Warhol silk screen, which would mean that the tear is actually on the image itself. Warhol's images usually cover the entire surface of the print."

You always should weigh the condition of a Contemporary print against its rarity and edition size.

"For example, prints from Rauschenberg's 1967 *Booster* series are rare on the market, so I would be

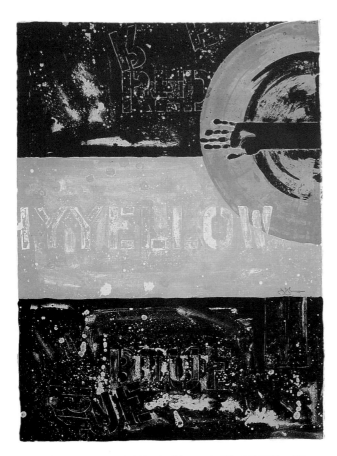

Jasper Johns, *Periscope I*, 1979, 7-color lithograph, 50" x 36". Edition: 65. $25,000 © Jasper Johns and Gemini G.E.L./Licensed by VAGA, New York, NY.

All criteria being equal, Contemporary prints in small editions tend to bring higher prices than prints of comparable subject matter by the same artist in large editions.

Since value determinants such as states, edition size, rarity, and condition vary from artist to artist, you should check catalogues raisonnés (publications that illustrate an artist's entire body of work) for specific information about an artist's prints. Price guides such as *Gordon's Print Price Annual* and Artnet's online price index will also help you to determine the current market value of the print on which you plan to bid. Of course, prints by the most-accomplished and internationally renowned artists will command the highest prices.

You can buy prints by noted Contemporary artists such as Frank Stella, Helen Frankenthaler, Robert Rauschenberg, Jasper Johns, and David Hockney for less than $2,000—for small, simple images—up to tens of thousands of dollars for their finest examples, depending upon the aforementioned criteria. Undervalued areas include prints by Contemporary artists such as Ellsworth Kelly and Claes Oldenburg, who have not worked consistently in this medium, as well as those by prolific printmakers such as Rauschenberg, whose prices are very affordable when weighed against his stature as one of the most influential artists of our time.

Whether it's a work on paper by Rembrandt, Matisse, O'Keeffe, or Rauschenberg that has piqued your interest, the more knowledgeable you are about the auction process, the more likely you are to make the best bid.

"People are often intimidated when they come to an auction house, but remember that the auction specialists are readily available to answer any questions you may have, both before and after the auction," Bialler says. "Don't be afraid to approach us during the auction preview, or feel that you are disturbing us. That's why we're there. Find a specialist with whom you have a rapport and build a relationship that can be helpful to you in the future. One of the aspects I most enjoy about my job is educating potential buyers about the artworks we offer for sale."

In addition to doing the necessary background research on the lot or lots that interest you and seeking the advice of experts prior to the auction, you should also determine your top bid price.

"It's all about what you know, and I don't mean just knowledge about the art itself," Peters notes. "You also have to know the marketplace and what you should expect to pay for works by specific artists in or-

more forgiving if one of those prints were not in pristine condition," Weyl says. "I would not be willing to compromise as much on the condition of a brand-new Rauschenberg print or on a print of similar quality from a large edition, say of 100 to 250. Generally, edition sizes today are of about 30 to 60 prints."

Unlike prints from earlier periods, the quality of an impression is not an issue with Contemporary prints. The publisher selects only the best impressions to be numbered, signed by the artist, and sold; therefore they display very little variation in quality. Similar to prints from earlier periods, Contemporary prints may exist in "states," which are the results of changes made by an artist during the printmaking process. For example, an artist may add some details to a printing plate after some prints have already been produced. Unlike with an Old Master print, the latest state of a Contemporary print is often more desirable than an early state because it displays the culmination of the artist's process. The type of printmaking technique used—whether woodcut, lithography, etching, screen-printing, or any combination of these techniques—usually does not affect the value of a print.

der to make the most of a buying opportunity. And remember that auctions can be emotionally charged events. Egos get involved. It's easy to get carried away if you haven't set your price limit beforehand."

"I make every effort not to go over my limit, because I know how easy it is to succumb to auction fever and overpay for a work that I really want. Similar examples will likely come up in future sales—if not that particular work itself—and you'll have other opportunities to bid. Be willing to let some things go," Schlossberg says. "I would also advise spending your alotted funds on one superb drawing rather than on three mediocre drawings."

But what if you are the only person in the saleroom bidding on your object of desire? Does that mean it's a dud? Don't panic. You should feel confident if you've done your homework.

"Trust your own judgment," Bialler counsels. "I remember once when I was a dealer, and I worried that no one was bidding on the Rembrandt print that I wanted. It turned out that the dealers I expected to be bidding against were interested in a print in a subsequent auction. External factors do come into play, and if you really know what you're doing, you can wind up with some bargains."

You also should trust your judgment enough not to be fooled by sometimes unrealistic auction estimates.

"You can't assume you're safe just because you're bidding at a big auction house," Weyl cautions. "You also have to look into what's being sold at galleries and make quality and price comparisons. Auction estimates aren't always an accurate indication of a work's value; they are sometimes set too low to lure buyers or too high to satisfy the sellers. Of course, one always hopes for a bargain, but it's just as easy to pay too much for a print as it is to pay too little. At auctions it's sometimes less about the work than it is about who wants it at that particular moment."

Whichever type of print or unique work on paper finds its way into your home, you will want to ensure the best possible conditions for their preservation.

"Make sure that your work on paper is matted on acid-free archival board and framed properly, so that it doesn't buckle," Weyman advises. "You also should not hang it in direct sunlight or shine a spotlight on it, which will cause fading. Color is most susceptible to light. It's a good idea to use special plexiglass that inhibits harmful ultraviolet rays, rather than glass, when framing a work on paper. You may want to rotate the works in your collection, so that no single one is overexposed to light. You should also keep consistently low temperature and humidity levels in your home to avoid buckling and rippling."

Michael Schlossberg on Sleuthing

One of the biggest thrills for me about collecting drawings is uncovering historical details about a work that had been previously unknown to me, whether its the relationships certain artists shared or the significance of their subject matter to their lives. I also like discovering works by little-known artists that others may have overlooked. It's intellectual detective work. One of my favorite auction discoveries was a Gauguin drawing that had another drawing by the artist, on the verso, that was unknown in the Gauguin literature. If you're looking for bargains, you may want to call the auction specialist immediately after the sale and inquire about lots that bought in, or didn't sell, during the auction. Generally, the best lots do sell, but you may be able to buy something that slipped through the cracks and negotiate a lower price than what it may have brought during the actual sale. I also like to investigate the small auction houses, where I've sometimes found treasures. Even external conditions such as bad weather can lead to buying opportunities. Fewer bidders in the saleroom, and therefore less competition, can mean lower prices. While I sometimes bid by telephone, I prefer to bid in person when I really want something, even if that means hopping on a plane. It's more fun and exciting to be in the saleroom, and then I don't have to worry about any technical glitches with the phone.

Market Watch
20TH-CENTURY ARTISTS'
EXHIBITION POSTERS

*E*xhibition posters by noted 20th-century artists, such as Picasso, Matisse, Duchamp, Cocteau, Warhol, and Lichtenstein, are a relatively untapped area of the art market that offer the opportunity to acquire original works of art from several hundred to several thousand dollars.

"Exhibition posters, designed by artists themselves throughout the 20th century both for exhibitions of their own art and for other cultural events, are not simply photographic reproductions of their paintings but individual works of art in their own right," says Susan Reinhold of New York's Reinhold-Brown Gallery, which specializes in 20th-century graphic-design posters. "There is often a lot of confusion about posters, which are made in multiples and intended to communicate a commercial message. While they can be reproductions, posters can also be 'original,' meaning that the artist's design was intended to be used specifically as a poster. The word 'original' in this case does mean that the poster was drawn by hand. Many of these unique poster designs appear in artists' catalogues raisonnés. They are still very undervalued for their quality and can only increase in value."

Poster, c. 1957, created by Jean Cocteau for a Paris gallery exhibition of posters by great painters. This poster is typical of the imagery of French Surrealist painter Jean Cocteau. $500. (Courtesy Reinhold-Brown Gallery, New York)

Exhibition posters printed on fine arches paper and issued in limited editions bring higher prices. Some artists signed their posters, which also enhances their value. Good auction venues include Poster Auctions International, in New York, and Swann, which recently began conducting auctions of modern graphic-design posters, a field that includes posters designed by artists, architects, and graphic designers of the Bauhaus, Art Deco, and Russian Constructivist periods.

SALES OF WORKS ON PAPER AT
SELECTED AUCTION HOUSES:

• SOTHEBY'S—Old Master Drawings: January and October; Prints: May and November

• CHRISTIE'S—Old Master Drawings: January; Prints: April and November; Impressionist and Twentieth-Century Works on Paper: May and November

• SWANN—Old Master Drawings: February; 19th- and 20th-Century Works of Art on Paper: March and September; Prints: May and November

• BUTTERFIELDS—Prints: April and October

RECOMMENDED MUSEUM COLLECTIONS:

• The Metropolitan Museum of Art, New York, NY
• The Art Institute of Chicago
• Museum of Fine Arts, Boston, MA
• Museum of Modern Art, New York, NY
• The National Gallery of Art, Washington, D.C.
• Fogg Art Museum, Harvard University, Cambridge, MA
• The Pierpont Morgan Library, New York, NY

Part Three

TYPES OF AUCTIONS

Chapter 1
LIVE AUCTIONS

Now that you know how to make the best bid, you may be wondering exactly where to find your object of desire and put your knowledge into practice. Perhaps you are in the market for a million-dollar painting or a modestly priced drawing by your favorite artist. Or you have decided to decorate your new home with antique American or Chinese furniture. Maybe you are responsible for dispersing the contents of a family estate or are searching for the best sale venue for your collection of 20th-century art glass. Perhaps you are beginning a collection of American folk art or looking for the perfect photograph to present as a gift.

You will be happy to know that there are hundreds of auction houses nationwide from which to choose, whether large or small, generalists or specialists. While the auction process itself is relatively consistent from house to house, the players occupy niches that can be broadly defined, for the sake of simplification, as international, regional, boutique or specialty, and country, with some crossovers. Geography, too, may dictate your auction house of choice. You may prefer either the convenience of attending an auction close to home or to weave an auction experience into your next weekend trip to the country or a holiday in New Orleans or New York City, for example, where you can also refine your eye at a host of renowned art galleries and antiques shops.

Since this chapter is intended as a map of sorts, let's begin our auction "roadtrip" (not to be confused with "roadshow," as in the highly popular PBS television series *Antiques Roadshow*) in New York City, the cultural epicenter of the universe according to some xenophobic New Yorkers. Here, you will find the heavyweight competitors Christie's and Sotheby's, whose operations are international in scope.

Founded in London in 1766, Christie's is a private company owned by French investor François Pinault with principal salerooms in London, New York (at Rockefeller Center), and Los Angeles. Sotheby's, which began as a book-auction house in London in 1744, is a public company trading on the New York Stock Exchange with principal salerooms in London and New York (on York Avenue). These two firms dominate the auction market, selling billions of dollars worth of merchandise annually in more than eighty collecting categories ranging from Impressionist paintings, Contemporary art and American furniture to jewelry, wine, and entertainment memorabilia. In addition to their principal salerooms, they also maintain offices and hold auctions in more than forty countries worldwide, in cities such as Geneva, Paris, Rome, Hong Kong, and Melbourne.

Christie's and Sotheby's hold sales in various categories during specific months, a practice followed by many large auction houses. For example, their American furniture sales usually take place every January and October, while their Asian-art sales are usually held every March and September. Prominent among the hundreds of auctions they conduct each year are their May and November sales of Impressionist and Contemporary art, which often grab headlines with record-breaking Monets and Picassos, as well as high-profile single-owner collections that also ignite their share of media attention.

Notable auctions in Christie's recent history have included the sales of van Gogh's *Sunflowers,* for $39.9 million, and *Portrait of Dr. Gachet* for $82.5 million, the most expensive work of art ever sold at auction; Leonardo da Vinci's *Codex Hammer* for $30.8 million, an auction record for any object other than a painting; the collection of Rudolf Nureyev; and the collection of Victor and Sally Ganz, one of the most important private collections of 20th-century artworks ever sold. Auction highlights at Sotheby's have included the sales of van Gogh's *Irises* for $53 million; Renoir's *Au Moulin de la Galette* for $78 million; the estate of Jacqueline Kennedy Onassis; the collection of the Duke and Duchess of Windsor; and Impressionist and Modern art from the estate of Mr. and Mrs. John Hay Whitney.

Given such stratospheric price tags, it is not sur-

Pair of ruby slippers worn by Judy Garland in M.G.M.'s classic 1939 film *The Wizard of Oz*. Sold for $666,000 at Christie's East, New York.

prising that Christie's and Sotheby's are regarded as the premier auctioneers of high-end works of art. Indeed, you'll rarely find items for less than $2,500 in their salerooms. In addition to the sheer volume and variety of objects offered at their auctions, these two houses are distinguished by their massive marketing and promotional resources. Their worldwide network of offices and salerooms enables sellers to reach a larger pool of buyers than most regional auction houses, while also taking advantage of national collecting habits and fluctuating exchange rates when determining the best sale venues for their property. (The Internet, however, is rapidly leveling the playing field; see the separate section on Internet auctions.) Consigned objects receive maximum exposure through broad catalogue distribution, traveling exhibitions, advertising and publicity in international media, and, depending upon consignment value, special invitation-only receptions.

Equally powerful in luring buyers and sellers to Christie's and Sotheby's is, of course, the glamour factor. Many of their highly publicized sales are also popular social events that take on the aura of a spectator sport. Here you can brush shoulders with the rich and famous, perhaps recalling a few lines from a famous poem by that most British of American poets, T. S. Eliot: "In the room the women come and go talking of Michelangelo." Before placing your first bid, you may also want to remember that "In a minute there is time for decisions and revisions which a minute will reverse," as Eliot also wrote.

Christie's and Sotheby's also provide a host of other services, including publication of their own scholarly art books and international magazines featuring objects of interest from upcoming sales; real-estate brokerage of prestigious properties; financing secured by artworks; private treaty sales of artworks; graduate programs in connoisseurship, the art market, and the arts; as well as art- and antiques-related lectures, seminars, and courses on subjects ranging from English furniture and Japanese decorative arts to jewelry and Scandinavian art and design. (For more information on these educational services, call Christie's Education at 212-355-1501 or Sotheby's Institute at 212 894-1111.)

For those on more modest budgets, both Christie's and Sotheby's hold sales devoted to lower-priced art, antiques, and collectibles. Christie's East, formerly located on East 67th Street in New York City and now based at Christie's Rockefeller Center headquarters, conducts sales in many of the same categories as its Rockefeller Center parent, including American paintings, photographs, Impressionist and Contemporary art, and European furniture. The big difference is that you might spend about $3,500 on an American painting here, versus the tens of thousands or more that you would likely spend at Christie's Rockefeller Center saleroom. You might also find a Contemporary print for $1,000 or an English dining table for $3,000 at Christie's East, which obtains the majority of its offerings from estates.

"Our affordable price ranges are ideally suited to beginning collectors. People feel comfortable here because we are smaller, less formal, and less intimidating than the big houses," says Richard Madley, president of Christie's East. "Being smaller allows us to be flexible and creative with our sales. For example, we recreated original room settings for our auction of furnishings from Hammersmith Farm in Newport, Rhode Island, which was known as 'the summer White House' during the Kennedy administration. We also try to make ourselves accessible with expanded preview hours on the weekends and by offering free Monday-evening 'walkabouts,' during which our specialists discuss highlights of upcoming sales."

Christie's East is particularly noted for its auctions of popular arts, a category comprising Hollywood and sports memorabilia as well as animation art, which often bring higher prices than those achieved by the art and antiques in its traditional estate sales. Popular-arts highlights at Christie's East have included Dorothy's ruby slippers from *The Wizard of Oz,* which brought

$666,000; Herman Mankiewicz's personal script of *Citizen Kane,* fetching $231,000; a scene setup from the 1934 Walt Disney movie *Orphan's Benefit,* which brought $286,000; and a rare Honus Wagner baseball card that sold for $640,500. The firm prides itself on anticipating new trends in collecting and design, and pioneering unique theme sales such as maritime and ocean-liner memorabilia. Christie's East is also one of the world's largest auctioneers of musical instruments.

Sotheby's also offers affordable fine arts, decorative arts, and jewelry priced from about $1,000 to $10,000 in its popular Arcade auctions, which traditionally have taken place on the ground floor (or arcade level) of its York Avenue headquarters.

Phillips, de Pury & Luxembourg, the world's third-largest auction house, has undergone a major restructuring with the hope of challenging the supremacy of Christie's and Sotheby's. Founded in London in 1796, Phillips was acquired in 1999 by the French luxury-goods group LVMH Moet Hennessy Louis Vuitton, whose owner Bernard Arnault is the business rival of Christie's owner François Pinault. Like Christie's and Sotheby's, Phillips maintains an international staff of specialists and conducts hundreds of auctions worldwide each year of everything from Impressionist and Contemporary art, jewelry, and European furniture to 20th-century Design and sports memorabilia. Its main salerooms are in London and New York. With its recent acquisition of Etude Tajan, France's largest auction house, Phillips also plans to open a saleroom in Paris. Its St. Louis, Missouri, saleroom at Phillips-Selkirk organizes mid-market sales of fine and decorative arts and jewelry as well as specialty auctions in such categories as wine, toys and collectibles, and Civil War memorabilia.

"Until now, Phillips has been a modest player, especially in New York. We plan to expand our international presence by increasing our staff, offering more high-end art and antiques and single-owner collections, and moving into larger, more upscale premises in New York, which will emerge as our largest theater of operation," says Christopher Thomson, chief executive officer of Phillips, U.K. "For buyers, the main advantage of an international auction house is having the opportunity to view and purchase merchandise

Gerhard Richter, *Apfelbaum,* oil on canvas, 1987. Sold for $1,652,500 at Phillips Auctioneers (now Phillips, de Pury & Luxembourg).

that is sourced globally. For sellers, the advantage is global exposure for the goods they are selling."

In addition to the major international auction houses, there are hundreds of smaller, regional auction houses nationwide that specialize mainly in selling estate and mid-market merchandise to a loyal local clientele as well as to increasing numbers of national and international buyers. With annual sales totaling from a few million to tens of millions of dollars, most of these auction houses are privately owned firms that receive the majority of their consignments from their own geographic regions.

Many of the larger regional houses such as Sloan's of North Bethesda, Maryland, and Miami; Butterfields of San Francisco and Los Angeles, the third-largest U.S. auction house; and Skinner of Boston and Bolton, Massachusetts, the fourth-largest U.S. auction house, employ numerous specialists in a variety of departments ranging from American and European paintings and furniture to jewelry, Asian art, prints, and stamps and coins. Some have become known for specialized areas of expertise. Skinner, for example, is a good source for American furniture and decorative arts, Oriental rugs and carpets, and toys and dolls. Butterfields has made a name for itself in such collecting categories as entertainment memorabilia, books and manuscripts, and arms and armor, and is one of the few houses that conducts natural-history auctions comprising such items as fossils, rare meteorites, dinosauria, and museum-quality gems.

Auction of "Treasures from the Hoi An Hoard"—thousands of rare 15th- and 16th-century Vietnamese ceramics recovered from an ancient shipwreck off the coast of Hoi An, Vietnam. Dragon on left $75,000; dragon jar on right $28,750. (Courtesy Butterfields, San Francisco).

Because they are smaller in size than the major international auction houses, many regional houses contend that they are more accessible and more responsive to the needs of a broad base of buyers and sellers, who might be interested in consigning a painting valued at $250,000 or looking to buy a piece of Chinese-export porcelain for a few hundred dollars.

"The big New York auction houses tend to focus more on higher value works and name artists, whereas many regional houses offer objects that span a wide price range. In addition to paintings, sculpture, antique furniture and fine china, we would also sell your grandmother's old Steinway piano, for example. That's not to say that we don't ever auction big-ticket items. We recently sold a Mary Cassatt painting and a Frederick Remington sculpture," says Lawrence Du-Mouchelle of the well-known Detroit auction house DuMouchelle Art Galleries. "While you may find fewer specialists at a lot of regional auction houses, they are usually well versed in a number of different subjects. When it comes to estate sales, the bulk of our business, we will not only hand-pick the best items for auction, we will also organize tag sales for the low-value items, so that you don't have to look for another sales venue, a service that the big houses don't provide. We can also be more flexible with our sales schedule, whereas buyers and sellers may have to wait for months until the appropriate sale comes up at Christie's or Sotheby's."

While they may be smaller in size, staff, and annual sales figures, many regional auction houses do a good job of marketing their consignments through catalogues, advertisements, and mailing lists. And what they may lack in international presence they make up for in a high degree of personalized service. A regional auction house is more apt to publicize a mid-market painting, for example, and may not charge for catalogue photography, insurance, or storage, with the hope of luring consignors. Their buyer's and seller's premiums also can be lower than those charged by the large auction houses.

"Smaller auction houses can be very cost-effective for the consignor. If you have a Modigliani painting to sell, I recommend the major New York houses. But for 99 percent of art and antiques in the $50,000 to $100,000 range, you will probably find that a regional house can bring you hammer prices comparable to what you would receive in New York," says Ronald Pook, owner of Pook & Pook Auctions in Downingtown, Pennsylvania.

When consigning objects for sale, particularly if you are liquidating an estate, you should consider not only the convenience of proximity but also whether the auction house has a particular strength that may enhance your chances for achieving high prices. The New Orleans-based Neal Auction Company, for example, is a good venue for selling 19th-century American and Southern furniture.

Many smaller houses pride themselves on their personal relationships with clients. They keep tabs on buyers' preferences, for example, and will notify them when an object of interest comes up for auction. They also may facilitate convenient shipping and payment options. While the large auction houses provide similar services, their high-end market niche, steep operational budgets, and the massive volume of merchandise that passes through their doors force them to be more selective in the relationships they cultivate. But don't always assume that you're going to make a steal at a regional house.

"Some buyers think they will pay less at regional auction houses because there may be less competition, or because the experts may not have enough knowledge about what they're selling. But that's a myth," says Carol Farley, owner, along with her husband,

Larry, of Pittsburgh-based Dargate Auction Galleries, which auctions fine art, antiques, and later furnishings and accessories for an average price of about $300 to $500. "It only takes two people who want something badly to drive up the price. And while most of our consignors are from the surrounding region, we have buyers from all over the country and the world, which increases competition. The fact that 80 percent of our lots are unreserved also stimulates bidding. We may have fewer specialists on staff, but that doesn't mean we have less expertise. If we don't know enough about a consigned item, we seek the advice of outside scholars, curators, collectors, and dealers."

Some auction houses are defying their traditional regional status with an increasing international presence in an effort to better serve their clients and attract new business. Butterfields, for example, has offices in Paris, London, Munich, and Brussels. Doyle New York, a thirty-seven-year-old family-owned business noted for its auctions of fine art, furniture and decorations, jewelry, couture, and 20th-century art and design, is part of an international marketing alliance with both the long-standing London auction house Bonhams (which merged in 2000 with Brooks of London, the world's premier auctioneers of vintage automobiles, to become Bonhams & Brooks) and the Paris-based auction house Boisgirard. The alliance enables the auction houses to conduct joint sales, pool marketing resources to promote each other's auctions, share specialist expertise and exhibition space for auction previews, link Web sites, receive maximum exposure for consignors' property, and offer buyers convenient access to the global auction market.

Doyle New York, which attracts a large number of private buyers, has made its mark with personalized service and exhibitions featuring roomlike "vignettes"

American sterling-silver presentation tankard and salver made by Joseph Lownes of Philadelphia, 1805. Sold for $35,725 at Dargate Auction Galleries, Pittsburgh.

1940 Packard Super 8 160, Model 1803, five-passenger four-door sedan. Sold for $43,700 at Dargate Auction Galleries, Pittsburgh.

that cater to both collectors and home decorators alike. Since the majority of the lots in its sales comes directly from estates, like many regional houses it provides comprehensive estate-liquidation services, including its trademark "broomclean" service in which it either purchases entire estates outright or takes them on consignment, then auctions appropriate items—everything from masterpieces to table lamps—and sends pieces of minimal value to charities for tax deductible contributions. The fifth-largest U.S. auction house, Doyle New York has auctioned the estates of such celebrities as Bette Davis, Gloria Swanson, and Louis Armstrong, but you don't have to be a star to do business here.

Like many established auctioneers, Doyle New

Howard Pyle, oil-on-canvas illustration for a story by William Makepeace Thackeray in *Harper's Monthly*, March 1907; owned by Norman Rockwell. Sold for $93,500 at Illustration House, New York.

York also holds free-appraisal days, when you can bring in paintings, furniture, and other objects to be appraised by its experts; offers lectures and seminars on art, antiques, and collecting (with the added attraction that they are free of charge); and also conducts auctions devoted solely to moderately priced items. Doyle New York's general Fine Furniture, Decorations and Paintings sales are similar to Skinner's Discovery auctions and Sloan's Attic auctions, where you can find everything from an 18th-century Georgian chair with a replaced leg and lesser-quality porcelain and glass by famous makers to paintings by little-known artists, all ranging in price from a few hundred to a few thousand dollars. You may even come across some higher-valued items from consignors who, for various reasons, did not want to wait for an important sale in a specific category. These auctions are not only fertile ground for treasure hunters but tend to be popular with new collectors on a limited budget.

New York City-based Swann Auction Galleries, which specializes in books, autographs and manuscripts, photographs, prints, vintage posters, and other works on paper ranging in price from several hundred to several hundred thousand dollars, also has gone international. Since 1993, Swann and seven other independent auction houses, including Butterfields; Lawsons of Sydney, Australia; the Dorotheum in Vienna and Prague; and Bukowskis in Stockholm and Helsinki, have participated in an alliance called International Auctioneers (IA), which allows them to market one another's sales through joint previews, simultaneous auctions with real-time Internet bidding, the exchange of specialist knowledge and client lists, and advertisements in their newsletters and catalogues—all with the aim of bringing a wider selection of items to their buyers, generating greater competition and higher prices for consignors, and, of course, attracting new clients from an ever-expanding worldwide audience.

Founded in 1941 as an auction house for rare and antiquarian books, Swann is what insiders typically refer to as a boutique (or specialty) auction house, which is noted for a particular area or areas of expertise and occupies a distinctive market niche. In addition to major auctions in the categories mentioned above, Swann also holds auctions devoted to such subjects as magic, cameras and viewing devices, and maps and atlases. Auction highlights during the firm's recent history have included the sale of the only known letter in English by Anne Frank, which fetched $165,000, and a signed vintage print of Imogen Cunningham's photograph, *Magnolia Blossom* (1925), which brought $211,500.

Like regional auction houses, many boutique houses offer added incentives to buyers and sellers such as lower premiums; the waiving of fees for catalogue photographs, storage, insurance, and bought-in lots; and in-house packing and shipping services. But what is the main advantage of buying and selling at boutique auction houses?

"Because we specialize in fewer areas, we know our material inside and out. You're more likely to get a lot of in-depth information about a particular object as well as guarantees on both authenticity and condition, whether it's a Stickley cabinet or a Grueby vase," says David Rago of David Rago Auctions in Lambertville, New Jersey, who specializes in American Arts and Crafts–period objects and modern design. "You don't have to know as much when you're dealing with a specialty house, particularly if you're a new collector. One of our primary goals is to educate our clients. Consignors can feel comfortable knowing that we are able to accurately identify, describe, and appraise their property and market it to a base of specialized collectors, which increases their chances of achieving high prices. And because we are smaller in size, you will have a lot of personal contact with me and our other specialists."

A high level of expertise is also the trademark of New York City–based Illustration House, the foremost U.S. auction house devoted to American illustration art, which holds twice-yearly auctions of paintings and drawings by such artists as Norman Rockwell, N. C. Wyeth, and Howard Pyle, among others, at an average price range from $3,000 to $10,000.

"We originally started out as a gallery specializing in illustration art, and began organizing auctions on the subject because we felt that the auction houses didn't have sufficient knowledge of the field to handle this type of art properly," says Roger Reed, co-owner, along with his father, Walt, of Illustration House, which continues to operate as a gallery. "Illustrations, which were made specifically for publication, have come into their own as a respected art form. Due to the small scale of our auction house, we can give our clients a lot of individual attention. It's a good atmosphere for beginning as well as veteran collectors. We'll send buyers a free catalogue, for example, when we know that an item of interest is coming up in one of our auctions. As an added convenience, we hold two absentee bid-only sales each year for which you can either e-mail or fax your bids."

Henri Matisse, Mimosa carpet, made by Alexander Smith and Sons, wool, 1951. Mimosa, which was Matisse's only design for a carpet, was made in an edition of 500 and is signed with a woven signature. Sold for $3,335 at Wright, Chicago.

Another combination of gallery and boutique auction house is the Chicago-based Wright, which specializes in 20th-century art and design. Established by Richard Wright, a dealer and consultant in postwar furniture, and his wife, Julie Thoma-Wright, an interior designer, this newcomer to the auction scene is located in Chicago's West Loop gallery district. The treasures you will find here include screens and chairs by Charles and Ray Eames, tables by George Nakashima and Isamu Noguchi, and prints by Louise Bourgeois, Andy Warhol, Robert Rauschenberg, and others, as well as numerous offerings by lesser-known artists and designers. Prices range from a few hundred dollars to tens of thousands.

Like other specialty auction houses, Wright offers buyers and sellers the advantage of expertise in a niche market and a high level of one-on-one service.

"Because our focus is more specific, we bring a depth of knowledge and market experience to certain fields that a lot of bigger auction houses don't have. And because we're small, we can afford to explore the market more and discover lesser-known artists and designers," says Wright. "While we still sell from our gallery and organize special exhibtions, we put a lot of our best material up for auction. For sellers, auctions offer an opportunity for higher prices. For buyers, particularly beginning collectors, galleries can be more intimidating. If you walk in cold off the street, you have to prove to a lot of dealers that you're serious."

There are, of course, many other boutique auction houses throughout the country. Los Angeles Modern Auctions (LAMA), founded in 1992 by Peter Loughrey, also specializes in 20th-century art and design, particularly the works of mid-century American designers such as the Eameses, George Nelson, Eero Saarinen, and Harry Bertoia. Run by the young Loughrey and his wife, Shannon, LAMA was once listed in *GQ* magazine as the "coolest place to buy a vintage Eames chair." In addition to the 20th-century-design icons with which the firm has made its mark, LAMA also auctions fine art by Alexander Calder, Jonathan Borofsky, Sonia Delaunay, and other noted 20th-century artists, as well as Native American artifacts. Prices range from several hundred to more than $100,000.

If you're in the market for moderately priced photographs, you'll find them at Be-hold, of Yonkers, New York, which has for the past twenty years been conducting absentee bid-only auctions of 19th- and 20th-century photographs, most of which sell for less than $5,000. Owner Larry Gottheim, who says he auctions photos that are "quirky, adventurous, and artistic," has sold works by such noted photographers as Carlton Watkins, Edward Curtis, Weegee, and Mathew Brady. Be-hold, which caters to both beginning and serious collectors, accepts bids by telephone, fax, or e-mail for its three annual sales. Catalogues are available by subscription and also can be viewed on the company's Web site, Be-hold.com. There are no buyer's premiums.

There is even an auction house devoted to waterfowl decoys. Guyette & Schmidt of West Farmington, Maine, the country's leading auction house specializing in decoys and related items, such as waterfowl paintings and duck and goose calls, holds three sales each year in Easton, Maryland; St. Charles, Illinois; and Ogunquit, Maine. Prices range from several hundred to hundreds of thousands of dollars. In an auction of the Dr. James M. McCleery collection of waterfowl decoys, conducted jointly by Guyette & Schmidt and Sotheby's, a *Sleeping Canada Goose* by Elmer Crowell fetched a record $685,400, proving that specialty auction houses also can have a major impact on the market for a specific collecting category.

Perhaps your tastes are more eclectic than specific, and you are more disposed to attending an auction with a low-key, informal ambience. There are numerous country auctions throughout the U.S. that offer everything from antique furniture, china and art glass to paintings, jewelry, and collectibles that sell from less than $100 to a few hundred thousand dollars. The term "country auction" generally refers to auctions conducted by individual owner-auctioneers, often in rural or suburban areas where there is a loyal local following. These auctions are usually not as extensively catalogued or marketed as those organized by the large houses, and many are not catalogued at all. While some country auctioneers may employ a small staff of specialists, the owners themselves are often the only experts identifying and authenticating objects for sale. The caveat "buyer beware" is particularly applicable here. You undoubtedly must rely more upon your own knowledge when bidding at country auctions, since most do not offer guarantees.

The auction process at country auctions is essentially the same as that which you will find at other auction houses, although a simple wave of the hand or a numbered card may substitute for official bidding paddles, and telephone and absentee bidding may not be available. Like the larger auction houses, many country auctioneers hold previews prior to their sales, so you can inspect objects before bidding. While the majority of merchandise offered at country auctions usually comes from local or regional estates, individual consignments are also welcomed. Sale schedules can be erratic. The setting is informal—a tent, a barn, or an old firehouse, for example—and the atmosphere is casual and relaxed, often entertaining, and at times even amusingly eccentric.

Mike Clum has been holding auctions of antiques, fine art, and collectibles, as well as newer household items, for the past thirty-two years in an 1850s log-frame barn in Rushville, Ohio, forty-five miles southeast of Columbus. Sometimes, his fifty to eighty yearly auctions take place at a local fairground or hall, or at the home of a consigned estate, and often attract hundreds of bidders.

"I try to have a little knowledge about everything," says Clum. "But I will consult outside experts if needed. I don't put reserves or presale estimates on anything I auction. This has proven to be a successful strategy out here in the Midwest. People like to know that they're the ones setting the price. They don't like price protection. One of the advantages to country auctions is the wide variety of merchandise, including lower-end items that the big houses can't afford to take. We don't charge buyer's premiums on items that sell for less than $100,000. The fact that we're in a rural area is also attractive. People like getting out of the city and spending the day in the scenic countryside. We even sell sandwiches and homemade pies to make the experience that much more enjoyable."

Like a lot of country auctioneers, Clum advertises in antiques-trade publications such as the venerable *Antiques and The Arts Weekly,* a bible for antiques aficionados also known as the "Newtown Bee," published by the Bee Publishing Company of Newtown, Connecticut. *Maine Antique Digest,* published in Waldoboro, Maine, is another bible of the antiques-and-auction industry. These publications are excellent sources for information about auctions nationwide.

"We have national as well as local customers," Clum notes. "People trust us. They know we're fair and can get good prices. But you have to earn their respect."

Perhaps you live in the Northeast, and you're planning a weekend trip to the Berkshires region of western Massachusetts, which is noted for its myriad cultural attractions. It is here that, for more than thirty years, Bradford Galleries of Sheffield, Massachusetts, has been conducting auctions of fine art, antiques, decorative accessories, and secondhand furnishings that sell for an average price from $300 to $500. Bradford, which has four full-time experts, produces catalogues for its weekend auctions that contain brief descriptions and estimated values of the items being offered (no photographs). Previews run from three to six days before each sale, and few lots carry reserve prices.

"It used to be that you could find quality art and antiques for lower prices at country auctions. But as people become more informed, they are attending auctions in greater numbers, and consequently there are fewer bargains out there," says Robert Emberlin, co-owner of Bradford Galleries. "People are tired of the mall mentality. They're discovering that auctions are a fun and entertaining way to shop and collect, and that the auction process is actually very simple. It's not like the hogs-and-commodities fast talk or 'the scratch of the nose and you own it' portrayals that you see on

television. The great thing about country auction houses is that we have more flexibility. I'll sell $200 candlesticks, whereas the big houses won't sell items valued at less than several thousand dollars. But don't think that you have to consign to a big house to get a good price. We have an established following. Country auction houses can also offer a less intimidating, more personalized experience as well as reduced costs. For example, we don't charge sellers for advertising, buy-ins, or shipping, which is included in the commission."

Canton Barn, which holds weekly auctions in a colonial barn in Canton, Connecticut, is unusual in that it is not a consignment auction house. Instead, it purchases outright all property that it offers for auction. Lots are unreserved, and there are no buyer's or seller's premiums or catalogues. Free verbal appraisals are available every Sunday. You may bid either by raising your hand or by leaving an absentee bid. Every Saturday evening at 7:30 P.M., hundreds of bidders gather to compete for a broad selection of European and American paintings, antique furniture, china, glass, and carpets, among other items. In winter, they are warmed by heat from a wood-burning stove. Previews are held two hours prior to each sale. The average sale price is about $50 to $300.

"Consignors like the idea of getting paid right away in one lump sum and not having to wait a month to get a check. It's much less complicated when all the property goes to one buyer. Of course, I

Hand-painted Austrian cucumber dish with tray; 1940s Waterford decanters; cranberry thumbprint cream pitcher; hand-painted Royal Vienna cake pedestal; all sold at Canton Barn for prices ranging between $60 and $220. Photography: © S. Wacht, GeminiEye Images.

Whim Plantation Museum Antique Furniture Auction, which takes place every March on St. Croix, U.S. Virgin Islands. Photography by Bruce Buck.

realize I'm taking a risk by operating this way, since I have to turn a profit," says Richard Wacht, auctioneer and co-owner of Canton Barn, along with his wife, Susan. "Buyers like the idea of having a wide selection of items, both expensive and inexpensive, from which to choose. And it's all fresh merchandise, coming mainly from estates. You won't find items that have been consigned by dealers who couldn't sell them. I describe the lot and its condition when it comes on the block. We don't have a staff of in-house experts, but I stand behind everything I sell. If I identify a vase as Qing Dynasty and it's proven to be otherwise, you'll get your money back. If a chest of drawers is Chippendale-style versus Chippendale, I will describe it as such. Of course, you should always have knowledge about what you're bidding on."

In addition to the thrill of the chase, and the casual, country-style setting at Canton Barn, complete with a resident poodle, you may find yourself returning for the homemade pies. Perhaps you're in the mood for something a bit more exotic. Then picture yourself sitting under a tent at a country auction on the grounds of the Whim Plantation Museum near Frederiksted on St. Croix in the U.S. Virgin Islands, with the turquoise waters of the Caribbean glistening in the distance. Presented every March by the St. Croix Landmarks Society to benefit its programs and the Whim Plantation Museum, home to one of the world's finest collections of West Indian antiques, the auction attracts a mix of both local and off-island collectors, antiques dealers, and enthusiasts who compete for colonial West Indian armoires, four-poster bedsteads, tables, chairs, and other furniture crafted during the 18th and 19th centuries by West Indian cabinetmakers working for wealthy European plantation owners. Made primarily of local mahogany, West Indian antiques blend European styles favored by the early colonists with whimsical African interpretations. (See European Furniture on page 71.)

On the 18th-century sugarcane plantation where the Whim Plantation Museum is situated, both the neoclassical great house (or planter's residence) that the museum occupies and the stone windmill (once used to grind cane into sugar) that stands nearby recall an era when sugar was gold and St. Croix was one of the wealthiest islands in the West Indies. The West Indian antiques offered at the Whim auction, which sometimes include pieces crafted on neighboring islands such as St. Thomas, Martinique, and Jamaica, come from dealers, collectors, and nearby estates. Prices range from several hundred to several thousand dollars. Long overlooked, these one-of-a-kind pieces have attracted growing interest in recent years. You can also buy fine European and American antiques here, often at exceptional prices. That completes our "auction roadtrip." May you succeed in finding your objects of desire, and may all your bids be best bids.

Chapter 2
INTERNET AUCTIONS

Unless you have been living on a desert island these past years, you probably have noticed that auction fever has gripped the Internet, transforming the way merchandise is being bought and sold. And the rarefied art and antiques industry, like many others, has succumbed to both the promise and perils of cyberspace. Since 1999, in a rush to capitalize on the potential of reaching an unprecedented number of bidders around the world at any given time, established auction houses, dealers, and e-commerce firms have launched scores of Internet auction sites that sell everything from vintage photographs and 19th-century American paintings to Tiffany lamps and Chippendale furniture.

The good news for these companies is that increasing numbers of consumers seem to feel comfortable making purchases through online auctions. The market leader **eBay** (**ebay.com**), for example, currently claims 15 million registered users, up from 2.2 million at the end of 1998. And Forrester Research in Cambridge, Massachusetts, predicts that online auction sales will grow from $1.4 billion in 1998 to $19 billion in 2003. But exactly how much of this projected revenue will be generated by the online art market remains to be seen.

Like all nascent industries, most online auction companies specializing in art and antiques are experiencing their share of growth pains as profits are slow to materialize and stock prices alternately peak and plummet, causing some to fold prematurely and others to regroup. In such a volatile marketplace, where new online-auction ventures must not only keep pace with rapid technological advances but also convince customers of their credibility and investors of their viability, it is difficult to predict which players will survive as the new millennium progresses. That's not to say, however, that there aren't some strong contenders who are negotiating the ground between the revolutionary fervor with which art-market visionaries first embraced the Internet and the cautious skepticism of those who believe that art and antiques are best ex-

SOTHEBYS.COM Web page

changed in the hallowed halls of traditional auction houses and galleries.

"The Internet has contributed greatly to the evolution of the art market. Our online auctions facilitate the exchange of quality art and antiques between tens of thousands of buyers and sellers from all over the world, more than we could ever bring together at one time in our salerooms," says Craig Moffett, who helped to launch **SOTHEBYS.COM,** the Internet arm of the 256-year-old international auction house that was among the first in its business to launch online auctions. "Volume plays a big role in the Internet marketplace. Traditional auction houses can handle only so much merchandise, which is offered in specific sales several times each year. Buyers like the convenience and flexibility of being able to bid on a much greater variety of objects in continuous online auctions at any time of the day or night, whether they live in New York or Hong Kong. The fact that we offer authenticated art, antiques, and collectibles online, just as we do in our live sales, adds an extra layer of comfort."

SOTHEBYS.COM initially auctioned only higher-end fine art and antiques online but has expanded its inventory to include collectibles such as sports and entertainment memorabilia, coins, and stamps that were formerly sold on its now-defunct sister site, Sotheby's.amazon.com. It also offers lower-priced art, antiques, and jewelry estimated in the $500 to $10,000 range that have found a devoted following in its live Arcade sales. Buyers can choose from among five thousand items at any given time. **Amazon.com,** one of the leading Internet retail sites that also runs its own online auctions, now provides a link to SOTHEBYS.COM and promotes the site to its users.

While most established bricks-and-mortar auction houses are using the Internet in some way to enhance their business, there are no signs that the art auction-going public wants to abandon the thrill of the chase at traditional live auctions. Sotheby's annual sales were $1.93 billion in 2000, while Christie's annual sales were $2.32 billion in 2000, up from $1.96 billion in 1998. Despite the Internet's enormous potential to bring more art to more people at lower transaction costs than those paid by buyers and sellers at live auctions, insiders agree that the Internet will not replace the immediate experience of personally viewing and handling a work of art.

"So far, our success in selling art and antiques online has been slow in coming. The art world isn't renowned for making changes quickly. There's still some resistance in the traditional dealer, collector, and auction community to doing business on the Internet. A lot of people still want to see the art in person be-

fore they buy it," says Geoffrey Iddison, general manager of **eBay Premier** (**ebaypremier.com**), formerly known as eBay Great Collections, an online auction site offering quality art, antiques, and collectibles that was established in 1999, when eBay acquired the 135-year-old San Francisco auction house Butterfields. "Online auctions will complement traditional live auctions. They won't replace them. Bricks-and-mortar auction houses will most likely remain the major venue for the highest-priced art and antiques. And the Internet will increasingly dominate the market with large quantities of middle-range items selling for a few hundred dollars to tens of thousands. That's the niche we want to occupy."

Whether you prefer the excitement and social buzz of a live-auction saleroom or are content to click and collect from the comfort of your own home, you might be surprised to discover that buying a painting or antique online is not as revolutionary as it appears.

"A large percentage of the items sold at live auctions go to telephone and absentee bidders who rely solely on conversations with auction specialists and the information and photographs provided in auction catalogues," Moffett says. "You can do the same thing in our online auctions, where you can inspect high-resolution digital images that are equal in quality to or better than auction-catalogue photographs. The digital images are accompanied by descriptions, estimates, and condition reports about each lot. And you can e-mail or call our experts if you have questions. Occasionally, we even exhibit some of the works we offer online in our salerooms."

In addition to the sheer volume of property, global reach, and convenience provided by online auctions, lower costs to both buyers and sellers are also challenging the status quo.

"It's cheaper to buy and sell online. Bricks-and-mortar auction houses charge higher buyer's and seller's commissions than most online auction companies because they have a bigger overhead, more staff to support, catalogues to produce, and shipping, handling, storage, and marketing costs," notes Iddison. "Online auction companies don't have to deal with the movement and handling of objects."

The combined buyer's and seller's fees at bricks-and-mortar auction houses can be as much as 40 percent of the hammer price of each lot sold. eBay Premier, for example, charges 10 percent a buyer's premium. Since its inventory is supplied by a network of vetted dealers and auction houses such as Butterfields, Vienna's Dorotheum, and other art-related e-

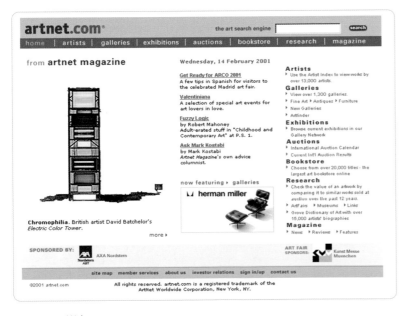

artnet.com Web page

commerce sites, individuals must consign objects to these parties, whose fees vary. SOTHEBYS.COM, the majority of whose inventory is supplied by a network of five thousand vetted dealers, charges a 15 percent buyer's premium on the first $10,000 and 10 percent on every amount thereafter. For Sotheby's live sales, buyer's premiums are 20 percent of the hammer price on items up to and including $15,000, 15 percent on the next $85,000, and 10 percent on any amount more than $100,000. Individuals may also consign objects for sale on SOTHEBYS.COM for a fee of 20 percent of the hammer price. Seller's commissions at Sotheby's live sales range from 2 to 20 percent based upon the value of the property sold.

Artnet (**artnet.com**), the New York-based online art portal (resource site) noted for its subscription-only illustrated database of international fine-art auction records, charged a 10 percent buyer's premium on items sold in its auctions of high-end fine art. Individuals could consign works through Artnet's eight hundred vetted dealer partners for negotiable fees. Early in 2001, however, Artnet suspended its online auctions in favor of focusing on its Fine Art Auctions Database and Gallery Network, which operates as an online marketplace where more than thirteen hundred dealers display their inventories and exhibitions.

"I am still an enthusiastic supporter of online art auctions, but our information-based products have always been the core of our business and have proven for us to be the more successful service to the art community as well as more profitable," says Artnet founder and chief executive officer Hans Neuendorf. "The cost and organization of selling high-end art online had become prohibitive. I do believe, however, that online art auctions will prevail."

While photographs, prints, and collectibles priced under $5,000 have been selling well on the Internet, online buyers are increasingly paying larger sums for more expensive works of art.

"We have sold many hundreds of lots in the $20,000 to $50,000 range," says Moffett. "I didn't expect that people would feel comfortable so soon buying higher-end art online. When you're buying a truly one-of-a-kind painting or antique, the seller's brand name becomes very important. Buyers need to feel a certain level of trust."

The most expensive work auctioned on the Internet to date is a rare first printing of the Declaration of Independence that sold for $8.14 million on SOTHEBYS.COM in the summer of 2000. Other top lots sold by SOTHEBYS.COM, whose average sale price

Paint-decorated miniature blanket chest made by J. Werrey, 1867. Sold for $41,800 on SOTHEBYS.COM.

Andy Warhol, *Marilyn*, screenprint, 1967. Sold for $34,650 on artnet.com.

is about $1,500, include Jasper F. Cropsey's *Portrait of Rose Cropsey*, a circa 1863 painting estimated at $10,000 to $20,000 that sold for $57,200 after sixty-nine bids, and an 1867 paint-decorated miniature blanket chest estimated at $2,000 to $3,000 that sold for $41,800 after ninety-nine bids. Top sales at Artnet, whose average sale price was $2,500, ranged from Lucio Fontana's 1959 painting *Concetto Spaziale, Attese,* which sold for $168,000, to Andy Warhol's 1967 screen-print, *Marilyn,* which brought $34,650 after four bids. eBay Great Collections (now eBay Premier) sold a historic gold watch owned by the sheriff who captured Billy the Kid for $62,000 after four bids while its parent site, eBay, sold an oil on canvas by the early-20th-century American artist Konrad Cramer for $15,000 after forty-two bids.

Whether you are a collector or searching for the perfect aesthetic accent for your new home, the online art market may seem intimidating if you haven't already taken the plunge. But insiders argue otherwise.

"Online auctions are very appealing to beginning collectors and art enthusiasts who are often intimidated by traditional galleries and auction houses, which have a reputation for being insular and elitist," says Karen Amiel, a vice president at Artnet. "They are intimidated because a lot of the information they need is not readily available, and they're embarrassed to ask questions. They don't know which art magazines and books to buy, or where to find price records, for example. And you often have to be an art student or professional to use the libraries at major museums. By contrast, the Internet democratizes the art world by making so much more information available to everyone. We realize that we have to do a lot more than post an image on the screen to sell art. Artnet offers a lot of educational support through its database of over two million auction records; an online art magazine with news of upcoming auctions and articles about collecting; and an online art library and bookstore that offers twenty-one thousand hard-to-find art books. All this extra information at your fingertips makes buying art a lot easier."

But how do you navigate this virtual brave new world, where there are so many different online auction sites from which to choose? You first have to decide whether you want to bid on person-to-person auction sites, such as eBay.com, **auctions.amazon.com,** and **auctions.yahoo.com,** which allow individuals to consign objects for sale but do not assume any responsibility for their authenticity, or business-to-consumer sites, such as SOTHEBYS.COM and eBay Premier, where the sellers are primarily art dealers or auction houses who guarantee the authenticity and condition of the works offered for sale.

Online auctions also vary in format. There are both silent and live Internet auctions. Silent Internet (online-only) auctions are time-based sales in which sellers post items for a limited period of time to attract the highest Internet bidder. Live Internet auctions allow online bidders to submit bids in real time during a traditional live auction, thereby enabling them to compete with bidders in the saleroom. Generally, person-to-person auction sites are based on the silent auction format while business-to-consumer sites employ either one or both of these formats. Additionally, many bricks-and-mortar auction houses offer you the convenience of submitting online absentee bids via e-mail prior to a live sale and post their catalogues on their Web sites free of charge.

eBay, the world's largest person-to-person auction site with four million items for sale at any time in more than four thousand categories, has served as a model for many other person-to-person sites that have adopted similar features. Although it may be best known for selling collectibles such as Pez dispensers and Beanie Babies, eBay, founded in 1995, also offers a significant number of art and antiques ranging from Arts and Crafts furniture and antique silver to turn-of-the-century American drawings and contemporary prints, many of which sell for less than $1,000. (Its main competitors, auctions.amazon.com and auctions.yahoo.com, offer mostly inexpensive collectibles and other consumer goods.)

You may be able to find a bargain in this cyber-flea market if you know the real thing when you see it and snap it up quickly. Although works by known artists do show up on eBay, you will have to scroll through numerous amateur paintings and reproductions of famous works to find them.

Sellers pay eBay listing fees based on the value of the item and up to 5 percent of the final sale price. Aside from the breadth of material offered, the good news is that there is no buyer's premium. The bad news about buying art and antiques on person-to-person auction sites like eBay, where individual sellers are fully responsible for providing information and delivery, is that there is ample opportunity for fraud when the items are only as good as the seller's word. So, *Buyer Beware!* You could wind up with a fake or damaged goods or no goods at all. There was considerable press coverage about a work listed as an "unauthenticated Monet" that garnered a bid of $1.77 million, but failed to sell against its reserve. There was also a $135,805 sale of a purported Richard Diebenkorn painting that eBay canceled when it discovered that the seller had been driving up bids on his own behalf, a practice known as "shilling."

If you've decided to try your luck on eBay, once you've located your object of desire, you'll want to inspect the digital image and description, take note of the bidding action and the seller's e-mail address, and read the user feedback posted by buyers who have previously purchased from the seller. You also can use this feature to register your own positive or negative comments once a sale has been consummated. Likewise, sellers can rate buyers. (Unfortunately, they also can adopt a new user name to dodge a negative rating, or intentionally build up a good record before offering something questionable.) As further protection against fraud, eBay offers free insurance on items up to $200 (with a $25 deductible), meaning that you will be reimbursed if the item you purchased was misrepresented or fails to arrive.

You also should e-mail your questions to the seller before you bid. As with most online auction sites, you will have to register to bid and provide a credit-card number. eBay's auctions usually last for about ten days from the time an item is posted by the seller. eBay notifies you by e-mail of the bidding progress and provides the convenience option of automatic bidding in which the system tops other bids by a minimal amount until your ceiling price is exceeded by another bidder or until you win the object. Beware of a practice known as sniping, whereby a bidder with rapid Internet access outbids you by a few cents or dollars during the final seconds of an auction. Free Web-based services, such as esnipe.com, use high-speed Internet connections to deliver your bid seconds before the auction closes. If you emerge as the highest bidder, the seller will contact you about payment and shipping arrangements. Most sellers prefer money orders or certified checks, although when possible you should try to pay by credit card, which gives you some recourse against fraud. As in live auctions, you should always honor your bid or run the risk of being barred from the site.

The Federal Trade Commission (FTC) reports that Internet-auction fraud is the number-one Internet-related complaint, comprising more than 50 percent of all Internet fraud complaints. And the overwhelming majority involve person-to-person auction sites in which individuals are responsible either for misrepresenting items for sale or for not sending items upon payment. While eBay and other person-to-person sites do not assume liability for the transactions they facilitate, they do provide consumers with links to the FTC and the National Consumer's League in Washington, D.C., which has an Internet Fraud Watch program. These organizations then forward complaints to law-enforcement agencies nationwide.

"We tell consumers to complain in as many places as possible. In addition to registering complaints with us, go to your local police department, your state attorney general's office, and to the same bodies in the jurisdiction where the seller is operating," says Delores Gardner, an FTC attorney specializing in Internet auction fraud. "In cooperation with local law-enforcement agencies, we have already prosecuted more than one hundred Internet auction fraud cases. Consumers got their money back, and disreputable sellers were banned from online auction sites. Of course, we monitor all complaints closely before taking action."

Until person-to-person online auction sites like eBay are forced to assume greater responsibility for their transactions, you can protect yourself by following a few cyber rules.

"First, try to get as much information as possible about the seller. Don't just settle for an e-mail address and a P.O. box; get his phone number and address. Check the online feedback from buyers who have purchased from the seller. And ask questions about the item you want to bid on. Has it been authenticated? Are there any repairs or condition problems? How did he obtain the item? Does he offer a money-back guarantee?" Gardner advises. "Know the value of what you're bidding on by doing some comparison shopping and consulting price guides. If you're buying art and antiques over $500, then consider using an online escrow service, which will hold your payment for a fee until you receive your purchase and are satisfied with it. Escrow services advertise on the auction sites."

Should you become an unfortunate victim of Internet auction fraud, register your complaint with the auction site itself and with the FTC on its Web site, **ftc.gov,** or by calling 877-FTC-HELP. You also can register Internet complaints with the National Consumers League on its Web site, **fraud.org,** or by calling 800-876-7060.

Dr. Michael Schlossberg of Atlanta, Georgia, who has amassed a world-class collection of French drawings and sculpture over the past thirty years, confesses to being an eBay convert. He could barely contain his excitement upon learning that he had won a Manet drawing for $4,500 after eight bids.

"I can't believe I found such a fantastic work of art on eBay, which has always seemed to me like a big junk shop. You have to sift through a lot of low-end items to find something good. When I discovered the drawing I immediately checked the Manet catalogue raisonné, and there it was," says Schlossberg. "It's a study for a painting by Manet in the Metropolitan Museum in New York—an 1860 sketch of his soon-to-be wife. And it was being sold by someone who didn't know its value. I was stunned to have been able to buy it for such a low price. It's worth at least $20,000 to $25,000. Of course, it's always best to inspect a work of art in person if you can, but I can't always hop on a flight to New York or Amsterdam when something I want turns up at a live auction. I've found that buying online is not all that different from bidding by telephone after I've looked at an auction catalogue, read a condition report, and asked questions of an auction specialist."

Schlossberg also sold some drawings on SOTHEBY'S.COM for a combined $15,000 when a move to smaller living quarters required that he streamline his collection.

"I liked the fact that there were no buy-in fees online and that I didn't have to pay for catalogue photography and storage as I would have for a live auction," Schlossberg observes.

Other collectors remain wary of buying art online.

"For me, it's essential to see the work in person. Digital images don't really give you a good feel for the subtleties of color, scale, texture, and condition," says Contemporary-art collector Robert Lehrman of Washington, D.C. "Particularly when you're buying high-end art, it's still a personal-service business."

While books are usually more prized for their historic interest than for their visual impact, English professor Matthew Bruccoli of Columbia, South Carolina, one of the world's foremost collectors of books and manuscripts by F. Scott Fitzgerald, concurs: "Collecting online is like kissing a girl through a screen door. I want to be able to hold the book in my hands."

If you are willing to spend significant sums for art and antiques online, then you will most likely feel more comfortable with business-to-consumer auction sites that offer specialized art expertise and authenticity and condition guarantees. Forrester Research predicts that business-to-consumer auctions, where there is less risk of fraud, will eventually eclipse person-to-person auctions in consumer demand and grow to represent 66 percent of total online auction sales by 2003.

Business-to-consumer auction sites specializing in art and antiques have been established by both bricks-and-mortar auction houses and independent online companies, many of which rely upon a global network of dealers and/or auction houses for their inventory, as well as individual consignors. While some features vary from site to site—including buyer's and seller's premiums, the comprehensiveness of lot descriptions, auction running times that range anywhere from a few days to more than a month, and the type

William Morris, *Canopic Jar, Fallow Deer*, glass sculpture, 1994. Sold for $150,650 on ewolfs.com.

and extent of accompanying educational resources and other art-related services—most business-to-consumer sites offer continuous online auctions, carefully screen their vendors, post online condition reports along with descriptions and images of each lot, provide buyers with e-mail and telephone access to art experts who can answer questions about the items being auctioned, offer refunds within a specific time period should the authenticity and/or condition of an item be misrepresented, and, in some cases, facilitate the financial transaction between buyer and seller.

Unlike Butterfields and Sotheby's, which have teamed up with person-to-person auction sites such as eBay and amazon.com, respectively, which allows them to tap into a vast, already existing online client base while vouching for the authenticity of objects posted on their own sites, the twenty-five-year-old auction house Wolf's Fine Art Auctioneers of Cleveland, Ohio, has pioneered another online auction model by moving its business entirely online. Since its inception in the spring of 1999, **ewolfs.com,** which offers midmarket fine and decorative arts averaging about $1,000 per lot, has reported a highly successful sales rate of 82 percent, confirming founder Michael Wolf's conviction that Internet auctions are the wave of the future.

"You can't assume that someone living in Nebraska is going to fly to Cleveland for an auction. The Internet has really opened up the traditional auction business and allowed it to reach people that it wouldn't have otherwise. Wolf's used to get around two hundred people at a live auction. Now ewolfs.com reaches thousands of buyers around the world," says Wolf. "The company is still doing business the same way and still stands behind everything it sells. Customers like the fact that, unlike other online auctions, many offerings do not carry reserve prices, a practice that encourages bidding. This was also true of Wolf's live sales. People like having full control over the price. The difference with online auctions versus live auctions is that the presentation has to be even better, the guarantees clearer, and the images better defined than catalogue photos. With online auctions there is also the convenience of knowing that the auction will close at a certain time, so you don't have to sit there for hours waiting to place your bid."

Whether you prefer the online or live auction experience, Wolf can't resist offering a few helpful tips. "I always tell buyers not to be afraid to trust the advice of experts at reputable auction houses. They know the merchandise, and they know good value. They are not trying to take you. As for sellers, remember that the biggest auction houses are not always the best choice if you are consigning middle-range works of art, a $20,000 painting, for example. Smaller auction houses like Wolf's are able to devote more attention to promoting them."

ewolfs closely approximates the traditional bricks-and-mortar auction process by accepting consignments from individuals, holding previews prior to each auction, and relying upon its in-house experts in Cleveland to personally inspect and vet all items of-

Charles S. Kaelin (1858–1929), *Harbor,* oil on canvas. Sold for $28,060 on ewolfs.com.

fered for sale. Its commission rates are 15 percent for buyers and up to 20 percent for sellers. Lots sold on ewolfs.com have included a piece of 19th-century glass by William Morris that brought $150,650 and a rare book by Marcel Duchamp that brought $55,200.

Some auction houses, however, have taken a more conservative approach. Christie's, for example, does not offer online auctions but uses the Internet to enhance its overall business by providing online catalogues of its sales, virtual tours of exhibitions, video lectures by auction specialists, interviews and studio

ewolfs.com Web page

visits with contemporary artists, and an online search service called Lotfinder that enables buyers to view specific works of art offered at Christie's auctions worldwide. Taking advantage of the latest technology, Christie's was the first auction house to broadcast live auctions in a video format on the Internet. Live Web casts on **christies.com** have included celebrity sales such as Eric Clapton's guitars and the personal property of Marilyn Monroe as well as the firm's annual evening sales of Impressionist and Contemporary art, for which buyers can place either telephone or absentee bids. You do not have to bid, however, to enjoy the auction entertainment of the Web cast.

Like Christie's, the London-based international auction house Phillips, de Pury & Luxembourg, which also conducts auctions of fine and decorative arts in its New York saleroom, does not offer online-only auctions. It has, however, broadcast a number of its traditional sales in cooperation with the Auction Channel, an Internet company founded in London in 1996 that televises live auctions on cable and enables bidders at home to place bids in real time through the Internet or by Touch Tone phone. At the Web site **theauctionchannel.com,** you can register and bid in live auctions around the world and receive news about upcoming sales and the auction market.

"Our live Internet auctions increased bidding competition by reaching more buyers. We will continue to work with the Auction Channel periodically to offer live Internet bidding, but our focus is really on our traditional auctions," says Christopher Thomson, chief executive officer of Phillips U.K., the world's third largest auction house. "It's too early to say that all auction business will migrate to the Internet. For high-end works of art especially, the traditional auction house will remain the preferred venue. The Internet can't replace the excitement of being in the saleroom."

Other auction houses have also tapped into cutting-edge technology to offer live Internet bidding. Doyle New York, a thirty-seven-year-old privately owned auction house that specializes in estate sales, was among the first to post its illustrated catalogues online at its Web site, **doylenewyork.com.** It was also a pioneer in broadcasting live auctions on the Internet in cooperation with the companies **livebid.amazon.com** and **ibidlive.tv,** which facilitate both online absentee and real-time bidding during live auctions. When bidding via the Internet during live auctions, you usually will see the lots and their accompanying descriptions and estimates, as well as all incoming bids, on your computer screen. In some

cases, there is also an audio link-up that allows you to hear the auctioneer's call. With a click of your mouse, you can enter your own bid. Ibidlive.tv also broadcasts live auctions via the PAX television network, making it possible for you to watch the auction while bidding online or by telephone.

Doyle New York's standing-room-only sale of the James Cagney estate, which featured the Hollywood star's 1961 Bentley and 1942 Academy Award for *Yankee Doodle Dandy,* attracted 450 people to its New York saleroom, while an additional 50,000 Cagney fans logged on to ibidlive.tv. Twenty-five percent of the 155 lots sold went to Internet buyers. Doyle New York also offers an online personal shopping service that alerts buyers when lots of interest are being auctioned, whether you're looking for a Sèvres porcelain dish or an English sideboard.

Butterfields has incorporated live Internet bidding into many of its sales, including American and European prints, vintage Hollywood posters, and the special collection "Treasures from the Hoi An Hoard," which comprised thousands of rare 15th-century Vietnamese ceramics recovered from an ancient shipwreck off the coast of Hoi An, Vietnam. During this live auction in Butterfields' San Francisco saleroom, cyberbidders were able to place real-time bids through ebaygreatcollections.com (now ebaypremier.com), which also hosted a six-month silent auction of a large portion of the Hoi An treasures. Of the 915 lots sold during the live sale, 10 to 12 percent went to real-time Internet bidders participating from the comfort of their own homes. Butterfields also offers a broad range of fine art, antiques, collectibles, and jewelry through continuous online-only auctions on ebaypremier.com, which offers live real-time bidding in selected auctions worldwide through a link-up with **ebayliveauctions.com.**

The Pittsburgh auction house Dargate also has added real-time Internet bidding to its traditional auction format. Dargate is part of a new alliance between eBay Premier and the art portal **icollector.com,** which offers eBay's Live Auctions technology to icollector.com's three hundred auction house partners worldwide.

"Broadcasting our sales live on the Internet simply expands upon our live auctions, which are more economically viable for us than continuous online auctions," says Dargate's owner, Carol Farley. "We are still devoted to our traditional estate auction business, but we like the exposure that the Internet provides."

Although live Internet auctions most closely approximate traditional auctions by providing online bidders with direct access to the saleroom action, silent Internet (continuous online) auctions offer a greater volume of material on which to bid. Live auctions usually comprise several hundred lots compared to the thousands offered at any given time in many continuous online auctions. Additionally, due to technical glitches in live Internet bidding, you may experience a delay of several seconds in receiving bidding information from the auction floor, a problem that should disappear as Internet bandwidth increases.

Another advantage to buying in continuous online auctions is that within one hour you can find numerous examples of the object you're looking for when you might otherwise spend days or weeks. That's assuming, of course, that you're not in the market for a one-of-a-kind work. Being able to make so many cost and quality comparisons mitigates the risk of buying online, and you have a better chance of finding something that may be underpriced. The downside of buying online is the potential for bidder fraud, since you can't prove bid rigging by someone who is trying to bid up or inflate the price of a legitimate object.

Other regional auction houses that specialize mainly in estate sales and midmarket art, antiques, and collectibles also benefit in various ways from the Internet's global reach, yet they are more committed than ever to their traditional bricks-and-mortar auctions. Skinner, one of the largest U.S. auction houses located in Boston and Bolton, Massachusetts, has teamed up with Lycos, a leading Internet portal, to develop the Web site **skinner.lycos.com,** which enables you to bid online on items in Skinner's upcoming live auctions. The winning Internet bid is then executed by a Skinner representative as an absentee bid. You may enter online bids beginning two weeks and up to four hours before the sale takes place and can change your bid while monitoring the competition, which is not possible when submitting a traditional absentee bid.

In addition to bidding online for paintings, American furniture, jewelry, ceramics, and other fine and decorative arts in Skinner's featured sales, you also can bid on lower-priced items such as postcards and designer luggage valued at less than $1,000 in the firm's online Kiosk sales, the Internet version of its popular live Discovery auctions.

"The Internet has allowed us to tap into a huge international audience that we weren't formerly able to reach. But we're taking a cautious approach," says Kerry Shrives, an auctioneer and appraiser at Skinner. "At this point, we're using the Internet more as a marketing tool to enhance our business rather than as a profit-making venue. It will never replace live auctions. There is nothing like the energy in the saleroom. But if I were going to buy art and antiques online, I'd feel much safer on a site affiliated with a reputable auction house that has a proven track record than on a person-to-person site, where there is a greater potential for fraud."

Sloan's, a 147-year-old auction house with salerooms in Miami, Florida, and North Bethesda, Maryland, uses the Internet like many other established auction houses to make its catalogues available free of charge and as a convenient venue for bidder registration and placing absentee bids for its live auctions. These services are available on **sloansauction.com.** Sloan's also holds monthly online auctions of lower-priced vetted property, including paintings, decorative arts, jewelry, and Asian art valued from $150 to $3,000.

"Initially, people thought the Internet would be the messiah of the art world, but it is really just an adjunct to our core business. You have to be skeptical when something new is touted as having the capacity to change your life. In reality, it's always somewhere in the middle," says Deborah Seidel, president of Sloan's. "Since there is an average 65 percent sell-through rate in the auction business, the Internet provides auction houses with the opportunity to sell the other 35 percent that for various reasons doesn't find buyers in traditional sales. But there will always be people who want to handle objects and inspect them firsthand. People come to traditional auctions to buy unusual, one-of-a-kind items. They feel more comfortable buying lower-priced items online that have been vetted and come from a source they trust."

Apart from the auction houses, independent business-to-consumer auction sites specializing in art and antiques are carving a niche for themselves in cyberspace. First, a note about the pioneers. One of these is the above-mentioned New York-based artnet.com, which began in 1989 as an auction-price database and grew to become an online art portal offering numerous art-related resources, including auctions of primarily 20th-century paintings, prints, drawings, photographs, and sculpture ranging in price from $1,000 to several hundred thousand dollars. Although recently suspended for reasons noted previously, artnet.com's auctions offered high-end art by brand-name artists such as Picasso, Chagall, Warhol, and Ansel Adams, and theme sales devoted to subjects

ehammer.com Web page

such as fashion photography, portraits, individual artists, and 20th-century design. Artnet's auctions, which ran from fourteen to twenty-one days, showed a 50 percent increase in sales during their first year of operation from 1999 to 2000.

Founded in 1994, London- and New York-based **icollector.com** is another pioneer of online art sales where you can purchase art at fixed prices from dealers, peruse catalogues for live auctions at three hundred participating auction houses, place absentee bids, consult a reference library and free-art price database (versus the monthly subscription fee for artnet.com's database), and participate in auctions of art, antiques, and collectibles through live real-time bidding made possible by icollector.com's alliance with eBay Premier. Like Artnet, however, icollector.com dropped its continuous online auctions in early 2001.

"Our online auctions were too time- and labor-intensive and were not cost efficient. The marketplace is moving toward live auction technology. We had numerous requests from auction houses and buyers to introduce live real-time bidding," says Clint Cantwell, executive vice president at icollector.com. "We've found that this model works well, because auction houses don't really have to change the way they operate. They can still conduct their traditional floor auctions, with the Internet providing additional bidders. Teaming up with eBay Premier allows us to offer this new service to our auction house partners and customers while eBay's customers will be able to bid on a broader selection of art from more auction houses."

The independent online auction site **ehammer.**

com of New Haven, Connecticut, founded by antiques-dealer Fred Giampietro, has developed a unique hybrid model that blends the successful person-to-person format pioneered by eBay with a business-to-consumer format. This easily navigated site offers art, antiques, and collectibles (with an emphasis on Americana) at an average sale price of $200 to $250. Both individuals and dealers can consign items in ehammer.com's person-to-person auctions, which specialize exclusively in quality art and antiques. Like other person-to-person sites, where there is no formal screening process, sellers are responsible for standing behind their descriptions. There are no buyer's premiums; sellers pay listing fees up to $2.75 as well as an additional 2.5 percent on the hammer price. Other features include an escrow service, a seven-to-eight day refund window, and buyer and seller profiles similar to eBay's feedback mechanism.

ehammer also organizes what it calls showroom auctions, whereby it actively seek items for consignment that are displayed in four showrooms in Connecticut and New York so that bidders can view them before bidding online. ehammer guarantees the items in its showroom auctions, oversees financial transactions and shipping, and maintains a staff of in-house specialists who are available to answer questions. It also conducts appraisals and organizes live estate auctions on location.

"We have tried to stay close to the traditional auction format, and have found that people feel comfortable with that," Giampietro says. "But there is a limit to the number of items that can be offered in live auctions, which also run on restrictive schedules, whereas you can buy or sell something online anytime. And most of the big auction houses won't accept consignments valued at less than $2,000, but online auctions have proven to be a good venue for this material. Our buyers and sellers range from nonexperts and beginning collectors to experienced dealers."

Other independent business-to-consumer sites on which you can buy art and antiques include **antiqnet.com,** which offers both auctions and fixed-price sales of quality antiques supplied by five thousand dealers, and **leftbid.com** and **eauctionroom. com,** which offer Internet bidding in live auctions worldwide.

Whichever auction format you prefer, buying art online is not as complicated as it seems. When it comes to business-to-consumer auctions you should look for sites that provide in-depth information about the work and the artist, including condition reports, and an easily navigable presentation that allows you to search for works by subject, artist, title, price, and other categories so you don't have to wade through thousands of lots. You also should have access to art experts who can answer your questions, whether by phone or e-mail. Money-back guarantees are another optimal feature when buying works online that you haven't inspected in person.

Ronald Capobianco of Long Island, New York, a professional photographer and photograph collector, is a fan of business-to-consumer auctions. He bought three photographs by the fashion photographer Helmut Newton priced from $2,750 to $6,600 and an Annie Liebovitz photograph of Michael Jordan for $2,200 from artnet.com before it pulled the plug on its auctions.

"My experience buying photographs online has been positive. I even discovered that I had paid $2,000 less than an associate had paid for the same photograph at a gallery. I'd buy even more if I had the wall space. I'm not keen on person-to-person auctions, though, because you don't know exactly what you're getting. Before I started bidding on Artnet, I consulted some dealers and collectors to make sure that its affiliated galleries were reputable. It was a comfort to know that the photographs were guaranteed and that I could call Artnet's specialists with questions. The problem with collecting online is that it is so convenient it could become addictive."

There has been a mixed reaction to buying and selling in cyberspace among art and antiques dealers, who have traditionally operated independently from auction houses and once comprised the bulk of their audience.

One of the first to participate in online auctions was New York dealer Mary-Anne Martin, a SOTHEBY'S.COM associate who specializes in Latin American art and who, like many dealers, also maintains her own gallery Web site.

"We're trying to sell lower-value works online, mainly prints and drawings under $10,000. I still believe that if you're going to buy serious paintings you should see them in person," Martin says. "So far, the Internet has been more effective for us as a marketing tool than as a vehicle for direct sales. Our Web site has brought us a lot of additional business."

Chicago's Richard Gray Gallery, which specializes in Modern and Contemporary art, has sold prints by Hockney, Picasso, and Rosenquist for less than $15,000 in Artnet's auctions.

"I don't think the Internet should be pigeonholed

Decoy, early 20th century, sold for $10,100 on ehammer.com.

as a source for only lower-end items. It has a lot of potential. Many sophisticated collectors are looking for higher-end art online because it's convenient for them," says the gallery's Paul Gray. "Not too long ago the fax machine became ubiquitous; the same thing is going to happen with the Internet."

Russ Goldberger, an Americana dealer in Rye, New Hampshire, has sold hundreds of items (mainly decoys and painted country accessories) on ehammer. com at an average price of $500.

"The Internet has been a strong, growing part of our business. It's very effective in reaching a lot of people who don't have convenient access to galleries, auctions, and art fairs. So far, our experience has been very positive in both selling and buying online, and the value of the items we're selling is increasing. But it's still an underdeveloped market," says Goldberger, who also has purchased items on ehammer.com, SOTHEBYS.COM, and eBay. "You can find some good bargains on the Internet if you know what you're doing and ask the right questions. The impersonal nature of the Internet puts even more of a burden on you to be knowledgeable about your area of interest. When I list an item on the Internet I personally guarantee it and describe it in painstaking detail, including condition. So many of my clients have bought objects from me based on black-and-white advertisements in trade publications. That's not so different from buying online, especially if you're buying from a reputable source."

Others in the trade remain skeptical. The American furniture dealers Bernard & S. Dean Levy of New

York have decided not to participate in online auctions.

"When you're buying three-dimensional objects like antiques you really need to look at them in person, especially the more valuable pieces. You don't get a feeling for the quality of the carving, depth of finish, dimensions, and condition details when you look at a digital image," explains Frank Levy. "And a lot of online sites are segmented into such broad categories that it takes awhile to find what you're looking for. The Internet is also a convenient place for dealers and collectors to unload objects of lesser quality."

New York's Dalva Brothers, dealers specializing in 18th-century French furniture and works of art, is also a staunch defender of tradition. "On the Internet it's too easy to skirt condition issues or to provide scanty information," says Leon Dalva. "You need to look at the piece in person. Digital images can be deceiving. You can't see the subtleties of grain on antique furniture, for example, or a chair leg that is warped. And a lot of people don't know enough to determine whether a piece has been reconstructed or repaired. Art is about subtlety, and that doesn't come across on the Internet."

So what does the future hold? Internet holograms that will enable you to beam a virtual Eames chair or Picasso painting right into your living room before you place your first bid? While the Internet is here to stay, it is still too soon to determine to what extent it will revolutionize the art and antiques industry. Like a cautiously optimistic parent witnessing a child's first bold steps, the art market will have to wait and see.

NOTE: *This chapter does not aim to list every online auction site, but rather to highlight those that have projected staying power. Given the infancy and constantly evolving nature of the Internet business, it is inevitable that new sites will continue to develop while others disappear from the screen.*

APPENDICES

U.S. AUCTION HOUSES

ALABAMA

FLOMATON ANTIQUE AUCTION
320 Palafox Street
Flomaton, AL
Tel: 334-296-3059; 334-296-3710
Fax: 334-296-3059

European and American fine and decorative arts, particularly from the Victorian period

ARIZONA

DAN MAY & ASSOCIATES
4110 North Scottsdale Road, #105
Scottsdale, AZ 85251
Tel: 480-941-4200 Fax: 480-941-4433
www.maygallery.com

Fine art

OLD WORLD AUCTIONS
671 Highway 179
Sedona, AZ 86336
Tel: 520-282-3944 Fax: 520-282-3945
www.oldworldauctions.com

Antique maps and prints

CALIFORNIA

A. N. ABELL AUCTION COMPANY
2613 Yates Avenue
Los Angeles, CA 90040
Tel: 323-724-8102; 800-404-2235 Fax:
323-724-9550
www.abell.com

Fine art, antiques, decorations; estates

BEVERLY HILLS AUCTIONEERS
9454 Wilshire Boulevard
Beverly Hills, CA 90212
Tel: 310-278-8115 Fax: 310-278-5567
www.bhauctioneers.com

Jewelry

BUTTERFIELDS
220 San Bruno Avenue
San Francisco, CA 94103
Tel: 415-861-7500 Fax: 415-861-8951

7601 Sunset Boulevard
Los Angeles, CA 90046
Tel: 323-850-7500 Fax: 323-850-5843
www.butterfields.com

Fine art, antiques, jewelry, and collectibles

I. M. CHAIT GALLERY AND AUCTION
9330 Civic Center Drive
Beverly Hills, CA 90210
Tel: 310-285-0182 Fax: 310-285-9740
www.chait.com

Asian art

CHRISTIE'S
360 North Camden Drive
Beverly Hills, CA 90210
Tel: 310-385-2600 Fax: 310-385-9292
www.christies.com

Vintage cars, jewelry, fine art, books and manuscripts, entertainment memorabilia, modern design

CLARK CIERLAK FINE ARTS
14452 Ventura Boulevard
Sherman Oaks, CA 91423
Tel: 818-783-3052 Fax: 818-783-3162
www.estateauctionservice.com

Fine art; estates

HARVEY CLARS ESTATE AUCTION
GALLERY
5644 Telegraph Avenue
Oakland, CA 94609
Tel: 510-428-0100 Fax: 510-658-9917
www.harveyclar.com

Fine art, antiques, jewelry; estates

LOS ANGELES MODERN AUCTIONS
(LAMA)
8057 Beverly Boulevard
Los Angeles, CA 90048
Tel: 323-904-1950 Fax: 323-904-1954
www.lamodern.com

20th-century art and design

MALTER GALLERIES INC.
17003 Ventura Boulevard
Encino, CA 91316
Tel: 818-784-7772 Fax: 818-784-4726
www.maltergalleries.com

Ancient art, coins, and collectibles

JOHN MORAN INC., FINE ART &
ANTIQUE AUCTIONEERS
735 West Woodbury Road
Altadena, CA 91001
Tel: 626-793-1883 Fax: 626-798-2079
www.johnmoran.com

Fine art and antiques, especially early American and Californian

PACIFIC BOOK AUCTION GALLERIES
133 Kearny Street
San Francisco, CA 94108
Tel: 415-989-2665 Fax: 415-989-1664
www.pacificbook.com

Rare books and manuscripts, prints

L. H. SELMAN LTD.
123 Locust Street
Santa Cruz, CA 95060
Tel: 831-427-1177 Fax: 831-427-0111
www.paperweight.com

Glass paperweights and related objects

SUPERIOR GALLERIES
9478 West Olympic Boulevard
Beverly Hills, CA 90212
Tel: 310-203-9855 Fax: 310-203-0496
www.superiorgalleries.com

Decorative arts, books, rare coins, stamps, jewelry; entertainment, sports, and space memorabilia

CONNECTICUT

CANTON BARN
75 Old Canton Road
Canton, CT 06019
Tel: 860-693-0601

Fine art and antiques; estates

CLEARING HOUSE AUCTION GALLERIES
207 Church Street
Wethersfield, CT 06109
Tel: 860-529-3344 Fax: 860-529-3021
www.clearinghouseauctions.com

Fine art and antiques; estates

ROBERT H. GLASS ASSOCIATES
Box 237
Sterling, CT 06377
Tel: 860-564-7318 Fax: 860-535-0657
www.robertglassauctions.com

Fine art and antiques; estates

MYSTIC FINE ARTS, LTD.
47 Holmes Street
Mystic, CT 06355
Tel: 860-572-8873 Fax: 860-572-8895
www.mysticfinearts.com

18th- to 20th-century fine arts

NADEAU'S AUCTION GALLERY, INC.
25 Meadow Road
Windsor, CT 06095
Tel: 860-246-2444 Fax: 860-524-8735
www.nadeausauction.com

Fine art and antiques; estates

WINTER ASSOCIATES
21 Cooke Street
Plainville, CT 06062
Tel: 860-793-0288 Fax: 860-793-8288

Fine art and antiques; estates

DELAWARE

MID-ATLANTIC AUCTIONS & APPRAISALS, INC.
P.O. Box 4365
Greenville, DE 19807
Tel: 302-633-9470 Fax: 302-633-9478
www.mid-atlantic.com

18th- and 19th-century fine and decorative arts

DISTRICT OF COLUMBIA

ADAM A. WESCHLER & SON, INC.
909 E Street NW
Washington, D.C. 20004
Tel: 202-628-1281 Fax: 202-628-2366
www.weschlers.com

Fine art, furniture, jewelry

FLORIDA

ARTHUR JAMES GALLERIES
615 East Atlantic Avenue
Delray Beach, FL 33483
Tel: 561-278-2373 Fax: 561-278-7633
www.arthurjames.com

Estates

JOSEPH'S AUCTION GALLERY
1116 Ninth Street North
St. Petersburg, FL 33705
Tel: 727-895-3249 Fax: 727-822-7227

Fine art, antiques; estates

SLOAN'S AUCTION GALLERIES
8861 NW 18th Terrace
Miami, FL 33172
Tel: 305-592-2575 Fax: 305-592-2426
www.sloansauction.com

Fine art, antiques, jewelry; estates. Also has a gallery/saleroom in North Bethesda, Maryland (Washington D.C. area).

GEORGIA

DEPEW GALLERIES
1860 Piedmont Road NE
Atlanta, GA 30324
Tel: 404-874-2286 Fax: 404-874-2285
www.depewauction.com

Antiques; estates

GREAT GATSBY'S
5070 Peachtree Industrial Boulevard
Atlanta, GA 30341
Tel: 770-457-8719; 800-428-7297 Fax: 770-457-7250
www.gatsbys.com

Fine art, antiques, jewelry, architectural artifacts, garden statuary

RED BARON'S AUCTION GALLERY
6450 Roswell Road
Atlanta, GA 30328
Tel: 404-252-3770 Fax: 404-257-0268
www.redbaronsantiques.com

Fine and decorative arts, collectibles, statuary, architectural artifacts, lighting

IDAHO

COEUR D'ALENE ART AUCTION
Box 310
Hayden, ID 83835
Tel: 208-772-9009 Fax: 208-772-8294

www.cdaartauction.com

Specializes in American Western and wildlife paintings

ILLINOIS

BUNTE AUCTION SERVICES, INC.
755 Church Road
Elgin, IL 60123
Tel: 847-214-8423 Fax: 847-214-8802
www.bunteauction.com

Antiques, jewelry, cars, American Indian artifacts, separate sales of fine art; estates

CHICAGO ART GALLERIES
3388 Commercial
Northbrook, IL 60062
Tel: 847-498-9949

Antiques, fine art; estates

JOY LUKE AUCTION GALLERY
300 East Grove Street
Bloomington, IL 61701
Tel: 309-828-5533 Fax: 309-829-2266
www.joyluke.com

Fine art, antiques, jewelry

BARBARA PECKHAM & ASSOCIATES
118 East University Avenue
Champagne, IL 61820
Tel: 217-344-3475 Fax: 217-351-7777

Antiques; estates

PICK GALLERIES INTERNATIONAL
886 Green Bay Road
Winnetka, IL 60093
Tel: 847-446-7444

Fine art, antiques; estates, real estate, horses

SOTHEBY'S
215 West Ohio Street
Chicago, IL 60610
Tel: 312-396-9599 Fax: 312-396-9598
www.sothebys.com

Wine, musical instruments, 19th- and 20th-century art and antiques

SUSANIN'S AUCTIONS
138 Merchandise Mart
Chicago, IL 60654
Tel: 312-832-9800 Fax: 312-832-9311
www.auctionsmart.com

Fine art, antiques; estates

JOHN TOOMEY GALLERY
818 North Boulevard
Oak Park, IL 60301
Tel: 708-383-5234 Fax: 708-383-4828
www.treadwaygallery.com

Twentieth-century art and design, especially American Arts and Crafts. Holds auctions in cooperation with Treadway Gallery of Cincinnati, Ohio.

WRIGHT
1140 West Fulton Street
Chicago, IL 60607
Tel: 312-563-0020 Fax: 312-563-0040
www.wright20.com

Twentieth-century art and design

INDIANA

KRUSE INTERNATIONAL
P.O. Box 190
5540 County Road 11A
Auburn, IN 46706
Tel: 219-925-5600 Fax: 219-925-5467
www.kruseinternational.com

Fine art, antiques, collectibles, vintage cars

IOWA

GENE HARRIS ANTIQUE AUCTION CENTER
203 South 18th Avenue
P.O. Box 476
Marshalltown, IA 50158
Tel: 641-752-0600; 800-862-6674 Fax: 641-753-0226
www.geneharrisauctions.com

Antiques, clocks, art glass, dolls, toys, collectibles; estates

JACKSON'S AUCTIONEERS & APPRAISERS OF FINE ART AND ANTIQUES
2229 Lincoln Street
Cedar Falls, IA 50613
Tel: 319-277-2256 Fax: 319-277-1252
www.jacksonsauction.com

Fine art, antiques, jewelry, Russian icons

LOUISIANA

NEAL AUCTION COMPANY
4038 Magazine Street
New Orleans, LA 70115
Tel: 504-899-5329 Fax: 504-897-3808
www.nealauction.com

Fine art, antiques; estates

NEW ORLEANS AUCTION GALLERIES, INC.
801 Magazine Street
New Orleans, LA 70130
Tel: 504-566-1849 Fax: 504-566-1851
www.neworleansauction.com

Fine and decorative arts; estates

MAINE

ANDREWS & ANDREWS
71 Cross Street
Northport, ME 04849
Tel: 207-338-1386 Fax: 207-338-2677

Antiques; estates

F. O. BAILEY ANTIQUARIANS
141 Middle Street
Portland, ME 04101
Tel: 207-774-1479 Fax: 207-774-7914
www.fobailey.com

Antiques, fine art; estates

BARRIDOFF GALLERIES
Box 9715
Portland, ME 04104
Tel: 207-772-5011 Fax: 207-772-5049
www.barridoff.com

American and European fine art

CYR AUCTION COMPANY
Route 100
Gray, ME 04039
Tel: 207-657-5253 Fax: 207-657-5256
www.cyrauction.com

Fine art, antiques, jewelry, Americana; estates

ROBERT FOSTER
Route 1, Box 203
Newcastle, ME 04553
Tel: 207-563-8110 Fax: 207-563-6590
www.fosterauctions.com

Antiques; estates

GUYETTE & SCHMIDT, INC.
P.O. Box 522
West Farmington, ME 04992
Tel: 207-778-6256 Fax: 207-778-6501
www.guyetteandschmidt.com

Decoys, waterfowl paintings, related objects

JAMES D. JULIA, INC.
Box 830, Route 201
Fairfield, ME 04937
Tel: 207-453-7125 Fax: 207-453-2502
www.juliaauctions.com

Fine art, antiques; estates

MORRILL'S AUCTIONS
Box 710
Gray, ME 04039
Tel: 207-657-3610 Fax: 207-657-3610

Antiques; estates

THOMASTON AUCTION GALLERIES
P.O. Box 300
Thomaston, ME 04861
Tel: 207-354-8141 Fax: 207-354-9523
www.kajav.com

Fine art, antiques

YOUNG FINE ARTS AUCTIONS
Box 313 North
Berwick, ME 03906
Tel: 207-676-3104 Fax: 207-676-3105
www.maine.com/yfa

American and European paintings and prints

MARYLAND

COCHRAN AUCTIONEERS & ASSOCIATES
7704 Mapleville Road
Boonsboro, MD 21713
Tel: 301-739-0538 Fax: 301-432-2844
www.cochranauctions.com

Fine art

ALEX COOPER AUCTIONEERS
908 York Road
Towson, MD 21204
Tel: 410-828-4838 Fax: 410-828-0875

Antiques; estates

HARRIS AUCTION GALLERIES, INC.
875 North Howard Street
Baltimore, MD 21201
Tel: 410-728-7040 Fax: 410-728-0449
www.harrisauction.com

Fine art, antiques, books

SLOAN'S AUCTION GALLERIES
4920 Wyaconda Road
North Bethesda, MD 20852
Tel: 301-468-4911 Fax: 301-468-9182
www.sloansauction.com

Fine art, antiques, rugs, jewelry, books

THERIAULT'S
Box 151
Annapolis, MD 21404
Tel: 410-224-3655 Fax: 410-224-2515
www.theriaults.com

Antique dolls

WAVERLY AUCTIONS
4931 Cordell Avenue, #AA
Bethesda, MD 20814
Tel: 301-951-8883 Fax: 301-718-8375
www.waverlyauctions.com

Fine art, books, autographs, maps

MASSACHUSETTS

AMERICAN HISTORICAL AUCTIONS
24 Farnsworth Street #605
Boston, MA O2210
Tel: 617-443-0033 Fax: 617-443-0789
www.auctioncentral.com

Stamps, autographs

ATLANTIC AUCTIONS
P.O. Box 631
Sagamore, MA 02561
Tel: 508-888-7220 Fax: 508-833-8703
www.antiquesandthearts.com (click on
"Sellers")

Antiques, fine art

JAMES R. BAKKER
236 Newbury Street
Boston, MA 02116
Tel: 617-262-8020 Fax: 617-262-8019
www.bakkerart.com

Fine art

BLACKWOOD/MARCH FINE ART AND
ANTIQUE AUCTIONEERS
3 Southern Avenue
Essex, MA 01929
Tel: 978-768-6943
www.blackwoodauction.com

Antiques, fine art; estates

BRADFORD GALLERIES, LTD.
Box 160, 725 Route 7
Sheffield, MA 01257
Tel: 413-229-6667 Fax: 413-229-3278
www.bradfordauctions.com

*Fine art, antiques, Americana, Oriental rugs,
books; estates*

DOUGLAS AUCTIONEERS
Route 5 South
Deerfield, MA 01373
Tel: 413-665-2877 Fax: 413-665-2877
www.douglasauctioneers.com

Antiques; estates

ELDRED'S AUCTIONEERS AND APPRAISERS
Box 796
East Dennis, MA 02641
Tel: 508-385-3116 Fax: 508-385-7201
www.eldreds.com

Fine art, antiques, Americana

GROGAN & COMPANY
22 Harris Street
Dedham, MA 02026
Tel: 781-461-9500 Fax: 781-461-9625
www.groganco.com

Fine art, antiques, Oriental rugs

WILLIS HENRY AUCTIONS
22 Main Street
Marshfield, MA 02050
Tel: 781-834-7774 Fax: 781-826-3520
www.willishenry.com

*Americana, Shaker furniture, Native Ameri-
can art*

F. B. HUBLEY & CO. INC.
364 Broadway
Cambridge, MA 02139
Tel: 617-876-2030 Fax: 617-876-2031
www.hubleys.com

Antiques, fine art, rugs; estates

LANDRY AUCTIONS
164 Main Street
Essex, MA 01929
Tel: 978-768-6233 Fax: 978-768-6233
www.landryauctions.com

Antiques, fine art; estates

JOHN MCINNIS AUCTIONEERS
76 Main Street
Amesbury, MA 01913
Tel: 978-388-0400 Fax: 978-388-8863
www.johnmcinnisauctioneers.com

Fine art, antiques, rugs

KEN MILLER & SON
141 Warwick Road
Northfield, MA 01360
Tel: 413-498-2749

Antiques

CARL R. NORDBLOM AUCTIONS
445 Concord Avenue
Cambridge, MA 02138
Tel: 617-661-9582 Fax: 617-661-1434
www.crnauctions.com

Antiques

RAFAEL OSONA
Box 2607
Nantucket, MA 02584
Tel: 508-228-3942 Fax: 508-228-8778

*Antiques, Americana, Nantucket art and
baskets*

PIONEER AUCTION OF AMHERST
169 Meadow Street, Box 9593
Amherst, MA 01059
Tel: 413-253-9914
www.pioneer-auction.com

Antiques; estates

SKINNER, INC.
The Heritage on the Garden
63 Park Plaza
Boston, MA 02116
Tel: 617-350-5400 Fax: 617-350-5429 357

Main Street Bolton, MA 01740
Tel: 978-779-6241 Fax: 978-779-5144
www.skinnerinc.com

Fine art, antiques, jewelry

CARL W. STINSON, INC.
293 Haverhill Street
Reading, MA 01867
Tel: 781-944-6488 Fax: 781-942-8892

*Antiques, Americana, Oriental rugs, col-
lectibles; estates*

SULLIVAN'S AUCTIONS & APPRAISERS
1125 Main Street
Acushnet, MA 02743
Tel: 508-999-3790 Fax: 508-991-3287

Antiques, household items

MICHIGAN

FRANK H. BOOS GALLERY
420 Enterprise Court
Bloomfield Hills, MI 48302
Tel: 248-332-1500 Fax: 248-332-6370
www.boos.com

Fine art, antiques, jewelry, collectibles; estates

DUMOUCHELLE ART GALLERIES
409 East Jefferson Avenue
Detroit, MI 48226
Tel: 313-963-6255 Fax: 313-963-8199
www.dumouchelles.com

Fine art, antiques; estates

SCHMIDT'S ANTIQUES
5138 West Michigan Avenue
Ypsilanti, MI 48197
Tel: 734-434-2660 Fax: 734-434-5366

Antiques

MINNESOTA

TRACY LUTHER AUCTIONS & ANTIQUES
2556 East 7th Avenue
North St. Paul, MN 55109
Tel: 651-770-6175 Fax: 651-770-6906
www.lutherauctions.com

Antiques, collectibles

ROSE GALLERIES
2717 Lincoln Drive
Roseville, MN 55113
Tel: 651-484-1415 Fax: 651-636-3431
www.rosegalleries.com

Antiques, fine art, jewelry; estates

MISSOURI

ROBERT MERRY AUCTION CO.
5501 Milburn Road
St. Louis, MO 63129
Tel: 314-487-3992 Fax: 314-487-4080

Antiques; estates

PHILLIPS-SELKIRK
7447 Forsyth Boulevard
St. Louis, MO 63105
Tel: 314-726-5515 Fax: 314-726-9908
www.phillips-
auctions.com/usa/selkirk.html

Fine art, antiques

BOB SLEEPER AUCTION SERVICE
924 Elm Street
Higginsville, MO 64037
Tel: 660-463-7828 Fax: 660-584-2239
www.biddersandbuyers.com/ads/sleeper.
htm

Antiques

MONTANA

ALLARD INDIAN AUCTIONS
Box 460
St. Ignatius, MT 59865
Tel: 406-745-2951 Fax: 406-745-2961

Native American and Western art

STAN HOWE & ASSOCIATES
4433 Red Fox Drive
Helena, MT 59601
Tel: 406-443-5658; 800-443-5658

Antiques; estates

NEBRASKA

KAUFMAN AUCTION SERVICE
1225 L Street
Lincoln, NE 68508
Tel: 402-489-9988

Antiques, collectibles, household items

NEVADA

STREMMEL AUCTIONS
4790 Caughlin Parkway #529
Reno, NV 89509
Tel: 775-787-7000

Fine art

NEW HAMPSHIRE

BOWERS AND MERENA GALLERIES
Box 1224
Wolfeboro, NH 03894
Tel: 603-569-5095 Fax: 603-569-5319
www.bowersandmerena.com

Rare coins

THE COBBS AUCTIONEERS
50 Jaffrey Road
Peterborough, NH 03458
Tel: 603-924-6361 Fax: 603-924-9098
www.thecobbs.com

Antiques, fine art

ED'S COUNTRY AUCTION HOUSE
West Main Street
Rindge, NH 03461
Tel: 603-899-6654

Antiques; estates

PAUL MCINNIS, INC.
155 Lafayette Road
Suite 8
North Hampton, NH 03862
Tel: 603-778-8989 Fax: 603-964-1302
www.paulmcinnis.com

Antiques, Americana, fine art; estates

NORTHEAST AUCTIONS
93 Pleasant Street
Portsmouth, NH 03801
Tel: 603-433-8400 Fax: 603-433-0415
www.northeastauctions.com

Antiques, Americana

RONALD J. ROSENBLEETH, INC.
AUCTIONEER & APPRAISER
Box 925
Henniker, NH 03242
Tel: 603-428-7686

Antiques, Americana

WILLIAM A. SMITH, INC. AUCTIONEERS
AND APPRAISERS
P.O. Box 49
Plainfield, NH 03781
Tel: 603-675-2549 Fax: 603-675-2227
www.wasmithauction.com

Antiques, fine art

NEW JERSEY

WM. BARRON GALLERIES, INC.
AUCTIONEERS AND APPRAISERS
504 Main Street
Asbury Park, NJ 07712
Tel: 732-988-7711 Fax: 732-774-5932

Antiques, fine art; estates

BERMAN AUCTION GALLERY
33 West Blackwell Street
Dover, NJ 07801
Tel: 973-361-3110 Fax: 973-361-3225

Antiques, fine art, jewelry

CASTNER'S
Box 920, 6 Wantage Avenue, Route 519
Branchville, NJ 07826
Tel: 973-948-3868 Fax: 973-948-3919
www.castnerauctions.com

Fine art, antiques, Americana; estates

DAWSON'S AUCTIONEERS & APPRAISERS
128 American Road
Morris Plains, NJ 07950
Tel: 973-984-6900 Fax: 973-984-6956
www.dawsonsauction.com

Antiques, fine art, Oriental rugs

DUTCH AUCTION SALES
356 Swedesboro Avenue
Mickleton, NJ 08056
Tel: 856-423-6800 Fax: 856-423-7857

Antiques; estates

IVY & MADER PHILATELIC AUCTIONS, INC.
775 Passaic Avenue
West Caldwell, NJ 07006
Tel: 973-882-0887 Fax: 973-882-5422
www.ivymader.com

Stamps

LINCOLN GALLERIES
225 Scotland Road
Orange, NJ 07050
Tel: 973-677-2000 Fax: 973-676-0129
www.lincolnmg.com

Antiques, fine art, jewelry; estates

GREG MANNING AUCTIONS, INC.
775 Passaic Avenue
West Caldwell, NJ 07006
Tel: 973-882-0004 Fax: 973-882-3499
www.gregmanning.com

Parent auction house of Ivy & Mader Philatelic Auctions; stamps, comic books, sports and entertainment memorabilia. The firm also runs continuous online auctions of the above-mentioned items, plus Contemporary prints, on its Web site, www.gregmanning.amazon.com.

NIXON AND NIXON AUCTION SERVICE
492 Red Line Road
Vincentown, NJ 08088
Tel: 609-859-2151 Fax: 609-859-2632
www.nixonandnixon.com

Estates

DAVID RAGO AUCTIONS, INC.
Lambertville Antique & Auction Center
333 North Main Street
Lambertville, NJ 08530
Tel: 609-397-9374 Fax: 609-397-9377
www.ragoarts.com

Twentieth-century decorative arts, especially American Arts and Crafts furniture and pottery, modern design

S & S AUCTION
Box 78A
Repaupo Station Road
Repaupo, NJ 08085
Tel: 800-343-4979 Fax: 856-467-5578
www.ssauction.com

Antiques, fine art, jewelry, rugs

NEW MEXICO

SKEEN AUCTION COMPANY, INC.
411 St. Michael's Drive
Santa Fe, NM 87505
Tel: 505-984-8007

Antiques, fine art; estates

NEW YORK CITY

ALICE (USA), INC.
630 Fifth Avenue
Suite 2000
New York, NY 10111
Tel: 212-332-3488 Fax: 212-332-3489
www.alice-auction.com

Sales in New York and Paris of 19th- and 20th-century fine art

ANTIQUORUM FIFTH AVENUE
609 Fifth Avenue
New York, NY 10017
Tel: 212-750-1103 Fax: 212-750-6127
www.antiquorum.com

Watches, jewelry

CHRISTIE'S
20 Rockefeller Plaza
New York, NY 10020
Tel: 212-636-2000 Fax: 212-636-2399
www.christies.com

Fine art, antiques, jewelry

CHRISTIE'S EAST
20 Rockefeller Plaza
New York, NY 10020
Tel: 212-636-2000 Fax: 212-636-2399
www.christies.com

Fine art, antiques, collectibles, entertainment and sports memorabilia.

DOYLE NEW YORK
175 East 87th Street
New York, NY 10128
Tel: 212-427-2730 Fax: 212-369-0892
www.doylenewyork.com

Fine art, antiques, jewelry

GUERNSEY'S
108 East 73rd Street
New York, NY 10021
Tel: 212-794-2280 Fax: 212-744-3638
www.guernseys.com

Collectibles, entertainment and sports memorabilia, carousels, cars

H. R. HARMER, INC.
3 East 28th Street
New York, NY 10016
Tel: 212-532-3700 Fax: 212-447-5625
www.hrharmer.com

Stamps

ILLUSTRATION HOUSE, INC.
96 Spring Street
New York, NY 10012
Tel: 212-966-9444 Fax: 212-966-9425
www.illustration-house.com

American illustration art

IRREPLACEABLE ARTIFACTS
216 East 125th Street
New York, NY 10035

14 Second Avenue New York, NY 10003
Tel: 212-777-2900 Fax: 212-780-0642
www.irreplaceableartifacts.com

Architectural artifacts, garden ornaments

KESTENBAUM & COMPANY
20 West 20th Street
New York, NY 10011
Tel: 212-366-1197 Fax: 212-366-1368
www.kestenbaum.net

Judaica, including books, manuscripts, paintings, sculpture

MORRELL & CO. FINE WINE AUCTIONS
665 Eleventh Avenue
New York, NY 10019
Tel: 212-307-4200 Fax: 212-247-5242
www.morrellwineauctions.com

Wine

PHILLIPS, DE PURY & LUXEMBOURG
3 West 57th Street
New York, NY 10019
Tel: 212-570-4830 Fax: 212-570-2207
www.phillips-auctions.com

Fine art, antiques, jewelry

POSTER AUCTIONS INTERNATIONAL
601 West 26th Street
New York, NY 10001
Tel: 787-4000 Fax: 212-604-9175
www.posterauctions.com

Vintage posters

ROBERT A. SIEGEL AUCTION GALLERIES
65 East 55th Street
New York, NY 10022
Tel: 212-753-6421 Fax: 212-753-6429
www.siegelauctions.com

Stamps, autographs

R. M. Smythe
26 Broadway, Suite 271
New York, NY 10004
Tel: 800-622-1880 Fax: 212-908-4047
www.smytheonline.com

Antique coins, autographs

Sotheby's
1334 York Avenue
New York, NY 10021
Tel: 212-606-7000 Fax: 212-606-7107
www.sothebys.com

Fine art, antiques, jewelry

Stack's Coin Co.
123 West 57th Street
New York, NY 10019
Tel: 212-582-2580 Fax: 212-582-5018
www.stacks.com

Rare coins

Swann Galleries
104 East 25th Street
New York, NY 10010
Tel: 212-254-4710 Fax: 212-979-1017
www.swanngalleries.com

Rare books, autographs, manuscripts, posters, photographs, prints, maps

Tepper Galleries
110 East 25th Street
New York, NY 10010
Tel: 212-677-5300 Fax: 212-673-3686
www.teppergalleries.com

Fine art, antiques, jewelry; estates

NEW YORK STATE

Absolute Auction & Realty
45 South Avenue
Pleasant Valley, NY 12569
Tel: 845-635-5140 Fax: 845-635-3169
www.absoluteauctionrealty.com

Antiques, fine art, collectibles

Amity Auction Galleries
11 Broadway
Amityville, NY 11701
Tel: 631-691-5836 Fax: 631-691-2682
www.amityauction.net

Antiques, fine art, Oriental rugs

Be-hold
78 Rockland Avenue Yonkers, NY 10705
Tel: 914-423-5806 Fax: 914-423-5802
www.be-hold.com

Photographs; absentee bid-only auction; previews held in New York City

Brzostek's Auction Service
2052 Lamson Road
Phoenix, NY 13135
Tel: 315-678-2542; 800-562-0660 Fax: 315-678-2579
www.brzostek.com

Antiques, fine art, collectibles; estates

Carlsen Gallery, Inc.
5098 Route 81
Greenville, NY 12083
Tel: 518-966-5068 Fax: 518-634-2467
www.carlsengallery.com

Antiques, fine art, Oriental rugs

Bob & Sallie Connelly
205 State Street
Binghamton, NY 13901
Tel: 607-722-9593 Fax: 607-722-1266

Antiques, collectibles; estates

Copake Auctions
Box H
Copake, NY 12516
Tel: 518-329-1142
www.copakeauction.com

Antiques, fine art, Americana, folk art, antique bicycles

F. E. S. Auctions
9 Park Lane
Rockville Centre, NY 11570
Tel: 516-764-7459

Antiques; estates and commercial sales

Gantz Auction Gallery
27 South Main Street
Portchester, NY 10573
Tel: 845-241-2262
www.gantzgallery.com

Antiques, fine art, Oriental rugs

Hesse Galleries
20 & 53 Main Street
Otego, NY 13825
Tel & Fax: 607-988-2523
www.hessegalleries.com

Antiques, Native American art; estates

William Jenack Estate Appraisers & Auctioneers
37 Elkay Drive
Chester, NY 10918
Tel: 845-469-9095 Fax: 845-469-8445
www.jenack.com

Antiques, fine art, jewelry, collectibles; estates

Donny Malone Auction Gallery
236 Main Street
Saugerties, NY 12477
Tel: 845-246-9928 Fax: 845-246-0386

Antiques, fine art

Mapes Auction Gallery
1729 Vestal Parkway West
Vestal, NY 13850
Tel: 607-754-9193 Fax: 607-786-3549

Antiques, fine art; estates

Morgansen's Ltd. Auctioneers & Appraisers
640 County Road 39
Southampton, New York 11968
Tel: 631-204-1600 Fax: 631-204-1157
www.morgansens.com

Antiques, fine art, collectibles, jewelry

Napanoch Auction Services
Huguenot Street
Napanoch, NY 12458
Tel: 845-647-6071 Fax: 845-647-6069

Antiques, fine art

Pleasant Valley Auction Hall
45 South Avenue
P.O. Box 1739
Pleasant Valley, NY 12569
Tel: 845-635-3169 Fax: 845-635-5140

Antiques, collectibles

Rinaldi Auctions & Appraisers
133 Bedell Road
Poughkeepsie, NY 12603
Tel: 845-485-5252 Antiques, fine art

Roberson's Auction Service
Route 52
Pine Bush, NY 12566
Tel: 845-744-9934 Fax: 845-744-2151
www.robersonsauctions.com

Antiques, fine art, collectibles; estates

Savoia's Auction, Inc.
Route 23
South Cairo, NY 12482
Tel: 518-622-8000 Fax: 518-622-9453

Antiques, Americana

South Bay Auctions
485 Montauk Highway
East Moriches, NY 11940
Tel: 516-878-2909 Fax: 516-878-1863
www.southbayauctions.com

Antiques, fine art, jewelry

H. R. TYRER GALLERIES
170 Glen Street
Glens Falls, NY 12801
Tel & Fax: 518-793-2244

Antiques, fine art

NORTH CAROLINA

LELAND LITTLE AUCTION & ESTATE SALES, LTD.
246 South Nash Street
Hillsboro, NC 27278
Tel & Fax: 919-644-1243
www.llauctions.com

Antiques, Americana, fine art; estates

MENDENHALL AUCTION
P.O. Box 7344
High Point, NC 27264
Tel: 336-887-1165 Fax: 336-887-1107

Antiques, fine art; estates, automobiles, office equipment. Also runs an auctioneering school.

SHELLEY'S AUCTION GALLERY
429 North Main Street
Hendersonville, NC 28792
Tel: 828-693-4305 Fax: 828-698-8485
www.shelleysauction.com

Antiques, collectibles

OHIO

MIKE CLUM
Box 2, Route #22
Rushville, OH 43150
Tel: 740-536-9220: 740-536-7242
www.clum.com

Antiques, fine art, collectibles

EARLY AUCTION CO.
123 Main Street
Milford, OH 45150
Tel: 513-831-4833 Fax: 513-831-1441

Fine art, antiques; specialty auctions of art glass

GARTH'S AUCTIONS, INC.
2690 Stratford Road, Box 369
Delaware, OH 43015
Tel: 740-362-4771 Fax: 740-362-0164

Antiques, American paintings; estates

TREADWAY GALLERY, INC.
2029 Madison Road
Cincinnati, OH 45208
Tel: 513-321-6742 Fax: 513-871-7722
www.treadwaygallery.com

Twentieth-century art, decorative arts, design

OREGON

O'GALLERIE
228 Northeast Seventh Avenue
Portland, OR 97232
Tel: 503-831-4833 Fax: 503-236-8211
www.ogallerie.com

Fine art, antiques, jewelry; estates

PENNSYLVANIA

ALDERFER AUCTION CO.
501 Fairgrounds Road
Hatfield, PA 19440
Tel: 215-393-3000 Fax: 215-368-9055
www.auction@alderfercompany.com

Antiques, Americana, collectibles

EARL P. L. APFELBAUM
2006 Walnut Street
Philadelphia, PA 19103
Tel: 215-567-5200 Fax: 215-567-5445

Stamps

NOEL BARRETT ANTIQUES & AUCTION, LTD.
Box 300
Carversville, PA 18913
Tel: 215-297-5109 Fax: 215-297-0457

Antique toys

DARGATE AUCTION GALLERIES
5607 Baum Boulevard
Pittsburgh, PA 15206
Tel: 412-362-3558 Fax: 412-362-3574
www.dargate.com

Antiques, fine art

FREEMAN'S—SAMUEL T. FREEMAN & CO.
1810 Chestnut Street
Philadelphia, PA 19013
Tel: 215-563-9275 Fax: 215-563-8236
www.freemansauction.com

Antiques, fine art

PENNYPACKER-ANDREWS AUCTION CENTER
1530 New Holland Road
Reading, PA 19607
Tel: 610-777-6121 Fax: 610-777-5890

Antiques, fine art

POOK & POOK, INC.
463 East Lancaster Avenue
Downingtown, PA 19335
Tel: 610-269-0695 Fax: 610-269-9274
www.pookandpookinc.com

Antiques, Americana, fine art

CHARLES A. WHITAKER AUCTION CO.
7105 Emlen Street
Philadelphia, PA 19119
Tel: 215-247-0850 Fax: 215-844-8283

Antiques; estates

SOUTH CAROLINA

HEATH HEIRLOOM AUCTIONS, INC.
P.O. Box 339 2352 Miles Road
Elgin, SC 29045-0339
Tel: 803-438-2724 Fax: 803-438-8144

Antiques, fine art; estates

ROUMILLAT'S
2241 Savannah Highway
Charleston, SC 29414
Tel: 843-766-8899 Fax: 843-766-0377
www.antiquesandauctions.com

Antiques, collectibles; estates

TENNESSEE

CLEMENTS ANTIQUES
7022 Dayton Pike
Hixon, TN 37343
Tel: 423-842-4177 Fax: 423-843-1416
www.clementsantiques.prodigybiz.com

Antiques

KIMBALL M. STERLING, INC.
125 West Market Street
Johnson City, TN 37604
Tel: 423-928-1471 Fax: 423-928-8697
www.outsiderauctions.com

Outsider (self-taught) art, antiques; estates

TEXAS

CLEMENTS ANTIQUES
Box 727
Forney, TX 75126
Tel: 972-564-1520 Fax: 972-552-9878

Antiques; estates

GARRETT GALLERIES
1800 Irving Boulevard
Dallas, TX 75207
Tel: 214-742-4343; 800-594-7933 Fax: 214-742-4342
www.garrettgalleries.com

Antiques, fine art

HART GALLERIES
2301 South Voss Road
Houston, TX 77057
Tel: 713-266-3500 Fax: 713-266-1013
www.hartgalleries.com

Antiques, fine art

HERITAGE NUMISMATIC AUCTIONS
Heritage Plaza
100 Highland Park Village
Dallas, TX 75205
Tel: 214-528-3500; 800-872-6467 Fax: 214-443-8425
www.heritagecoin.com or www.currency auction.com

Coins

VON REECE AUCTIONEERS
7200 Harry Hines
Dallas, TX 75235
Tel: 214-352-4343; 800-454-3443
Fax: 214-352-7887

Antique automobiles

U.S. VIRGIN ISLANDS

WHIM PLANTATION MUSEUM ANTIQUE FURNITURE AUCTION
52 Estate Whim
St. Croix
Frederiksted, VI 00840
Tel: 340-772-0598 Fax: 340-772-9446
www.stcroixlandmarks.com

West Indian and European antiques

VERMONT

DUANE MERRILL & CO. AUCTIONEERS
262 Eagle Mountain Harbor Road
Milton, VT 05468
Tel: 802-878-2625 Fax: 802-878-1624

Antiques, fine art

VIRGINIA

LUPER AUCTION GALLERIES
2933 West Cary Street, #201
Richmond, VA 23221
Tel: 804-359-2493 Fax: 804-359-8721

Antiques, fine art

WISCONSIN

BARRETTS AUCTION CENTER
4120 Eighth Street South
Wisconsin Rapids, WI 54494
Tel: 715-423-2252 Fax: 715-325-7171

Antiques

MILWAUKEE AUCTION GALLERIES
1718 North First Street
Milwaukee, WI 53212
Tel: 414-271-1105 Fax: 414-271-1934

Antiques, fine art

SCHRAGER AUCTION GALLERIES
2915 North Sherman Boulevard
Milwaukee, WI 53210
Tel: 414-873-3738 Fax: 414-873-5229
www.schragerauction.com

Antiques, fine art

The preceding list is only a sampling of the thousands of auction houses, both large and small, and independent auctioneers nationwide.

Contact the following organizations for more information on auctioneers and auction houses near you:

NATIONAL AUCTIONEERS ASSOCIATION
8880 Ballentine
Overland Park, KS 66214
Tel: 913-541-8084 Fax: 913-894-5281
www.auctioneers.org

Publishes an annual membership directory of thousands of auctioneers and auction houses nationwide

INTERNATIONAL AUCTION HOUSE DIRECTORY
Gordon's Art Reference
306 W. Coronado Road
Phoenix, AZ 85003
Tel: 800-892-4622; 602-253-6948
www.gordonsart.com

One of five art-and-auction price-reference directories published by Gordon's Art Reference; others include Gordon's Print Price Annual, Gordon's Photography Price Annual, Davenport's Art Reference and Price Guide, and Lawrence's Dealer Print Prices.

www.collectors.org

Listing of auction houses nationwide

ART AND ANTIQUES RESOURCES

1. **Antiques and the Arts Weekly**
   (Newtown Bee)
   www.antiquesandthearts.com
   The Bee Publishing Company
   P.O. Box 5503
   Newtown, CT 06470-5503
   Tel: 203-426-3141
   Fax: 203-426-1394

   This weekly publication is one of the nation's foremost resources for information about art and antiques, auctions, and art and antiques fairs.

2. **Antiques Roadshow**
   www.pbs.org/wgbh/pages/roadshow

   On this popular PBS television program, which airs Monday nights at 8 P.M. Eastern Standard time, auction-house specialists and dealers travel the country appraising art and antiques. The Web site version provides tips on collecting and lists upcoming shows.

3. **Antique Trader Weekly**
   www.csmonlinecsm.com/antique trader
   100 Bryant Street
   Dubuque, IA 52004-1050
   Tel: 800-482-4150
   Fax: 800-531-0880

   A weekly publication with articles on antiques and collecting and news of upcoming auctions and exhibitions.

4. **Art & Antiques**
   www.artantiquesmag.com
   2100 Powers Ferry Road
   Atlanta, GA 30339
   Tel: 770-955-5656
   Fax: 770-952-0669

   This monthly magazine offers news of the art world; in-depth features on art, antiques, and design; and profiles of artists, dealers, curators, and other art-world personalities.

5. **Art & Auction**
   www.artandauction.com
   11 East 36th Street, 9th floor
   New York, NY 10016
   Tel: 212-447-9555
   Fax: 212-447-5221

   This magazine provides up-to-date information on the art market, with an emphasis on the auction scene.

6. **Artfact.com**
   www.artfact.com

   This online database of nearly four million auction records over the past fifteen years, accompanied by images and catalogue descriptions, is available for an annual subscription fee.

7. **Art Forum**
   www.artforum.com
   350 Seventh Avenue, 19th floor
   New York, NY 10001
   Tel: 800-966-2783
   Fax: 212-529-1257

   This magazine publishes exhibition reviews, art and cultural criticism, and features on contemporary art.

8. **Art History Resources**
   on the Web
   http://witcombe.sbc.edu/ARTH Links.html

   This substantial art-history portal also links to artist directories, image banks, and museums. Users can click on any subject or art-historical time period to receive information.

9. **Art in America**
   575 Broadway
   New York, NY 10012
   Tel: 212-941-2800
   Fax: 212-941-2885

   This magazine is noted for its comprehensive coverage and criticism of contemporary art.

10. **Artivents**
    www.artivents.com
    526 West 26th Street #1023
    New York, NY 10001
    Tel: 212-620-0571
    Fax: 212-620-0949

    Developed by the Manhattan art public-relations firm FITZ & CO, this online calendar of upcoming art-world events including art fairs, museum exhibition and gallery openings, auctions, biennials, lectures, and symposia, is available for an annual membership fee.

11. **Artnet.com**
    www.artnet.com

    This online art portal charges a monthly subscription fee for access to its database of more than two million auction results over the past ten years from five hundred auction houses worldwide. Its excellent online magazine covers the international art market, including auctions and museum and gallery exhibitions.

12. **ARTnews**
    www.artnewsonline.com
    48 W. 38th Street
    New York, NY 10018
    Tel: 212-398-1690
    Fax: 212-819-0394

    This monthly magazine features in-depth articles about the art world, artist and collector profiles, and exhibition reviews. Its online version also provides links to sites that offer art for sale.

13. **ARTnewsletter**
    www.artnewsonline.com
    48 West 38th Street
    New York, NY 10018
    Tel: 212-398-1690
    Fax: 212-819-0394

This biweekly newsletter, a division of ARTnews, provides up-to-date coverage of the art market, including prices realized at auctions.

14. *The Art Newspaper*
www.theartnewspaper.com
80 East 11th Street
New York, NY 10032
Tel: 212-475-4574
Fax: 212-475-4615

This international newspaper is a leading source of information about the art market.

15. *Artprice.com*
www.artprice.com

An online database of more than two million auction results from the past thirteen years, this site charges $1.00 per search. Sales schedules from more than two thousand auction houses are also listed.

16. *The Auction Channel*
www.theauctionchannel.com

This Internet portal broadcasts live auctions on cable television and facilitates Internet bidding. It also provides informative articles, reviews, and updates on current auctions.

17. *AuctionWatch.com*
www.auctionwatch.com

This site supplies an enormous amount of auction-related information, including thorough reviews of Internet auctions and daily news about upcoming auctions and current market trends. It also offers online appraisal services and functions as an auction aggregator, allowing buyers and sellers to post or search for specific lots on multiple auction sites.

18. *Biddersedge.com*
www.biddersedge.com

Like auctionwatch.com, this Internet portal to more than one hundred fifty auction sites allows buyers and sellers to post and search for specific items across multiple sites.

19. *Boulay 300*
www.dir-dd.com/boulay300.html
64 Sloane Street
London SW1X 9SH, 9S England
Tel: 44-171-245-6826
Fax: 44-171-235-0577

This magazine is a guide to the top three hundred lots being sold by the world's foremost auction houses.

20. *Collectorshighway.com*
www.collectorshighway.com

This Internet portal is a vast storehouse of information on how to collect art, antiques, jewelry, and numerous types of collectibles. It was launched by Auction Index, publisher of *Leonard's Price Index of Art Auctions,* which lists North American auction results from 1980 to 1998 and is still available for sale in both printed and CD-ROM versions.

21. *Ebrick*
www.ebrick.com

New York-based Ebrick provides a listing of the best e-commerce sites in cyberspace, including those selling fine art and antiques.

22. *Eppraisals.com*
www.eppraisals.com

Founded by former Chicago auctioneer Leslie Hindman, who sold her firm to Sotheby's in 1997, this Web site provides appraisals of fine and decorative arts by a network of one thousand appraisers. For a $20 fee, customers can submit digital images of an object and receive an estimate of its value within three days. Most objects appraised range from $5 to $5,000.

23. *Grove Dictionary of Art*
www.groveart.com

This online version of the renowned multivolume publication by Grove Publishers of Great Britain has more than 45,000 articles about fine art, decorative arts, and architecture that are also linked to other sources. It also provides numerous biographical and bibliographical references as well as access to 100,000 online images. There is an annual subscription fee.

24. *Icollector.com*
www.icollector.com

This London-based Internet art portal maintains a free database of more than one million auction results since 1987, a reference library, and catalogue for auctions worldwide.

25. *Kovels' Antiques and Collectibles*
www.kovels.com
P.O. Box 22900

Beachwood, OH 44122
Tel: 800-571-1555 (books);
800-829-9158
(newsletters) Fax: 216-595-9702

Antiques-and-collectibles experts Ralph and Terry Kovel publish a well-respected monthly newsletter with information on the antiques-and-collectibles market, including collecting tips and "fake" alerts. They also publish books on a variety of topics in the field as well as a yearly price guide. Excerpts from these publications as well as a substantial price database are available online at Kovels' Web site.

26. *The Magazine Antiques*
575 Broadway
New York, NY 10012
Tel: 212-941-2800

This monthly magazine contains in-depth, scholarly articles about antiques.

27. *Maine Antique Digest (MAD)*
www.maineantiquedigest.com
911 Main Street
P.O. Box 1429
Waldoboro, ME 04572
Tel: 800-752-8521; 207-832-7534

Along with *Antiques and the Arts Weekly* (Newtown Bee), this monthly newspaper is a bible for art-and-antiques aficionados and offers comprehensive up-to-date reporting on the field, including auction news. The online version has a free illustrated price guide.

28. *Mayer International Auction Records*
Tel: 800-252-5231

This annual two-volume resource, published by Acatos in Switzerland, lists worldwide auction results for fine arts. It is distributed in the United States by Antique Collector's Club of Wappingers Falls, New York, a publisher of books on fine and decorative arts.

29. *Web Gallery of Art*
www.kfki.hu/~arthp

This extensive online database contains high-resolution images of European art from the 12th through the 18th centuries. It is searchable by artist, subject, title, time period, and country.

BIBLIOGRAPHY

Chapter 1

For more information on American folk art, see:

American Painted Furniture 1790–1880. Cynthia V. A. Schaffner and Susan Klein. New York: Clarkson Potter, 1997.

American Painted Furniture 1660–1880. Dean A. Fales, Jr. New York: E. P. Dutton, 1972.

The Art of the Weathervane. Steve Miller, Exton, PA: Schiffer Publishing, 1984.

The Flowering of American Folk Art. Jean Lipman and Alice Winchester, Whitney Museum of American Art. New York: Viking, 1976.

Girlhood Embroidery. Betty Ring. New York: Alfred A. Knopf, 1993.

Glorious American Quilts: The Quilt Collection of the Museum of American Folk Art. Elizabeth V. Warren and Sharon L. Eisenstat. New York: Penguin Studio in association with the Museum of American Folk Art, 1996.

Quilts of Illusion. Laura Fisher. New York: Sterling Publishing, 1988.

Chapter 2

For more information on American furniture, see:

American Furniture in the Henry Francis du Pont Winterthur Museum, Volume I, The Queen Anne and Chippendale Periods. Joseph Downs. New York: Macmillan, 1952.

American Furniture, The Federal Period, in the Henry Francis du Pont Winterthur Museum. Charles F. Montgomery. New York: Viking Press, 1966.

Fake, Fraud or Genuine? Myrna Kaye. Boston: Little, Brown, 1987.

Four Centuries of American Furniture. Oscar Fitzgerald. Radnor, PA: Wallace-Homestead Book Company, 1995.

The New Fine Points of Furniture: Early American—Good, Better, Best, Superior, Masterpiece. Albert Sack. New York: Crown Publishers, 1993.

Chapter 3

For more information on books and manuscripts, see:

ABC for Book Collectors. John Carter. New Castle, DE: Oak Knoll Press, 1995.

Bibliography of American Literature. Jacob Blanck. New Haven, CT: Yale University Press, 1991.

Book Collecting 2000. Allen and Patricia Ahearn. New York: G. P. Putnam's Sons, 2000

Collected Books: The Guide to Values. Allen and Patricia Ahearn. New York: G. P. Putnam's Sons, 1997.

Collecting Autographs and Manuscripts. Charles Hamilton. Santa Monica, CA: Modoc Press, 1993.

Chapter 4

For more information on Chinese ceramics, see:

Chinese Ceramics: A New Comprehensive Survey. He Li. New York: Rizzoli International Publications, 1996.

A Handbook of Chinese Ceramics. Suzanne Valenstein. New York: The Metropolitan Museum of Art, 1989.

Hare's Fur, Tortoiseshell and Partridge Feathers: Chinese Brown- and Black-Glazed Ceramics, 400–1400. Robert D. Mowry. Cambridge, MA: Harvard University Art Museums, 1997.

Chapter 5

For more information on Chinese furniture, see:

Chinese Furniture: Hardwood Examples of the Ming and Qing Dynasties. Robert H. Ellsworth. New York: Random House, 1971.

Chinese Domestic Furniture. Gustave Ecke. Rutland, VT, and Tokyo: Charles E. Tuttle Company, 1962.

Classic Chinese Furniture: Ming and Early Qing Dynasties. Wang Shixiang. Hong Kong: Joint Publishing Company, 1986.

Splendor of Style: Classical Furniture from the Ming and Qing Dynasties. Curtis Evarts. Taipei: National Museum of History, 1999.

Chapter 6

For more information on Contemporary art, see:

The American Century, Volume Two, 1950–2000. Barbara Haskell. New York: Whitney Museum of American Art, 1999.

Art at the Turn of the Millenium. Lars Bang Larsen, et al. Burkhard Riemschneider and Uta Grosenick, Eds. Cologne, Germany, and New York: Taschen, 1999.

Art periodicals such as *Art Forum, Art in America, Artnews.*

Catalogues from the Biennial exhibitions organized by the Whitney Museum of American Art.

Chapter 7

*For more information
on European ceramics, see*

The Book of Meissen. Robert E. Rontgen. Easton, PA: Schiffer Publishing, Ltd., 1984.

Eighteenth-Century English Porcelain. Geoffrey A. Godden. London: Grenada Publishing, 1985.

An Illustrated Encyclopedia of British Pottery and Porcelain. Geoffrey A. Godden. London: Jenkins, 1966.

The Wallace Collection Catalogue of Sèvres Porcelain, three volumes. Rosalind Savill. London: Wallace Collection, 1988.

World Ceramics: From Prehistoric to Modern Times. Hugo and Marjorie Munsterberg. New York: Penguin Studio, 1998.

Chapter 8

*For more information
on European furniture, see:*

The Dictionary of Antiques and the Decorative Arts. Louise and Batterson Boger. New York: Scribner, 1967.

The Dictionary of English Furniture. Ralph Edwards. London: Country Life, 1964

A Directory of Antique French Furniture, 1735–1800. Lewis Hinckley. New York: Crown, 1967.

Chapter 9

*For more information
on Japanese art, see:*

The Arts of Japan, two volumes. Seroku Noma. John Rosenfield, Tr. Tokyo, New York, San Francisco: Kodansha, 1978.

Edo: Art in Japan 1615–1868. Exhibition catalogue. Washington, D.C.: National Gallery of Art, 1998.

Images from the Floating World. Richard Lane. New York: G. P. Putnam's Sons, 1978.

Chapter 10

For more information on paintings, see:

Art Across America, three volumes. New York: Abbeville Press, 1990.

Census of Pre-19th-Century Italian Paintings in North American Public Collections. Burton B. Fredericksen and Federico Zeri. Cambridge, MA: Harvard University Press, 1972.

A Guide to Dutch Art in America. Peter C. Sutton. Washington, D.C.: Netherlands American Amity Trust, 1986.

The History of American Art. Daniel Marcus Mendelowitz. New York: Holt Rinehart & Winston, 1970.

The History of Impressionism. John Rewald. New York: Museum of Modern Art, 1973.

Latin American Art in the 20th Century. Edward Sullivan. London: Phaidon, 1996.

Leonard's Price Index of Latin American Art at Auction. Susan Theran. Newton, MA: Auction Index Inc., 1999.

Modern Art. Meyer Shapiro. New York: G. Brazillier, 1978.

Chapter 11

*For more information
on photographs, see:*

Looking at Photographs: A Guide to Technical Terms. Gordon Baldwin. Los Angeles: J. Paul Getty Trust Publications, 1991.

Looking at Photographs: One Hundred Pictures from the Museum of Modern Art. John Szarkowski. New York and Boston: Museum of Modern Art and Bullfinch Press, 1999.

World History of Photography. Naomi Rosenblum. New York: Abbeville, 1997.

Chapter 12

*For more information
on Pre-Columbian art, see:*

The Art of Pre-Columbian Gold: The Jan Mitchell Collection. New York: The Metropolitan Museum of Art, 1985.

Painting the Maya Universe: Royal Ceramics of the Classic Period. Dorie Reents-Budet. Durham, NC: Duke University Museum of Art, 1994.

Sweat of the Sun and Tears of the Moon. Andre Emmerich. Seattle, 1965.

Chapter 13

*For more information
on rugs and carpets, see:*

Great Carpets of the World. Yves Mikaeloff. New York: Vendome Press, 1996

Oriental Carpets: A Complete Guide. Murray Eiland. Boston: Bullfinch, 1998.

Oriental Carpets from the Tents, Cottages and Workshops of Asia. Jon Thompson. New York: Penguin Books, 1993 (first published in 1983 as *Carpet Magic*)

The Oriental Rug Lexicon. Peter Stone. Seattle, WA: University of Washington Press, 1997.

Woven Structures. Marla Mallett. Atlanta, GA: Christopher Publications, 1998.

Chapter 14

For more information on ancient Greek and Roman sculpture, see:

Greek Sculpture: An Exploration. Andrew F. Stewart. New Haven, CT: Yale University Press, 1990.

Hellenistic Sculpture I, The Styles of ca. 331–200 B.C. Brunilde Sismondo Ridgway. Bristol, Eng.: Bristol Classical Press, 1990.

Roman Sculpture. Diana E. E. Kleiner. New Haven, CT: Yale University Press, 1992.

*For more information
on African sculpture, see:*

Africa: The Art of a Continent, exhibition catalogue. New York: Solomon R. Guggenheim Museum, 1996.

African Art in American Collections. National Museum of African Art. Washington, D.C.: Smithsonian Institution Press, 1989

African Art in the Cycle of Life. Roy Sieber and Roslyn Walker. Washington, D.C.: Smithsonian Institution Press, 1987.

The Art of Africa. Jacques Kerchache. New York: Harry N. Abrams, 1993.

Chapter 15

*For more information on
20th-century decorative arts, see:*

American Arts & Crafts: Virtue in Design.
Leslie Green Bowman. Los Angeles: Los
Angeles County Museum of Art, 1992.

Art Deco Style. Bevis Hillier and Stephen
Escritt. London, Phaidon, 1997.

Design 1935–1965, What Modern Was.
Martin Eidelberg. New York: Harry N.
Abrams, 1991.

Eames Design. John Neuhart, Marilyn
Neuhart, and Ray Eames. New York:
Harry N. Abrams, 1989.

In the Deco Style. Dan Klein, Nancy A.
McClelland, and Malcolm Haslam. New
York: Rizzoli, 1986.

Masterworks of Louis Comfort Tiffany. Alastair
Duncan, Martin Eidelberg, and Neil
Harris. New York: Harry N. Abrams,
1989.

*Treasures of the American Arts and Crafts
Movement, 1890–1920.* Todd M. Volpe
and Beth Cathers. New York: Harry N.
Abrams, 1987.

Chapter 16

*For more information on
works on paper, see:*

*The Contemporary Print from Pre-Pop to Post-
Modern.* Susan Tallman. London:
Thames and Hudson, 1996.

A History of Engraving and Etching. Arthur M.
Hind. Boston and New York: Houghton
Mifflin, 1923.

Monographs and catalogues raisonnés on
individual artists

*Prints and Printmaking: An Introduction to the
History and Techniques.* Antony Griffiths.
London: The British Museum Publica-
tions, 1996.

*Thinking Print: Books to Billboards,
1980–1995.* Deborah Wye. New York:
Museum of Modern Art, 1996.

INDEX

Page numbers in *italics* refer to illustrations